MILITARY LEADERS
IN THE CIVIL WAR

Books by Joseph B. Mitchell

Decisive Battles of the Civil War

Decisive Battles of the American Revolution

Twenty Decisive Battles of the World
(*based upon Creasy*)

Discipline and Bayonets:
The Armies and Leaders in the War
of the American Revolution

The Badge of Gallantry

MILITARY LEADERS IN THE CIVIL WAR

By JOSEPH B. MITCHELL

EPM Publications, Inc.
McLean, Virginia

Library of Congress Cataloging-in-Publications Data

Mitchell, Joseph B. (Joseph Brady), 1915-
  Military leaders in the Civil War.

  Reprint. Originally published: New York: Putnam,
1972.
  Bibliography: p.
  Inclides index.
  1. United States--History--Civil War, 1861-1865--
Biography. I. Title.
E467.M68 1988   973.7'3'0922 [B]   88-24681
ISBN 0—939009-13-7

EPM Publications, Inc. , 1003 Turkey Run Road
Mclean, VA 22101
Printed in the United States of America

Cover design by Tom Huestis

In Memory of
GEORGE EWELL SCHROEBEL

Contents

	Foreword	11
1.	George Brinton McClellan	15
2.	Thomas J. Jackson	37
3.	Robert E. Lee	62
4.	James Longstreet	88
5.	Ulysses S. Grant	108
6.	George G. Meade	133
7.	William Tecumseh Sherman	152
8.	Joseph E. Johnston	174
9.	John Bell Hood	193
10.	George H. Thomas	215
	Epilogue	236
	Bibliography	238
	Index	243

Illustrations appear after page 128

List of Maps

The Peninsular Campaign   20
Jackson's Valley Campaign   43
The Campaign of Second Manassas   79
The Capture of Harpers Ferry   84
The Battle of Fredericksburg   94
The Vicksburg Campaign   118
The Gettysburg Campaign   145
The Campaign to Atlanta   161
The Battles Around Atlanta   203

Military Leaders in the Civil War

Foreword

THIS volume is a companion piece to my book *Discipline and Bayonets: The Armies and Leaders in the War of the American Revolution*. The former contained ten chapters on ten leaders of the war, six American and four British. This book on the Civil War is equally divided with five leaders from each side.

As in *Discipline and Bayonets*, a major battle or campaign was chosen as the high point of each officer's military career. With these events arranged in order, the leaders are presented in sequence. Thus General George B. McClellan is the first subject, emphasizing the reasons for his failure in the Peninsular campaign. His first opponent, General Joseph E. Johnston, does not, however, appear next in line because the Atlanta campaign was the high point of his career, so he is the subject of the eighth chapter. In like manner Stonewall Jackson appears before Robert E. Lee because the Valley campaign was fought before any of General Lee's famous battles.

This volume, like its predecessor, is designed as a study of the reasons for military success or failure. Those who fought strictly "by the book" at all times, never daring to break the rules, generally came off second best. The one exception is General George H. Thomas, but his case, it will be seen, was somewhat exceptional. His opponent, John Bell Hood, is presented in a better light than by most historians. General Grant is not the butcher he is reputed to have been, nor is General Lee perfect in all respects. There is no point whatever in writing another book about the War Between the States unless something new can be added. It could be said that this volume is the result of more than twenty years of study, thought, and research, combined with many hours of enjoyable discussion with others who have studied military history all their lives. A similar book could have been written on leaders of other wars, but for the American reading public the Civil War was chosen because more people could be expected to know more about it than they might know about other American wars or European conflicts.

Only generals who commanded armies for a considerable length of time were selected, with one exception. General James Longstreet could hardly be overlooked because he played such a prominent role. With this criterion, a genius in the art of war had to be omitted with regret. General Nathan Bedford Forrest should have been an army commander, and it was one of the great misfortunes of the South that he was not entrusted with high command a great deal earlier in the war. Some may ask why Braxton Bragg was not one of the ten; the answer is simply that General Hood illustrated far better the purposes for which this was written.

This work assumes that the normal reader has a fair knowledge of the greatest conflict ever waged in American history. Therefore references in the text to various battles by either their Northern or their Southern name (Bull Run or Manassas, Antietam or Sharpsburg, etc.) should not be confusing. In general, the Northern name has been used when discussing Union leaders, the Southern name when describing Confederate leaders.

This volume may not appeal to those persons who have such fixed opinions that they are unwilling to see the other side of the coin. Just as *Discipline and Bayonets* was perhaps unpopular with people who have been brought up on the myth that the American militia won the Revolution and are unwilling to give due credit to the Continental soldier who actually won that war, at least one chapter in this book may not appeal to certain Southerners. The "March to the Sea" was not nearly the atrocity that many people have been led to believe.

In like manner, this book may not be popular with those persons who are unwilling to admit that the Northern Army of the Potomac contained a great number of leaders who, following in General McClellan's footsteps, were satisfied throughout the war with what I have chosen to call "halfway measures." If readers are irritated, they would probably also be annoyed by the praise I have given in *Discipline and Bayonets* to the British Army, which was a very worthy opponent indeed, although this fact runs directly counter to the popular utterings of many public-spirited authors and politicians of that time and today.

Because these chapters are personality studies as well as military lessons, I tried to select photographs that would show something of the character of the leaders discussed. General Lee's portrait as superintendent at West Point is far more illustrative of his daring, bold spirit than the benign, bearded photographs taken during the war. Grant's photo in the Wilderness and Sherman's grizzled picture show them well. McClellan, with his wife, was purposely chosen because his letters to her were so revealing of his grandiose ideas and his unstable fears. In the other six cases there was little choice. I tried to select the best from among the Civil War photos, but almost all have long, flowing beards, are therefore featureless, and show little character.

If this volume accomplishes its purpose of demonstrating, by example, that very few can be successful in their chosen field (whether it be of a military or civilian nature) unless they are creative, willing to take risks when a crucial need arises, and possessed of the power of their own convictions, the purpose will have been achieved. The fear of failure or of losing popularity is all too evident in the world today.

The first five maps in this book were prepared and designed by me as pencil drawings, then submitted to Janice Downey, who executed them with great care and precision. When she was unable to continue with the work, the last four pencil drawings were then given to the Alexandria Drafting Company, which completed them in final form in a very professional manner.

I would like to express my appreciation to Mr. Charles Dwoskin of G. P. Putnam's Sons for his editorial assistance, helpful criticism, and enduring patience. Neither of us realized that too great a knowledge of the subject would be a handicap and would tend to delay completion. The problem was to simplify the presentation in order to emphasize the most important lessons and not become involved in telling too much. A great amount of detail had to be avoided and omitted to prevent this from becoming a history, instead of a study of personalities.

In addition, I would like to express my gratitude to my good friend H. Paul Porter, Commander-in-Chief of the Order of Stars and Bars, for his constructive, critical appraisal of this work.

A special acknowledgment is due also to Scott Hart, to whom I dedicated my *Decisive Battles of the American Revolution,* for introducing me to Farmville, Virginia, its people, and its history.

Finally I wish to thank my wife, Vivienne, and my family for their encouragement, interest, and enthusiasm while this book was being written.

JOSEPH B. MITCHELL

1

------◆◀◼▶▶------

George Brinton McClellan

QUOTED below are excerpts from telegrams sent to Washington, D.C., by Major General George B. McClellan, *for the benefit of the President of the United States:*

June 25, 1862—6:15 P.M.
"I incline to think that Jackson will attack my right and rear. The rebel force is stated at 200,000, including Jackson and Beauregard. . . .

"I regret my great inferiority in numbers, but feel that I am in no way responsible for it. . . . I will do all that a general can do with the splendid army I have the honor to command, and if it is destroyed by overwhelming numbers, can at least die with it and share its fate. But if the result of the action, which will probably occur to-morrow, or within a short time, is a disaster, the responsibility cannot be thrown on my shoulders; it must rest where it belongs."

The same day, 10:40 P.M.
"If I had another good division I could laugh at Jackson."

One day later, June 26—noon.
"I have just heard that our advanced cavalry pickets . . . are being driven in. It is probably Jackson's advance guard. . . . Do not believe reports of disaster, and do not be discouraged if you learn that my communications are cut off, and even York-town [50 miles to the rear] in possession of the enemy."

7:40 P.M.

"A very heavy engagement in progress just in front of me."

9:00 P.M.

"The firing has nearly ceased. . . . Victory of today complete and against great odds.

"I almost begin to think we are invincible."

On the third day, June 27, 8:00 P.M.

"Have had a terrible contest. Attacked by greatly superior numbers. . . . Had I 20,000 fresh and good troops we would be sure of a splendid victory to-morrow."

Just after midnight:

"I now know the full history of the day. On this side of the river (the right bank) we repulsed several strong attacks. On the left bank our men did all that men could do, all that soldiers could accomplish, but they were overwhelmed by vastly superior numbers, even after I brought my last reserves into action. The loss on both sides is terrible. I believe it will prove to be the most desperate battle of the war.

". . . Had I 20,000 or even 10,000 fresh troops to use to-morrow I could take Richmond. . . .

"I again repeat that I am not responsible for this, and I say it with the earnestness of the general who feels in his heart the loss of every brave man who has been needlessly sacrificed to-day. . . .

"I feel too earnestly to-night. I have seen too many dead and wounded comrades to feel otherwise than that the Government has not sustained this army. If you do not do so now the game is lost.

"If I save this army now, I tell you plainly that I owe no thanks to you or to any other persons in Washington.

"You have done your best to sacrifice this army."

The supervisor of military telegrams in Washington was so shocked by the last two sentences that, on his own responsibility, he deleted them from the telegram so that they would not be read by President Abraham Lincoln. It was not until some months later that either Secretary of War Edwin M. Stanton or the President knew the full contents of General McClellan's hysterical message.

It is appalling to think that a general commanding a great army would talk like this to the President of the United States. For the most part, his messages were addressed to the Secretary of War, but he knew they would be carefully read by the President. And there is absolutely no doubt that it was the President personally whom he was blaming for the lack of support given his army. At six o'clock in the evening he predicts disaster and disclaims all responsibility. Four hours later he is ready to laugh at his enemies, if he had just one more division. On the very next day he tells them not to be discouraged if they receive reports of disaster. By evening he is almost invincible.

On the evening of the third day he describes an attack by greatly superior numbers, yet irrationally talks of a splendid victory tomorrow, although this time he needs 20,000 fresh troops, not just one division.

The climax comes at midnight when half of his army is overwhelmed, but 10,000 fresh troops would suffice to take Richmond. This impossible conclusion is followed by tears for his dead and wounded comrades, whom he never saw at all because he had not been outside his headquarters while the battle was in progress. The last two sentences of this particular message are almost treasonable. Perhaps it is just as well that telegraphic communications were soon cut, so McClellan could not send any more messages for history to record.

On June 30, three days later, when communications were restored, McClellan spoke of trying to save his men by abandoning all his matériel and equipment. On the following day, July 1, if given 50,000 more men, he would retrieve everything. Two days later he wants 100,000 men to put an end to the rebellion.

How did it happen that a person who could send telegrams like these to his superiors in Washington could have been placed in command of the largest army that the United States had ever raised and sent to battle?

From the Northern point of view the first large battle of the war had been a great mistake, almost a disaster. On April 15, 1861, the day after the fall of Fort Sumter, President Lincoln had issued a proclamation calling for 75,000 volunteers to serve for three months. Then, as the time approached when the terms of service of these three-month men would expire, the newspapers and the public had begun to clamor for action or these men would return to their homes without having fired a shot at the enemy. These insistent demands could not very well be ignored. The President was forced to overrule the objections of his principal military adviser, Lieutenant General Winfield Scott, hero of two wars and the commanding general of the Army. Scott contended correctly that these men were not sufficiently trained to conduct an offensive campaign. The result was the Confederate victory at the First Battle of Bull Run, known to the South as the First Battle of Manassas, fought on July 21, 1861.

No one in authority particularly blamed the unfortunate officer, Brigadier General Irvin McDowell, who had been in command at this battle. However it seemed essential for morale purposes that a new commander should be selected to restore the confidence of the troops. At this time there was only one man who had a record of success on the battlefield. Troops under the command of Major General George Brinton McClellan had won two minor battles in West Virginia, at Rich Mountain on July 11 and Carrick's Ford on July 13. The President telegraphed McClellan to come immediately to Washington.

It is doubtful if the President could have made a more popular choice. General McClellan's reputation was of the highest. At thirty-five years of age he had been successful in every endeavor. In 1846 he had been graduated from the United States Military Academy at West Point, second in his class. During the Mexican War he had served with distinction on General Winfield Scott's staff as an engineer officer, where he had received two brevet promotions. When the Crimean War occurred in Europe, McClellan had been sent abroad with two other officers to study the European armies. Then in 1857 he had resigned from the Army to become chief engineer of the Illinois Central Railroad and subsequently vice-president, then president, of the Ohio and Mississippi Railroad. Upon the outbreak of the Civil War he had been commissioned a major general of volunteers to command the state troops furnished by Ohio, then accepted as a major general in the United States Army. Thus, when McClellan was personally called to Washington by the President of the United States, immediately after the defeat at Bull Run, he arrived knowing that the eyes of the entire country were upon him. He believed that he had been called as the savior of his country in its hour of greatest need. For a man inclined to be ambitious and arrogant, this could be a very dangerous idea.

Great things were expected of McClellan, and for a time he appeared capable of fulfilling the highest expectations. Thousands of recruits were pouring into Washington. McClellan promptly began the enormous task of organizing and training this army, and he soon proved that he had a genius for this sort of work, as well as boundless energy. Public confidence, shaken by the defeat at Bull Run, was soon restored. The men in training quickly learned that their new commander was an officer who knew the business of training, organizing, and administering an army. They learned to respect his judgment, have confidence in him, and even grew to have affection for him. If he had never been forced to lead troops into battle, McClellan's place in history would have been assured, for during the summer and fall of 1861, by working energetically, almost feverishly, he created a splendid army, capable of going into battle and giving a good account of itself.

Slowly, however, as the months passed, doubts began to arise. McClellan seemed most reluctant to employ the army that he

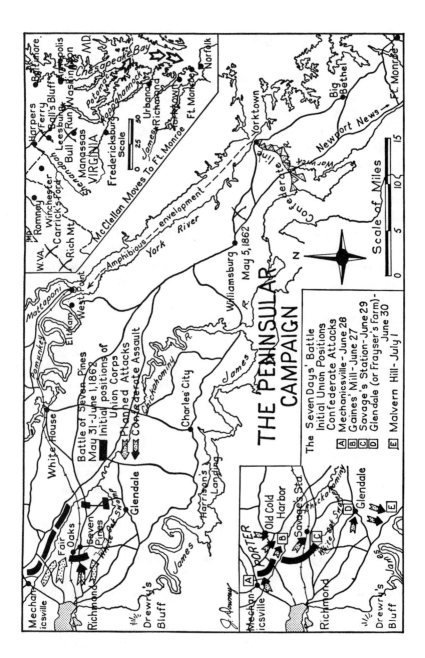

THE PENINSULAR CAMPAIGN

The Seven Days' Battle
Initial Union Positions
Confederate Attacks
[A] Mechanicsville - June 26
[B] Gaines' Mill - June 27
[C] Savage's Station - June 29
[D] Glendale (or Frayser's Farm) - June 30
[E] Malvern Hill - July 1

Battle of Seven Pines
May 31 - June 1, 1862
Initial positions of
Union Corps
Planned Attacks
Confederate Assault

Scale of Miles
0   5   10   15

Scale
25   50

N

had created and trained. It began to appear as if he had fathered a child whom he loved so much that he would take no risks with it.

Following their victory at the First Battle of Manassas, the Confederates, commanded by General Joseph E. Johnston, had moved their outposts closer to Washington, almost within sight of the unfinished dome of the Capitol. Although these outposts proved very annoying, McClellan took no action against them. He seemed fearful of provoking the enemy army, which he consistently appraised as being far stronger than it really was. In fact, the Confederate army was very much understrength and persistently troubled with shortages of supplies and equipment of all types. When, late in September, 1861, a Confederate outpost less than ten miles from Washington was evacuated, it was discovered that the formidable guns emplaced there had been nothing but "Quaker guns," wooden logs painted black.

Even this embarrassing incident did not spur McClellan into taking action. Only once during the fall did he permit any activity which might bring his troops into contact with the Confederates. The result was the Battle of Ball's Bluff, October 21, 1861. A Union brigade crossed the Potomac River near Leesburg, Virginia, and was nearly annihilated by a Confederate brigade commanded by Brigadier General Nathan G. Evans. Union losses were 900 killed, wounded and missing, while the Confederates had only 150 casualties.

The Union brigade commander, Colonel Edward D. Baker, was among those killed in the battle. He had been a prominent Senator from Oregon and a personal friend of President Lincoln but was totally untrained to command a brigade in battle. Immediately thereafter a storm broke on Capitol Hill. The many friends of former Senator Baker instituted an investigation to find a "scapegoat." They chose the division commander, Major General Charles P. Stone, who had been in no way responsible for the disaster. Poor Stone was thrown into jail and kept there for months without charges being preferred against him. General McClellan did nothing to help or protect his subordinate. He deserted Stone completely. This was a forbidding omen.

General Stone's case is one of the most remarkable miscarriages of justice in the history of the United States. Yet in the early stages of the war, he had done more to save the nation's capital from falling into Southern hands than any other individual. Stone resigned from the service in 1864, embittered and in disgrace in the eyes of the public. Subsequently he served as Chief of Staff of the Egyptian Army, but, ironically, when the Statue of Liberty was to be erected in New York harbor, Charles P. Stone was chosen as the engineer in charge of the project.

Not only did General McClellan fail to lift a finger to help Stone clear his name, but three weeks later, when a regimental commander on his own initiative made a successful raid across the Potomac south of Washington, McClellan placed the colonel in arrest. Was it because the colonel had taken too great a risk? Did McClellan object to initiative on the part of a subordinate? Or was it because his approval had not been sought in advance? Yet this raid had been directed against Confederate batteries which had closed the Potomac to navigation and were a great source of annoyance to the Northern government.

On November 1, 1861, Lieutenant General Winfield Scott retired. McClellan was appointed to succeed him as Commanding General of all the armies of the United States. Many people must have marked the contrast between the venerable seventy-five-year-old gentleman and his young successor who was so reluctant to engage the enemy. General Scott's combat record in the War of 1812 had been outstanding, and his 1847 campaign leading to the capture of Mexico City had been one of the supreme achievements of American arms.

As the month of November passed, people really began to wonder about their new general. His specialty now seemed to be conducting parades and reviews of his troops, culminating in a tremendous review of 70,000 men. If the army was so large, why was not something done to atone for the insult of the

"Quaker guns," to restore prestige lost at the disaster of Ball's Bluff, or at least to reopen the Potomac to navigation? Granted that McClellan did not feel that he should yet commit his army to battle at this stage until it was properly organized, equipped and trained; the result of attempting a campaign with an unprepared army had been demonstrated all too recently in July, 1861, at Bull Run.

Yet something could have been done to encourage the public. Someone, shortly after his arrival in Washington, had given McClellan the name "The Young Napoleon." This obviously brought him pleasure, and he loved the cheering of the troops as he galloped back and forth in front of them at the various reviews. However, this apparent disinclination to engage in battle of any sort contrasted strongly with what people knew of the reputation of the real Napoleon. Also there were rumors (which happened to be true) that his victories in West Virginia had been due more to the capabilities of good subordinate leaders than to McClellan's own efforts.

Then came winter and the army set about making itself comfortable until the coming of spring. By March, 1862, the people were so impatient that President Abraham Lincoln was showing signs of acute distress. The war had been in progress for nearly a year. Bases had been seized along the Atlantic Coast in North Carolina, South Carolina, and off the coast of Mississippi in the Gulf of Mexico. In January a Confederate force had been defeated in eastern Kentucky. Union troops in Missouri were threatening Arkansas. In February a great victory had been gained in Tennessee when Forts Henry and Donelson had been captured. On every front, Northern forces were on the move with one exception, the largest army of them all, the Army of the Potomac, which continued to sit idle in front of Washington, D.C.

One trouble was that McClellan vastly overestimated the strength of the army opposing him. Dissatisfied with the regular reports received through normal information channels, he employed the Pinkerton Detective Agency to furnish information concerning the enemy. The results were all the South could have wished for. The reports given him by his detectives usually doubled the actual strength of the Confederate army and led McClellan to believe that the Confederates had more than twice as large a force as they actually possessed.

If McClellan truly believed the reports furnished him, and his correspondence of the period would seem to indicate that he did, the plan of campaign he developed was peculiar, to say the least. In the first place, he knew that President Lincoln was greatly worried about the safety of Washington, D.C., and that the President would insist on a large number of troops remaining in the area to ensure its protection. Yet McClellan's first plan was to take the majority of his army by water to land at Urbana on the Rappahannock, then make a quick advance on Richmond. And his final plan was to proceed to Fortress Monroe and advance up the Peninsula between the York and the James rivers toward Richmond from the east. The assumption in both cases was that General Joseph E. Johnston, commanding the Confederate army near Manassas, would retreat southward to protect Richmond. This is exactly what Johnston did because his force was greatly outnumbered, but if Johnston had actually possessed an army anywhere near as large as McClellan believed him to have, Johnston would have been a great menace indeed to Washington. President Abraham Lincoln saw the possibilities much more clearly than McClellan. The North could not afford to take a chance on losing its capital city. The capture of Washington, D.C., would have almost certainly resulted in the recognition of the Confederacy by England and France, and that could mean the loss of the war by the North.

McClellan should have paid a great deal more attention to the wishes of the President. The latter made it completely clear that he was unhappy about a campaign where the troops would be moved away to a distant field. If, however, McClellan had moved directly southward toward Richmond, he would have had many more troops at his disposal than he was permitted to take to Fortress Monroe, for it would not have been necessary to leave a large garrison behind to guard Washington. Whereas, by moving to Fortress Monroe, large bodies of troops were taken from him for the purpose of protecting the capital city from attack.

There was another extremely important factor that McClellan chose to ignore. It had been assumed that operations up the Peninsula would be supported on both flanks by the United States Navy moving up the James and York rivers. But now the James River was closed because of the presence of the ironclad *Merrimack* waiting in Norfolk harbor after her memorable clash with the *Monitor* on March 9. With this menace to be guarded against constantly, the Navy could hardly be expected to undertake the additional task of reducing Confederate river batteries. Initially the troops would have to depend almost entirely on their own resources.

Considering all these factors, it would have been far better if McClellan had chosen the direct path southward toward Richmond. It is true that, later, General Grant eventually reached a position even farther south than McClellan was aiming for, but in those later years conditions were totally different in all respects. As far as McClellan was concerned, one cannot help but wonder if he was not just plain anxious to get away from the control of President Lincoln. His attitude toward the President had been peculiar from the very beginning. He seemed to look upon him as some sort of strange country bumpkin who, by a weird accident, had been elected to the office of President and that it was his, McClellan's, duty to educate the President not only in military affairs, but in political matters as well. Some of his letters to Lincoln seem patronizing, condescending, almost insulting. The contrast between the humility of the President and the arrogance of his general is remarkable indeed.

It probably came as a great surprise when, shortly before he left for Fortress Monroe to conduct his new campaign, General McClellan was relieved from command of all the armies of the United States except the Army of the Potomac. However, even

McClellan must have seen the justice in such a change. For how could a general absent in command of an army at Fortress Monroe remain in command of all the other armies of the United States? McClellan seems to have made no complaint when he received the order, but it did nothing to change his attitude. He continued to treat the President as his equal, or less. But it simultaneously gave him a chance to complain that he was not being supported when he did not receive more than his share of troops.

Almost from the moment when he reached his new sphere of activity in Virginia, he began to complain about the lack of support he was receiving. The plan had been to take the whole army to Fortress Monroe, but President Lincoln had ordered the First Corps (commanded by Irvin McDowell, the unfortunate victim of First Bull Run) to remain to help guard Washington. One might ask why this had been done. The President had approved McClellan's plan to attack Richmond by the way of the Peninsula. Why then had he taken away one of his corps? The answer was that the plan had been approved with the condition that Washington be left secure from attack. As Mr. Lincoln understood it, McClellan had disobeyed this order and had not left enough troops to guard the capital. Therefore the President had been forced to take appropriate action himself to ensure the safety of the city.

There has been a tremendous amount of discussion, pro and con, as to whether or not the number of troops which McClellan left behind was, in fact, adequate. Considering the fact that Washington was, by this time, well fortified by a chain of more than forty forts, it would appear that enough men were left in place, but whether or not this is true is entirely immaterial. McClellan had flagrantly disobeyed the President's orders. The President could have immediately relieved him from command with every justification but did not do so.

It would have been better for the United States, for the Northern cause, for the Union Army of the Potomac, and for McClellan himself if the President had promptly relieved him from command. Any one of the senior major generals present could have conducted a better campaign than McClellan conducted after his arrival at Fortress Monroe. The Peninsular campaign could have been won by the Union and the war brought to an early ending. McClellan's reputation today would have been that of a general who had, over a period of several months, trained a very efficient army. For there is no question but that the army he brought to the Peninsula with him was well trained, superbly equipped, and ready to fight. And for this McClellan could justly claim credit. Instead of being known today as a battlefield failure, he would have gone down in history as an extremely successful organizer and trainer of troops. His place in history might have been alongside Baron Frederick von Steuben of Revolutionary War fame, who trained the Continental Army at Valley Forge, and Lieutenant General Lesley J. McNair, who did such a superb job of training our World War II armies for battle.

George B. McClellan personally arrived on the Peninsula on the afternoon of April 2. Two days later he sent the equivalent of two strong army corps, about 60,000 men, marching toward Yorktown, which was defended by a very small garrison of considerably fewer than 15,000 men. Now, the distance from Fortress Monroe to Yorktown is about thirty miles. Outnumbered over four to one, Confederate General John Bankhead Magruder was responsible not only for the defense of Yorktown, but also for the establishment of a defense line entirely across the Peninsula from the James River to the York River. The main Confederate army that had been at Manassas was still moving toward Yorktown.

This was a splendid opportunity for McClellan. The Confederate line was extremely thin and lightly held. General Magruder, known as Prince John in the old Army, put on a splendid show of force, but if a strong attack had been launched, his line would surely have been broken, for 13,000 to 15,000 men could hardly be expected to hold fourteen miles against odds of over four to one.

[27]

Although McClellan constantly overestimated the strength of his enemy, a bold reconnaissance in force would soon have shown how lightly the Confederate line was held. General Joseph E. Johnston later wrote: "No one but McClellan could have hesitated to attack."

This is a terrible indictment but justly deserved. Here were his troops marching toward Yorktown, getting always closer to the enemy. The moment of truth had arrived. Unless something happened quickly, McClellan would be personally responsible for precipitating a battle. Just then he received the message that McDowell's First Corps had been taken from his command to ensure the safety of Washington. This was exactly the excuse McClellan needed for delay, and he could blame not only the enemy but also President Lincoln. Instead of attacking with his army, he decided that Magruder's works were too strong and could be taken only by siege. Then as the days passed, Johnston's Confederate troops began to arrive from Manassas; McClellan's army also grew larger. The Union Army of the Potomac now numbered more than 100,000 men, while the Confederates could count fewer than 60,000. Yet McClellan still did nothing but ask for more men and heavier siege guns. Finally the attack was set for May 5. The guns were ready to fire, and it was confidently expected that the Confederates would be unable to hold their lines. But the attack was never launched. On the night of May 3, Johnston withdrew, executing his retreat with perfect timing. By a simple show of force Magruder, then Johnston, had accomplished far more than either could reasonably have expected. McClellan had been held to a gain of only thirty miles in thirty days, an average of one mile a day.

As the Confederate forces withdrew toward Richmond, Union cavalry, closely followed by infantry, took up the pursuit. Near Williamsburg a brisk battle occurred. It began as a rearguard action on the afternoon of May 4 and continued nearly all the next day, the fifth of May, when the Confederates disengaged their troops and continued the march toward Richmond, where General Johnston intended to stand and fight.

McClellan was not present on the battlefield until near the end. He had, instead, been supervising the embarkation of a division at Yorktown. This division had been assigned to McDowell's corps, but the President, doing all he could to help McClellan, had sent it along to the Peninsula anyway. (Later he permitted the sending of a second division, giving McDowell others to take their places.) McClellan was using this division to attempt an amphibious envelopment up the York River. However, Johnston had foreseen such a move long before and had troops of his own all ready to attack the landing force. McClellan, as army commander, should have been present at the Battle of Williamsburg, not doing the work of a staff officer supervising the details of a secondary operation.

Two weeks after the action at Williamsburg the Union forces were leisurely moving forward toward the Chickahominy River, which they reached on May 20. The President had now decided that McDowell could move to McClellan's assistance without endangering the safety of the city of Washington. By this date McClellan had established his base of operations at White House on the Pamunkey River, an arm of the York River, and was expecting to be joined by McDowell's corps marching southward from Fredericksburg. By this time also the Confederate army had retreated across the Chickahominy into positions designed to protect Richmond. Expecting to be joined soon by McDowell's troops, McClellan, whose army had been recently reorganized into five corps, sent two corps south of the river, retaining three on the north bank. This position astride the Chickahominy placed his army in an extremely disadvantageous position. Although numerous bridges were built across the river, the area along both banks was swampy, full of marshes, and was liable in the event of a heavy rain to become a serious obstacle. The whole region could become inundated and the bridges swept away by high water. Even if the bridges were not carried away, the two wings on each side of the river would have difficulty supporting each other rapidly in the event of an attack on either one.

Surely a general of McClellan's intelligence must have recognized this fact, but even when he received word that McDowell's advance to join him had been suspended for the second time, due to an attack by Stonewall Jackson in the Shenandoah Valley, he did nothing but wait in place for further developments. His opponent, Joseph E. Johnston, had a much greater sense of the value of time. He saw immediately the disadvantageous position of the Union army and determined to take advantage of McClellan's faulty dispositions. The Confederate army had been reinforced to a strength of about 63,000 men, although this had meant the evacuation of Norfolk, the destruction of the *Merrimack,* and the opening of the James River to the Union Navy. Johnston could not hope to defeat the entire Army of the Potomac facing him on the Peninsula. It now numbered some 110,000 men, but he could attack one of the isolated wings. He chose to launch his assault on the two corps south of the Chickahominy. The result was the inconclusive Battle of Seven Pines, or Fair Oaks, as it is often called in the North.

On the first day of the battle, May 31, General Johnston was severely wounded. On the second day General Robert E. Lee was assigned to command. From that date forward the name Lee would forever be inseparably linked with the Confederate Army of Northern Virginia.

The Battle of Seven Pines had one other significant result, which has often been overlooked by many historians. Prior to the battle General McClellan had moved slowly and carefully whenever he came close to the enemy. The closer he came, the more cautiously and fearfully he acted. Instead of attacking at Yorktown, he had settled down to conduct siege operations. Then for nearly another month his army had moved very leisurely forward while he sent messages to the President, talking about a great impending battle, saying how hard he would fight when that time came, but continually complaining of the need for more reinforcements.

He had always claimed that the Southern army facing him had been far larger than it actually was. Then that army had attacked his. To McClellan's mind this was proof positive that the enemy's forces must be far stronger than his own. He could not conceive of the Confederates attacking without overwhelming numbers. Eventually he began to talk of Lee's being strengthened to 200,000 men. This was ridiculous, but McClellan seemed to believe what he was saying. He began to fear for the safety of his men. For the first time in his life he had seen a great battlefield with many killed, dying, and badly wounded, although he had not been present when the guns were firing. The army which he had trained for so many months was going to be slaughtered by an overwhelming force. The men for whom he had come to have such a great affection were going to be killed. Surely he could not be held responsible; the President and the Secretary of War must shoulder the blame for not having supported him.

A general has no business becoming so affectionate toward his men that he cannot bear the thought of sending them into a battle where they might get killed. McClellan was acting like a mother hen with a large flock of little chicks. He flooded the wires with telegrams requesting reinforcements. Additional troops were sent to him, but he never considered that they were near enough. Also McClellan filled the air with rumors of Lee's receiving large reinforcements, even including the totally impossible idea that General Pierre Beauregard was coming with some of his troops all the way from Mississippi to Richmond, Virginia.

The Battle of Seven Pines so unnerved McClellan that, although he talked loudly of advancing against Richmond, he made no plan whatsoever to do so. The only action taken by his army during the first three weeks of June was the movement of two more corps south of the Chickahominy, leaving only one corps north of the river extending a hand toward McDowell in the event that he might someday join.

Many historians have noted the fact that General McClellan was more popular with the men of the Army of the Potomac than any other commander they ever had. It is small wonder that this should be the case, for no man really wants to get himself killed, and all the soldiers knew that General McClellan would not risk their lives in battle, if it could possibly be avoided or unless victory was certain. But wars are not won this way, and in a few short days another battle would occur that would reduce McClellan to a state of near hysteria.

When he took command of the Army of Northern Virginia, General Robert E. Lee promptly set his men to digging entrenchments. At this point in his career General Lee was not popular. The Southern newspapers and the people began to criticize his fortification efforts. Undoubtedly they were afraid that the South had now acquired a McClellan who would dig but not fight. Quite the contrary was true. Lee's purpose was to make it possible to defend Richmond with a comparatively small force, thus freeing the major part of his army for an assault on the enemy.

With the help of President Jefferson Davis reinforcements were obtained from Georgia and the Carolinas. In addition, Lee planned to bring Stonewall Jackson's troops from the Shenandoah Valley. To gain information of the Union positions General J. E. B. Stuart was sent with 1,200 cavalrymen on a raid against McClellan's right (northern) flank. The redoubtable "Jeb" amazed both armies by riding completely around the Union Army of the Potomac. His raid turned out to be one of the most profitable and romantic exploits of the war. Lee was now ready with an increased force and adequate information of the enemy's positions. He called General Jackson to come secretly to join him. The plan was first to strike the right flank of the Union army, the one isolated Union corps north of the Chickahominy. It might be crushed before it could retreat across the river. Then there was the further possibility that the Union army might be separated from its line of communications and supply, for it was still being supplied from the base at White House on the Pamunkey River.

The series of battles that resulted is known to history as the Seven Days' Battle. It was on the first day, June 25, which was primarily devoted to preliminary operations, that McClellan sent the first of the series of telegrams quoted: estimating the enemy at 200,000, including Jackson and Beauregard; regretting his inferiority in numbers; offering to die with his troops; and disclaiming all responsibility for disaster. Of course Mc-Clellan actually outnumbered the Confederates about to attack him. The total effective strength on each side in this series of battles was 105,000 Union to 85,000 Confederates.

Then the second telegram was sent the evening before the first large battle took place, announcing that he could laugh at the enemy if he just had one more good division.

The Battle of Mechanicsville was fought on June 26. It consisted of a series of attacks launched against the isolated Union corps north of the Chickahominy commanded by Major General Fitz-John Porter. The attacks were repulsed, and Porter withdrew to a new position. The effect upon McClellan was remarkable indeed. He began by telling his superiors not to worry about disaster even if his communications were cut and Yorktown captured. He ended by boasting that his men were almost invincible.

On the next day, June 27, at the Battle of Gaines' Mill, Porter's men were attacked again and again. Finally their line was broken. The Confederates gained the positions, although large numbers of the Union troops managed to withdraw across the river under cover of darkness. After saying early in the evening that 20,000 troops would bring him victory, by midnight McClellan was weeping verbally over his dead and wounded comrades, whose desperate struggles he had not witnessed because he had stayed away from the battlefield. He had spent the entire day in his headquarters.

Some thoughtful students of McClellan have suggested he was afraid of the sight of blood. Whether this be true or not, he took no further part in the Seven Days' Battle. His subordinates were left to their own devices. There were thousands of Northern soldiers south of the Chickahominy who had not yet been engaged; McClellan made no use of them at all but decided to retreat. Fortunately for his superiors in Washington, when this was done, the telegraph was cut, so no more frantic messages could be sent.

Without any direction from their commanding general, the Union division and corps commanders retreated and fought the battles of Savage's Station (June 29) and Glendale, or Frayser's Farm (June 30), as best they could. As for McClellan, one can only assume that, instead of acting as army commander, he was concerned more with the logistical problems of the day, *i.e.,* changing his base from White House on the Pamunkey to the James River—from the extreme right to the extreme left flank. If ever a commanding general demonstrated a misplaced sense of duty, this was the occasion. And to cap the climax, when the final battle was fought at Malvern Hill on July 1, 1862, McClellan, instead of dying with his troops, was sitting safely on a gunboat in the James.

Among those present on the Southern side in the Peninsular campaign the names Robert E. Lee and Joseph E. Johnston are particularly worthy of mention, but of the commander on the Northern side the less said the better. As the creator of the Army of the Potomac he deserves every credit and every word of praise that has ever been written about him in connection with this achievement. However, as its commander in battle it is difficult to find even one good word to say about him. McClellan set such a poor example—multiple excuses, timidity, lack of appreciation of the value of time, caution, and apprehension—that his army never completely recovered from the effects of his leadership until the very last days of the war when General Grant was in charge of its operations. The contrast between it and the Confederate Army of Northern Virginia, where rapidity and quick action were the rule rather than the exception, is startling. There were notable occasions such as General John Sedgwick's remarkable march of thirty-four miles to Gettysburg, but all too often somebody was too slow, or stopped to rest, or waited for orders. After creating a magnificent army ready to fight, McClellan then taught its leaders to be satisfied with halfway measures. Some refused to agree with this doctrine, but far too many accepted it.

When every factor is taken into consideration, it seems only proper to conclude that President Lincoln's worst military mistake of the entire Civil War was to leave McClellan in command of the army that he had trained, yet the President had no way of knowing in advance what a failure McClellan would be. Yet Mr. Lincoln recalled him for the Antietam campaign, where McClellan again failed. With a copy of General Lee's famous "Lost Order," Special Orders No. 191, in his possession, McClellan failed to destroy Lee's army. He was present at the Battle of Antietam, but he acted as if he were not. He left the fighting to subordinates, letting them deliver five separate and uncoordinated attacks. He withheld two corps completely from the battle, so they stood idle all day, and of course failed to attack again on the following day, although Lee remained in place with the greatly outnumbered Confederate army and practically invited the Union army to attack.

It would appear that the principal reason McClellan failed was that he was abnormally afraid of failure.

Finally, no chapter on General McClellan would be complete without mention of Secretary of War Edwin M. Stanton, whom McClellan regarded as his archenemy and who he believed was engaged in a conspiracy against him. Mr. Stanton has been severely criticized by almost every student of the war for his arbitrary, opinionated and often unfair treatment of practically every senior general in the United States Army, including McClellan. This criticism is justly deserved, since

Stanton had no military training or experience which would qualify him to exercise opinions of any sort concerning matters involving military tactics or strategy. Yet there is one great excuse to be offered in his behalf. The first general with whom he had been forced to deal had been George B. McClellan.

2

Thomas J. Jackson

LET us turn now to an officer who was the exact antithesis of General McClellan in almost every respect. Whereas McClellan dearly loved pomp and ceremony, parades and grand reviews, this Confederate soldier cared nothing about such appearances. His trademarks were a well-worn old cap pushed forward over his eyes and an old uniform coat, usually rather dirty. As for galloping back and forth to impress his soldiers, he cut a poor figure on a horse and was totally disinterested in the plaudits of the multitude.

In contrast to McClellan, who loved the nickname The Young Napoleon, here was an officer who had studied Napoleon's battles and campaigns thoroughly and repeatedly. The great emperor's advice to "read and re-read the eighty-eight campaigns of Alexander, Hannibal, Caesar, Gustavus, Turenne, Eugène and Frederick" had not been lost on this man. He had spent the greater part of his adult life doing exactly that.

Completely serious, almost devoid of humor, profoundly religious, ungainly, awkward, he was at first a sort of joke to his men, but there were exceptions. Those who had looked into his piercing eyes, under that old worn cap, felt the power of his just wrath, or seen the light of battle flashing in those sharp, blue eyes instantly revised their opinion. They spread the word that this man was not to be trifled with. Later, someone gave him the nickname Old Blue Light, not because of his strict puritanical behavior, but for the battle light that shone in his eyes when, in an instant, he would be transformed from an ungainly figure into one of heroic mold.

In fact, his soldiers had three nicknames for him. They most often referred to him as Old Jack, but he is far better known to history by a different name, acquired in the heat of battle near Manassas, Virginia, where he and his brigade, standing "like a stone wall," formed a rallying point for the army, firmly repulsed all assaults of their enemies, then delivered a powerful counterattack.

"Stonewall" Jackson, christened Thomas Jonathan Jackson, was born January 21, 1824, in Clarksburg, Virginia (now West Virginia). By the time he was seven years old both of his parents had died; he, an older brother, and a sister were reared by their father's half-brother. Schooling was not of the best in this semi-frontier region, and as a result, when Jackson entered West Point, there was grave doubt that he would be able to graduate. The first year was a grim struggle, but by the last year, many of his classmates were prone to remark that if the four-year course were extended to five years, Jackson would stand first in his class. There were 59 graduated, while 52 failed. Despite the fact that the lower standings of his earlier years were averaged with his later higher marks, Jackson stood 17 in the West Point Class of 1846. General McClellan was number two in the same class.

During the Mexican War, Jackson served as a lieutenant in "Prince John" Magruder's battery and made such a splendid record that he received two brevet promotions. Three years after the war, he resigned from the Army to accept the position of professor of natural and experimental philosophy, and artillery instructor, at Virginia Military Institute. As a professor of mathematics and physical sciences he was probably not an inspiring teacher, but those years at Lexington, Virginia, were a God-given opportunity for him to study. When war came, Jackson was as ready as any man in the nation to fulfill his destiny.

His first command was as a colonel at Harpers Ferry, where the Shenandoah River flows into the Potomac, a place long renowned for its natural beauty and charm. Not quite a year and a half later, Jackson would make it militarily famous as the place where he would capture 12,500 Union soldiers during the Antietam campaign of September, 1862.

In recognition of the outstanding part that he and his brigade had played in the First Battle of Manassas, Stonewall Jackson was promoted on October 7, 1861, from brigadier to major general. Later in the same month he was assigned to command the Confederate forces in the Shenandoah Valley. Although the troops he commanded were few in number, on the very first day of the new year, January 1, 1862, Jackson marched northward from Winchester toward the Potomac. Undaunted by bitter cold, snow, hail and sleet storms that turned the mountain roads into sheets of ice, Jackson led his men onward. By his orders the railway and telegraph lines were destroyed for many miles, effectively cutting all direct communications between Maryland and West Virginia. Then the column turned west to seize the town of Romney, which was hurriedly evacuated by the Union garrison upon his approach.

It had been a very short campaign, lasting only ten days, but an important section of the country had been recovered from the enemy and large quantities of military supplies and equipment captured. Then Jackson left the town of Romney to be garrisoned by Brigadier General W. W. Loring's division and returned to Winchester with the Stonewall Brigade.

Shortly after his return to Winchester, General Jackson received an order from the Confederate Secretary of War, Judah P. Benjamin, directing him to recall Loring's division from Romney. The men of that division were unhappy with their new assignment. Their officers had complained to friends in Richmond, and General Loring had forwarded a letter to Mr. Benjamin expressing their unhappiness. It need hardly be said that, by sending this letter of complaint, Loring not only effectively demonstrated that his officers and men were poorly trained and disciplined, but at the same time proved his unfitness to command them.

Yet the reaction of the Secretary of War when he received the complaint was just the opposite of what should have been expected from a responsible Secretary of War. Without any reference to General Joseph E. Johnston, who was the commander of all the forces in northern Virginia, an order was sent to Jackson to recall Loring's division. Like a good soldier, Jackson promptly complied, although the order completely nullified almost everything that had been gained by his extraordinarily difficult winter campaign.

General Johnston did not learn what had happened until he received Jackson's letter of resignation addressed to the Secretary of War. Jackson's letter was clear, direct and explicit. The order to recall Loring had been complied with, but with such interference in his command, Jackson wrote that he could not be expected to be of much service in the field; his resignation was respectfully submitted.

War, to Jackson, was a serious business. It could not be conducted in such a way that a commander's orders in the field could be countermanded whenever somebody was unhappy. Any responsible officer knew that action of this sort, catering to the whims of subordinates, would not only ruin discipline, but destroy morale and produce an army full of chaos. Fortunately for the South, through the efforts principally of Governor John Letcher of Virginia, Secretary Benjamin was made to see the error of his ways in this instance, although the military damage was done. Romney could not be recovered. General Loring was subsequently transferred to another command, his division broken up and dispersed to other districts. About a month later, before active campaigning began, Benjamin became Secretary of State and George W. Randolph succeeded him as Secretary of War.

Thus when March, 1862, arrived, Jackson's name was well known to the Confederate authorities in Richmond. The people of the South had heard of him as a general who, among others, had served with distinction at Manassas. Some of the generals up North had known him personally as a cadet at West Point or as a junior officer in the Mexican War. They undoubtedly remembered him as a very determined, serious young man, soft-spoken, studious and precise. They may also have recalled that he was deeply religious, seldom smiled, and did not make friends easily. However there was no way for them to judge, as yet, how good Jackson might be as a general, for they had never known him in that capacity. To the people of the North his name meant little or nothing.

At this time, when he was making his plans to take his large army to the Peninsula, General Jackson's West Point classmate, McClellan, certainly could not have given Jackson much more than a passing thought. He surely knew that Jackson's little command in the Shenandoah Valley was very small indeed. McClellan's mind was fully occupied, to the exclusion of everything else, with making preparations for his grand move to the Peninsula. He certainly felt confident that there were more than enough Northern troops available to chase Jackson out of the Shenandoah Valley. In fact, as far as McClellan was concerned, this little problem was, for all practical purposes, already resolved. Late in February Union troops had crossed the Potomac and seized Harpers Ferry. On March 12 the leading division of General Nathaniel P. Banks' corps of 23,000 men had occupied Winchester. Jackson, who had far too few soldiers to oppose this advance, had been forced to withdraw the evening before, southward up the Valley.

General McClellan can hardly be blamed for his optimism. It was thoroughly reasonable to suppose that Banks would pursue Jackson until he had cleared the Valley. Then, according to McClellan's plan, Banks was to move east with one of his two divisions to guard the Washington area. The other division was to remain in the Shenandoah region until the railroad was repaired. After that work had been completed, only one brigade was to be left to guard the Valley. In his computations of the number of troops remaining behind to defend the capital,

McClellan had counted on the great majority of Banks' troops being available for that purpose. He had every reason to expect that Banks' entire corps, less only one brigade, would arrive soon at Manassas to help guard the city of Washington from attack.

The fame of Stonewall Jackson's name rests to a considerable degree on his famous Valley campaign, one of the most remarkable in world history. It certainly deserves inclusion in any list of outstanding military achievements of history. In its entirety it lasted almost exactly three months, from the middle of March to mid-June, 1862. Some students of the Civil War have portrayed the Valley campaign as covering only the latter half of this period, but those who do so are taking into account only the period when General Robert E. Lee was involved. Perhaps they are too ardent admirers of General Lee, but in stressing his part, they fail to give Stonewall Jackson the great credit that he, and he alone, deserves. In fact, Jackson's operations in the first half of the campaign pointed the way for the strategy undertaken in the second half.

To understand the development of this most famous campaign, it is necessary first to picture Jackson early in March at Winchester in command of a little army composed of only 4,200 men (3,600 infantry and artillery, plus 600 cavalry). This was an extremely small drop in the bucket when compared with the great numbers comprising the Northern hosts and small even by comparison with the outnumbered Confederate forces. Furthermore, Jackson's little detachment was stationed in an extremely exposed position near the northern end of the Shenandoah Valley, far from any hope of support by friendly forces and out at the end of a long supply line. It may be safely assumed that the average general left in such a position would have thought that he was more than adequately performing his duty just by staying there until a larger force drove him away. Certainly the average general would have begun to contemplate retreat as soon as the Northern forces crossed the Potomac and seized Harpers Ferry. Then when he received word that the

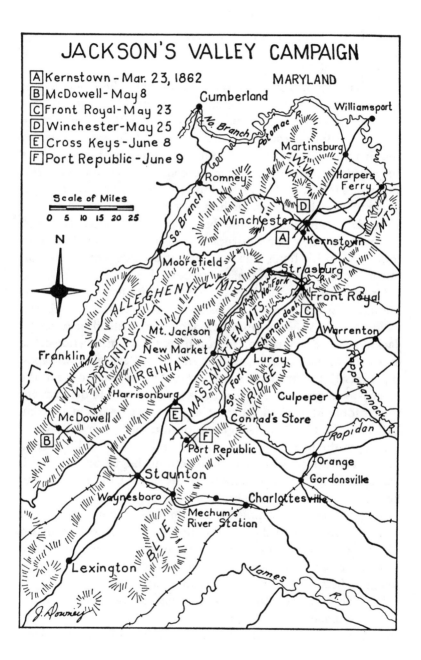

JACKSON'S VALLEY CAMPAIGN

- [A] Kernstown - Mar. 23, 1862
- [B] McDowell - May 8
- [C] Front Royal - May 23
- [D] Winchester - May 25
- [E] Cross Keys - June 8
- [F] Port Republic - June 9

MARYLAND

Scale of Miles
0 5 10 15 20 25

N

Cumberland
Williamsport
No. Branch
Potomac R.
Martinsburg
Romney
Harpers Ferry
W.VA.
VA.
[D]
Winchester
[A]
Kernstown
Moorefield
Strasburg
Front Royal
So. Branch
ALLEGHENY MTS.
MASSANUTTEN MTS.
No. Fork
Shenandoah R.
Warrenton
W. VIRGINIA
VIRGINIA
Mt. Jackson
New Market
Luray
BLUE RIDGE
So. Fork
Rappahannock
Franklin
Harrisonburg
Culpeper
[E]
Conrad's Store
McDowell
Rapidan R.
[B]
[F]
Port Republic
Orange
Staunton
Gordonsville
Waynesboro
Charlottesville
Mechum's River Station
BLUE
Lexington
James R.

J. Downey

other Confederate troops on his flank were retreating, or were about to retreat, his first thought would assuredly have been to start his own withdrawal.

Yet as soon as Jackson received word that the Confederates adjacent to him were moving back, he wrote a letter to his commander, Joseph E. Johnston, proposing that those very troops be sent to him instead. This letter reached Johnston on the day that his army was evacuating Manassas. The very idea of such a suggestion at this time must have come to Johnston as a real surprise. Here was General Jackson isolated in an advanced position at Winchester, the farthest outpost of the Confederacy in Virginia, suggesting that he be reinforced so that he could threaten the enemy and disrupt the Northern battle plans. Furthermore, in his letter Jackson did not divulge what he had in mind. He only hinted at benefits to be derived.

Great credit is due here to General Johnston. Reinforcements could not possibly be spared when Johnston himself was facing greatly superior numbers. However, instead of ordering Jackson also to join him, Johnston sent him instructions: "to endeavor to employ the invaders in the Valley, without exposing himself to the danger of defeat, by keeping so near the enemy as to prevent him making any considerable detachment to reinforce McClellan, but not so near that he might be compelled to fight." Thus General Johnston, although fully occupied with the problems of the troops under his own direct command, saw the possibility that something might be done with Jackson's small force, perhaps to divert other Union troops and keep them occupied elsewhere, not helping McClellan.

Johnston could not possibly have guessed what Jackson had in mind, but he had the good sense not to demand lengthy explanations of Jackson's plans. There was only the caution not to place his army in such a position that he might be compelled to fight a battle, against his will, against superior numbers.

No one will ever know exactly what Jackson had in mind when he made his initial proposal that reinforcements be sent to him, nor for how long he had been formulating his plans.

Jackson did not survive the war and, even if he had, probably would not have written his memoirs or become engaged in postwar controversies. It would have been contrary to his nature to do so, just as now he did not discuss his thoughts, ideas or hopes with his subordinates. Closemouthed at all times, he usually left his officers in the dark to surmise what his battle plans might be, until they were revealed in his orders or in battle action that suddenly occurred.

When reinforcements were not sent to him and the Union troops advanced, Jackson was forced to evacuate Winchester on the evening of March 11. On the next day the town was occupied by General James Shields, commanding Banks' leading division. The loss of Winchester was a disheartening blow to Jackson's men, but there was little they could do to prevent it. One might think that the retreat up the Valley and the loss of Winchester would have discouraged Jackson. It seems almost certain that a lesser general would then have done what his Northern opponents expected. For within a few days the Union cavalry reported that Jackson had gone. Never doubting this information, General Banks, feeling certain that his mission of chasing Jackson out of the Valley had been accomplished, started one of his divisions marching eastward, in accordance with his instructions.

In fact, Jackson had not left the Valley, although he had retreated a great distance, forty-five miles, as far as Mount Jackson, possibly in the hope of luring Banks into following him or, as happened, deluding his opponents into believing that he had gone. As soon as he learned that Banks was moving eastward, Jackson advanced. On March 23, 1862, he struck the Union forces near Kernstown, just south of Winchester. For once, his cavalry failed him. The enemy had been reported as consisting of only four regiments of infantry with guns and cavalry, but, as the battle developed, the Confederates discovered that they were outnumbered two to one. Shields' whole division had been left in place. The result was a Confederate repulse, a tactical defeat.

That evening Jackson has been quoted as saying that he was "satisfied" with the Battle of Kernstown. His attack had been repulsed. Surely this was not very *satisfactory*, even though his little army had been heavily outnumbered in the battle.

It is impossible to know exactly, and completely, what any person has in his mind at any given moment by quoting his words. When Stonewall Jackson said that he was "satisfied" with what had happened at Kernstown, one cannot help but wonder how much he foresaw, how much was hope, or how much was sheer genius that could penetrate the "fog of war" into the minds of his enemies.

Since General McClellan had been relieved from command of all the armies of the North, Jackson's principal enemy was Secretary of War Edwin M. Stanton. It cannot be asserted that, at this early stage in the proceedings, General Jackson was well enough acquainted with Mr. Stanton's peculiarities to have predicted what the latter's reaction might be when the Battle of Kernstown was reported to him. On the other hand, Jackson did know that he was dealing with amateur soldiers, not only in the person of Secretary Stanton but also General Banks and General John C. Frémont, who had just been appointed to command in West Virginia. Both Banks and Frémont were political appointees. President Lincoln, burdened with all the affairs of all branches of the government, had no one in the War Department capable of advising him properly. Therefore Jackson's three most senior opponents in the campaign were to be the trio of Stanton, Banks, and Frémont.

To return to the Battle of Kernstown, when Jackson attacked Shields at that point, he certainly had good reason to expect that Banks would be forced to return to the Valley. If so, Banks would be prevented from reinforcing the defenses of Washington and thereby releasing other Union troops for service with McClellan in the Peninsula. Thus Jackson would be complying with his instructions: "to endeavor to employ the invaders in the Valley . . . by keeping so near the enemy as to prevent him making any considerable detachment to reinforce McClellan. . . ."

Shields at Kernstown could not believe that Jackson would have dared attack unless the Confederates had at least equal numbers. Certainly, in addition, Jackson must also be expecting reinforcements. Shields called for help. Banks hastily returned with two of the three brigades of his other division (the third brigade had already marched too far away to be recalled).

This was only the beginning. The President's War Order No. 3, relieving McClellan from command of all the military departments except the Potomac and simultaneously creating the Mountain Department, which included West Virginia, had been issued on March 11. The new department commander, General Frémont, had not yet taken over his new duties when Jackson launched his attack at Kernstown. However, in the meantime Frémont's political friends had been busily engaged in exerting pressure on Lincoln to give Frémont more troops so that his assignment would appear more important. During this preliminary period prior to McClellan's sailing away for the Peninsula, the President told McClellan that pressure was being exerted on him to send General Blenker's division to Frémont but that he would not take these troops away from McClellan's army.

Then came Kernstown. Blenker's division was pulled away from McClellan's army and sent to join Frémont in West Virginia. There can be no question whatever that Mr. Lincoln did this, after vigorous urging by Stanton, not because of increased political pressure, but as a direct result of the news of Kernstown. This is clearly indicated by the fact that General Banks was authorized to stop the division en route if it was needed by him to fight Jackson.

Two days later the President made the discovery that McClellan had not complied with the Presidential order as to the size of the force to remain in the Washington area for the defense of the city. With their attention drawn to the Shenandoah Valley and with the defense of Washington uppermost in their minds, Secretary Stanton and President Lincoln directed that McDowell's First Corps not embark for the Peninsula but be held back to protect the capital.

Thus in the first act of the drama that was to become known to history as Jackson's Valley Campaign the Confederate attack at Kernstown had been repulsed. It was the only battle that Jackson ever lost, and it had these astounding results. First, instead of one Union division (later supposed to be reduced to one Union brigade) guarding the Shenandoah Valley, almost all of General Banks' corps was now employed there. It can be recorded that the Northern plan of campaign was exactly reversed by Jackson. Instead of one brigade remaining, only one brigade, with some other troops and attached cavalry, got away.

Of General Banks' force of 23,000 men, 17,000 were retained in the Shenandoah region, and 7,000 of these were kept there as a result of Jackson's vigorous, aggressive action which had led everyone on the Northern side to overestimate vastly his strength. Mr. Stanton, for example, would never have believed that Jackson had only 4,200 men. The Battle of Kernstown had also been the deciding factor in the decision to take Blenker's division (10,000 more men) from McClellan and dispatch it posthaste to West Virginia. And, for the moment, McDowell's First Corps (38,500 men) had been held in the Washington area. Directly, or indirectly, Jackson's little 4,200-man battle had the extraordinary result of changing the marching orders, radically altering the troop dispositions, or temporarily immobilizing 55,500 of his opponents.

Following the battle, although he was strongly urged to take vigorous action, Banks' pursuit after Kernstown was hardly worthy of the name. He feared that Jackson had been strongly reinforced. His Union cavalry was unable to obtain information for him since they were no match for the superb Confederate cavalrymen who guarded Jackson's lines. Two days after the battle Banks reached Strasburg, where he halted for a week, then moved forward a day's march to Woodstock, where he stayed in place for two more weeks.

It is difficult to attach a specific date to the beginning of the second half of the Valley campaign, nor is it completely essential to do so. There are certain factors, however, that were different. More troops were involved; more battles were fought; the stage was the entire Valley not just the northern (lower) end. Stonewall Jackson was still the executive officer in charge of all operations. However, with Joseph E. Johnston on the Peninsula, General Robert E. Lee, who had been appointed military adviser to President Jefferson Davis, supervised the planning from Richmond. It was the beginning of that great, unbeatable Lee-Jackson combination.

Stanton, Banks and Frémont would be just the first of many to learn that they were no match for this combination. It is hardly to be wondered at that a lawyer and two politicians would find themselves unable to defeat such men, thoroughly trained in their profession, who were to prove not only skillful, but also geniuses in the art of war.

Finally, on April 17, General Banks again moved south. To date, operations had been confined almost exclusively to the lower (northern) section of the Valley, but this advance now threatened, for the first time, the central and upper portions.

Lying between the Blue Ridge Mountains on the east and the Allegheny Mountains on the west, the Shenandoah Valley is an extremely fertile region. Although it averages only forty miles in width, it was the most productive area in Virginia, both for cattle and for grain, and thus of extreme importance to the Confederacy.

Due to the fact that it ran in a southwest-northeast direction, the Valley did not afford a favorable route of invasion for a Northern army because it diverged away from, rather than toward, Richmond and led to no other objective of military importance. On the other hand, it offered a very favorable invasion route for the South to strike into the region above Washington and east of Baltimore. Thus occupation of the Shenandoah area by the North not only would materially reduce the flow of a tremendous quantity of food supplies to the Southern armies, but also would effectively block the most likely means of approach for Southern troops to move into Northern territory.

The geography of the Shenandoah region is of supreme importance to an understanding of the second half of the campaign that was to follow. Along the western side, the Allegheny Mountains offer only a very few points where large bodies of troops can be moved into or out of the Valley. Along the eastern side, the Blue Ridge Mountains contain a number of passes, or gaps, where armies can cross, although the majority of these can be easily defended by a small force against a much more numerous enemy.

The Shenandoah River, which drains the region, flows from southwest to northeast. For the first two-thirds of its course the river is divided into two forks. The North Fork was by far the better-known route and contained the famous Valley Turnpike, the best road in the area, which was macadamized throughout a large part of its length. The North and South forks join just north of the town of Front Royal; from thence the river flows to the Potomac, meeting it at Harpers Ferry.

The upper and lower sections of the Valley contain no outstanding geographic features of any great magnitude, but in the central part there rises between the two forks of the Shenandoah a great high ridge of mountains called the Massanuttens. Except for a few woodsmen's trails and one good east-west road, the Massanutten Mountains were heavily forested, filled with steep ravines and sharp ridges. They presented an almost impenetrable wall fifty miles long, stretching from near Harrisonburg at the southern end northward to Strasburg and Front Royal. At both ends, the Massanuttens fall off precipitously. The only good road across was that leading from New Market in the wider valley of the North Fork eastward to Luray.

When General Banks moved south on April 17, he did so with more confidence than he had ordinarily displayed in the past. Perhaps by this time he had begun to obtain an inkling of how few troops Jackson really had. The Union forces seized New Market and advanced a large detachment over the vital road crossing the Massanuttens to Luray. Troops were also sent forward to Harrisonburg, which Banks occupied in force a few days later.

Thus threatened, Jackson made a forced march eastward to Conrad's Store, where, by means of Swift Run Gap, one of the better passes in the Blue Ridge, he was in communication with General Lee in Richmond, with General Johnston, and with a division commanded by Major General Richard S. Ewell, which Johnston had left on the upper Rappahannock in the event that Jackson might need help in combating Banks.

General Ewell was directed to join Jackson. Their joint command was now in a splendid position to attack the left flank of Banks' troops if the latter made a further move south toward Staunton.

However, from the Confederate point of view, this was only a partial solution to one of three problems. The second was that McDowell's large corps was at last on the march toward Richmond. If it reached there and joined forces with McClellan, it seemed almost impossible that the Confederates would be able to save their capital from capture. In fact, some of McDowell's troops had, by this date, reached Fredericksburg, the halfway point, and were just awaiting orders to cross the river and capture the place, which was held by only a very few Confederate soldiers.

The third problem was a threat from the west, where General Frémont was approaching Staunton, guarded by only 2,800 men commanded by Brigadier General Edward Johnson. Frémont was reported to have a strength of 15,000 men available to attack Staunton, although they were strung out for many miles along the road, with Blenker's division still passing Winchester en route to Moorefield.

Lee and Johnston had arranged to send Ewell's Division to aid Jackson, and Lee now made some suggestions as to how

Jackson might use his two divisions. But the decision was left entirely to Jackson's discretion as to how he should deal with the various threats.

Lee was hopeful that a diversionary operation would stop McDowell from joining McClellan at Richmond. However, it is extremely doubtful that Lee expected such a dynamic, brilliant campaign as actually followed.

First, leaving Ewell to guard Conrad's Store and Swift Run Gap, prepared to attack Banks if the latter should march toward Staunton, Jackson took the road to Port Republic. Telling no one where he planned to go, extremely secretive as always, he then doubled back eastward over the Blue Ridge as if going to Richmond. His troops thought he was leaving the Valley, where most of their families lived, and were sickened at the prospect. However, when reaching Mechum's River Station, there were railroad cars which moved not east toward Richmond, but westward back to Staunton. Overjoyed, the troops pressed forward, joined the command of Edward Johnson, and met the advanced forces at Frémont's command at the Battle of McDowell. The date was May 8, 1862, and marks the first of the five battles of the second half of the famous Valley campaign. The Union troops, though outnumbered, bravely attacked the superior Confederate forces and did not withdraw until after nightfall. On the next day Jackson followed, but the enemy had set the woods on fire, delaying his pursuit.

The retreating forces were soon met by Frémont with Blenker's division and other troops. Perhaps Frémont should have then come back to try odds again with Jackson. An aggressive, knowledgeable leader might well have done so, but Frémont made no such effort, and therein lies the importance of the Battle of McDowell. Frémont with 15,000 men was put out of action for more than two weeks. Jackson was now free to attack Banks.

It seems strange that the significance of the Battle of McDowell was completely lost on the federal authorities in Washington, as it has been on a number of reputable historians since then, on both sides, after the war. This is possibly because of the comparatively small numbers of troops involved: 2,500 Union soldiers, with some 250 casualties, against 6,000 Confederates, with 500 casualties. But when 6,000 Confederates with only 500 casualties can completely put 15,000 soldiers out of action for more than two weeks, while they turn to strike at other enemies, the action can by no stretch of the imagination be called insignificant.

Obviously Mr. Stanton thought it was a minor affair. On May 1 he ordered Banks to withdraw to Strasburg and to send Shields' division to Fredericksburg to join McDowell's corps. It would appear that he no longer considered Jackson a threat, although all common sense should have led to the opposite conclusion after the engagement at McDowell. With Frémont out of the picture and Ewell now with Jackson, also strengthened by the soldiers of Edward Johnson who had fought at McDowell, Banks was in far greater danger than ever before.

On May 12 Banks moved back to Strasburg, also occupying Front Royal with a reinforced regiment, while Shields departed with his division for Fredericksburg. During this period, while awaiting Jackson's return from McDowell, General "Dick" Ewell, at Conrad's Store, was placed in an extremely perplexing, confusing situation. He was receiving contradictory orders from Jackson, from Joseph E. Johnston, his army commander, and from General Lee, the President's military adviser, each based on different information received at different times at the various headquarters concerned.

Although Ewell had, at one time or another, called Jackson "crazy" because of some of Jackson's idiosyncracies, Dick Ewell was an excellent soldier and could see very clearly that Jackson's plan offered the greatest possibilities for crushing their common enemy, Banks. Yet Ewell could not disobey his other orders. "Old Baldy," as his men affectionately styled him, immediately rode to confer with Jackson. This was on May 18.

[53]

The two decided to go ahead with their attack plans to defeat Banks, driving him to the Potomac, hoping that their marching orders, which they promptly issued, would be confirmed at the last moment. They could not afford to lose their great opportunity. Confirmation of their hopes, plans and orders finally came on May 20. Three days later their attack burst upon the Union position at Front Royal.

Sometimes fortune smiles on the intelligent, the daring, and the brave. Shields' division had reached Fredericksburg on May 22. McDowell was under orders to march toward Richmond on May 26. Then on May 23 Jackson struck at Front Royal. The timing of the attack, as it had been at Kernstown, was fantastically perfect. And Jackson had used to full advantage the peculiar characteristics of the Massanutten Mountains. With Brigadier General Richard Taylor's Louisiana brigade of Ewell's troops in the lead, then his own division, followed by Edward Johnson's troops, which after his wounding at McDowell had been absorbed into Ewell's Division, Jackson had marched along the west side of the Massanuttens, then turned east at New Market. Again none of his troops knew his destination until they reached Luray, where they were joined by the remainder of Ewell's Division. There the column turned and marched north to Front Royal, to burst suddenly upon the little command there, who resisted bravely and stubbornly but were completely overwhelmed, losing 900 killed, wounded, captured, and missing. The Confederate loss was fewer than 50 casualties.

For this assault Jackson had assembled an overwhelming force. He had his division of 6,000 men. Ewell's had been increased to 10,000 with the addition of Johnson's former command, and there were also some 1,600 cavalry and artillery, a total of about 17,600 troops. This may seem like a tremendous concentration to overwhelm one reinforced regiment, but Jackson's real target was Banks at Strasburg.

Yet Banks at first refused to believe it was more than a raid. When urged to retreat, he made the classic retort: "By God, sir,

I will not retreat! We have more to fear, sir, from the opinions of our friends than the bayonets of our enemies!"

Nevertheless Banks did retreat and made a useless stand on May 25 at Winchester. With about 7,500 men left after the disaster at Front Royal, Banks had small chance against the combined forces of Ewell and Jackson. By midnight Banks was hurrying back across the Potomac, his losses totaling more than 2,000 more, or well in excess of 3,000 casualties for the battles of May 23-25. Jackson and Ewell's losses for the same period came to only 400 men.

On May 24 and 25 there was great excitement in Washington, not so much on the part of President Lincoln, who was, as usual, cool and level-headed; but certainly Stanton was panic-stricken. His actions were reminiscent of the oft-repeated stories of his staring frantically out the windows of his office expecting to see the Confederate ironclad *Merrimack* steaming up the Potomac River after the news of its sinking of the *Cumberland* and the *Congress* had reached him. On that day Stanton had sent excited telegrams to the major port cities on the eastern coast predicting complete disaster.

It is likewise easy to picture Stanton's excitement when the news of Jackson advancing to the Potomac reached his desk. Again startling, panic-stricken telegrams poured forth to the governors of the Northern states. Although the panic was short-lived, it was extreme.

In this emergency President Lincoln and Secretary Stanton evolved a plan, which was entirely unworkable, to try to capture Jackson's little army. McDowell, with 41,000 troops near Fredericksburg, with another brigade in support near Manassas, was ordered to send 20,000 men to the Shenandoah to try to capture Jackson and Ewell. Both McClellan and McDowell objected; McDowell called the decision a "crushing blow" and said bluntly that the scheme would not work. Both generals knew that the forces available to Frémont and to Banks should be adequate to cause Jackson's return to the Valley. But, though protesting, McDowell immediately sent back Shields' division, then Ord's division (recently assigned), and later King's division. This decision completely stopped for the second time McDowell's march to join McClellan.

Simultaneously, as McDowell was ordered to try to cut Jackson off at Front Royal, Frémont was ordered to Harrisonburg for the same purpose. For various reasons Frémont moved instead toward Strasburg. It may be suspected that Frémont, having once crossed swords with Jackson, was not too eager to go to Harrisonburg, where he would be facing Jackson alone, but preferred to march to Strasburg, where he would be closer to Shields and to Banks. Banks was also slow to return to come to grips with the Confederates. For, except for a garrison which had been hastily assembled at Harpers Ferry, he himself had just been forced to flee ignominiously across the Potomac. Only Shields and Ord appear to have moved with any speed to try to intercept the Confederates.

Thus Jackson's army, which with Ewell's Division and attached cavalry and artillery could never have amounted to more than 17,600 men, was occupying the attention of Banks' field army, the garrison under his command at Harpers Ferry, Frémont, with 15,000 more, and more than 20,000 (later 30,000) of McDowell's. At the same time Jackson and Ewell were temporarily immobilizing McDowell's fourth division of 11,000 more. Truly a magnificent achievement—a total of from 60,000 to 70,000 Union troops held immovable or vainly chasing some 17,600 Confederates around the country with little or no chance of capturing them.

When Jackson learned that Shields had reached Front Royal, he made all haste to return from his excursion to the Potomac. Although Shields had only eleven or twelve miles to go to close the trap at Strasburg and Jackson's main body had twice that distance to cover, while the rear guard had to march four times that far, Jackson had the better Valley Turnpike on which to march. And it was not for nothing that his men had earned the proud title of "foot cavalry." Furthermore, neither Shields nor Frémont was in direct communication with each other, and both were naturally cautious in their approach toward their common enemy, whom they had learned to treat with the greatest respect.

Plans of this sort, as concocted by Mr. Lincoln and Mr. Stanton, which look so promising on paper, seldom succeed when put to the test against a master of the art of war. With the stalwart Dick Ewell holding off Frémont's approach from the west, all the Confederate column passed through Strasburg with comparative ease, escaping with most of their prisoners and large quantities of captured supplies, particularly guns, ammunition and badly needed medical equipment.

In Lincoln's favor, one thing should, however, be said. If he had not tried to capture Jackson but had permitted McDowell to join McClellan, he still would have had no assurance whatever that McClellan would use these troops for their intended purpose upon arrival. With his increased strength McClellan might still have done nothing but ask for more reinforcements. Whereas, if a Grant or a Sherman had been in command on the Peninsula, President Lincoln could have let McDowell proceed, knowing that upon arrival his corps would go into action. If such had been the case, the futile effort to try to capture Jackson in the Valley might never have been attempted.

Turning back to the Valley, did Frémont or Shields ever catch up to Jackson? The answer is yes, but only when he chose to wait for them and offer battle on his own terms. He could have escaped from the Valley with little difficulty and thus have avoided further conflict with his enemies, who greatly outnumbered him. But to do so while there was still the possibility of inflicting damage on his pursuers was not Stonewall's way.

The Union forces pursued southward in two columns, Frémont west of the Massanuttens along the Valley Turnpike, Shields on the road following up the South Fork of the Shenandoah, east of the Massanuttens. First, Jackson, in his retreat, destroyed the bridges north of Port Republic on the South Fork to make it difficult for the two columns, already separated by the Massanutten Mountains, to act effectively together. Heavy rains had caused the waters to rise, so it was impossible to construct temporary bridges quickly. Thus the two Union columns advanced with little or no coordination or knowledge of each other's movements. Then Jackson sent a detachment to hold the bridge at Port Republic for his own use.

Frémont's pursuit was energetically conducted but tempered with a proper sense of caution, knowing that he was facing such an aggressive, energetic opponent. However Shields, to the eastward, somehow gained the impression that Jackson was fleeing, almost panic-stricken. Although his corps commander, McDowell, had specifically cautioned him on the fifth of June to have all his force "well in hand, with the parts in supporting distance of each other," Shields in his eagerness to catch his enemy stretched his command out over twenty-five miles of road. The head of his column as it approached Port Republic offered a tempting target.

On June 8 Frémont, advancing from Harrisonburg toward Port Republic, found his way barred by General Ewell at Cross Keys. Although Frémont strongly outnumbered Ewell's Division, he was uncertain of the whereabouts of General Shields and the other Union column and was afraid that he might be facing all of Jackson's army. As a result his attack was delivered timidly, in a halfhearted manner. "Old Bald Head" and his men firmly repulsed the attack.

On the following day, June 9, the Battle of Port Republic was fought. There were only two Union brigades on the field commanded by Brigadier General Erastus B. Tyler. They were isolated far in advance of the remainder of Shields' division. Jackson's plan was to overwhelm these two brigades quickly, then turn to fall upon Frémont with his entire force. The plan was well conceived, but at Port Republic the Confederates met such extremely stiff resistance and a strong counterattack that, although Ewell and a large part of his division were brought into the fray, for several hours the issue was in doubt. Finally the two heavily outnumbered Union brigades were forced to retreat almost to Conrad's Store, where they were met by Shields with the remainder of his command.

The remarkably stubborn resistance of General Tyler prevented Jackson from carrying out his plan of turning against Frémont. However, the twin battles of Cross Keys and Port Republic for the third time prevented McDowell from moving against Richmond. There was only one division (McCall's) still in position at Fredericksburg able to move to McClellan's assistance. The remainder were scattered from Warrenton westward to the Valley, beyond hope of early recall. McCall's division actually did join and took a prominent part in the Seven Days' Battle, but it was the only division to do so.

Following the battles of Cross Keys and Port Republic, both Frémont and Shields retreated. Jackson moved to Richmond to take part in the Seven Days', but none of the major units that had fought against him in the Valley reached the Peninsula in time to fight with McClellan in that battle. Shields' division was found to be in such poor condition that it was broken up. A part of it was indeed sent to McClellan. It arrived after the battle was over and took part in some minor skirmishing that followed. On June 26, the day that Mechanicsville, the first large battle of the Seven Days', was being fought, the troops of Frémont, Banks and McDowell were consolidated into a new army to be called the Army of Virginia and placed under the command of Major General John Pope. Although the order announcing the consolidation certainly did not say so, it was for all practical purposes a public admission that these troops would not be able to go to McClellan's aid in the near future.

It hardly seems necessary to summarize the Valley campaign. The facts speak all too clearly for themselves. Jackson, with a little army varying in size from 4,200 men to a maximum strength of 17,600 men, had for a period of three months, from the middle of March to the middle of June, 1862, occupied the attention of many thousands more of his opponents, baffling and bewildering them at every step.

The qualities of a commander possessed by Stonewall Jackson are rare, so rare indeed that those in American history who have possessed them could be counted on a person's fingers. Only once in his entire career did he appear to falter and that was at the beginning of the Seven Days' Battle. Because he was so superb on every other occasion historians have undertaken hundreds of hours of research and written thousands of words on the subject to try to explain why. It would seem that a quick review of Jackson's activities on the days immediately preceding provide a simple ready answer. Like everyone else, in the long run, Jackson too was human—and the answer must be, and can be no other than, sheer exhaustion.

Second Manassas and the Antietam campaign both will be discussed later, but since Chancellorsville will not, a remark concerning the planning of that battle should not be out of place. Just as the biographers of General Lee are inclined to emphasize the second half of the Valley campaign, to the detriment of the first half, whenever the question arises as to which of the two, Jackson or Lee, suggested the bold, daring envelopment of the Union right flank at Chancellorsville, one can hardly blame Lee's biographers for claiming the credit.

Either Lee or Jackson could have suggested it, but Jackson had been the first to arrive on the scene. He was better acquainted with the ground and the tactical situation. It seems more logical that it was Jackson rather than Lee who proposed the startling plan and then further elaborated on it, explaining to his superior that he planned to take his entire corps. This uniquely daring scheme was then approved by General Lee. Because of Jackson's being wounded and then dying of pneumonia, no other similar bold maneuvers were again attempted by General Lee. The reasons why are best expressed in Lee's own words: "Such an executive officer the sun never shone on. I have but to show him my design, and I know that if it can be done it will be done. No need for me to send or watch him. Straight as the needle to the pole he advances to the execution of my purpose."

Thomas J. Jackson

Some writers have compared Stonewall Jackson to Oliver Cromwell. In military genius the two are comparable. Both were deeply religious; both have been called religious fanatics. However, unlike the Lord Protector, Jackson never attempted to force his religious beliefs on another. His was a simple trust in an all-wise Providence. When told that he was dying, he simply said, "Very good, very good; it is all right."

3

Robert E. Lee

WHEN General Robert E. Lee assumed command of the Confederate army near Richmond, it was a great moment in American history, but it is safe to say that very few people, if any, recognized the significance of the occasion. It was June 1, 1862, the second day of the Battle of Seven Pines. On the first day, General Joseph E. Johnston had been severely wounded. President Jefferson Davis had then appointed Lee, who at the time was serving as the President's chief military adviser.

When General Lee decided to draw his sword in defense of Virginia, he brought with him a military reputation second only to that of the venerable Lieutenant General Winfield Scott, then Commanding General of the United States Army, who had led the Army in its victorious campaign to capture Mexico City in 1847.

Robert Edward Lee was born at Stratford, Westmoreland County, Virginia, on January 19, 1807. At the age of three his family had moved to Alexandria, Virginia, where he had lived until he was eighteen, when he entered the United States Military Academy at West Point. Four years later, on July 1, Lee was graduated number two in the class of 1829. From that time forward his career had been uniformly successful with two outstanding highlights.

In the Mexican War he had served as a captain of engineers on General Scott's staff. In this capacity he had performed some extraordinary exploits. At Cerro Gordo he made a daring reconnaissance around the enemy left flank, almost getting captured in the process. Then he had guided the American troops around the enemy position to put them and their artillery in position to make the assault which had resulted in an American victory and opened the way to a continued advance against Mexico City. Upon reaching the approaches to the Mexican capital and in the attack upon its fortifications, Captain Lee had performed similar outstanding services with equal success. For his conduct at Cerro Gordo, at Chapultepec, where he had been wounded, and at Churubusco, Lee received three brevet promotions and the highest possible praise from General Scott, who considered him "the very best soldier that I ever saw in the field."

Five years later Lee became superintendent of the United States Military Academy at West Point, a position of responsibility of quite a different nature but which he performed in a superior fashion for a period lasting two and one-half years.

Shortly before the outbreak of the Civil War, Colonel Lee was asked to call on General Scott at his office in Washington. Although neither officer ever revealed what was said at this meeting, it is probable that Scott, realizing that at the age of seventy-five he was too infirm to lead troops into battle, unofficially offered the command of the Army to Lee. Later, after the firing on Fort Sumter, Lee was again invited to Washington. There he was informed by Francis P. Blair, Sr., that President Lincoln and Secretary of War Simon Cameron wanted to know if Lee would accept the command. This offer was respectfully declined because, as Lee explained, "though opposed to secession and deprecating war, I could take no part in an invasion of the Southern States."

However, when Virginia passed an ordinance of secession, a decision was forced upon him. With a heavy heart, Lee tendered his resignation from the United States Army because his first duty must be to Virginia. Therefore, when Governor John Letcher asked him to come to Richmond, Lee promptly obeyed. It is indicative of his fame and popularity that, while on this trip, crowds of citizens met his train and insisted on his coming out to greet them.

Upon arrival in Richmond, Lee was commissioned as commander of the military and naval forces of Virginia with the rank of major general. For the next seven weeks, until the state forces were transferred to the Confederacy, Lee was responsible for the mobilization and defense of Virginia, a sort of thankless task for which he received little public credit and no acclaim.

During this period he was also commissioned a brigadier general in the regular army of the Confederacy, the highest rank then existing in that new army. After the Confederate victory at the First Battle of Manassas he was commissioned a full general, then was assigned the almost hopeless task of trying to save what had not already been lost in West Virginia. From this unsuccessful and thankless duty he emerged with his public reputation damaged and the far from complimentary nickname Granny Lee.

It is small wonder therefore that when he assumed command of the army near Richmond, his first orders when read to the troops were received with something less than enthusiasm. Nor did he gain any popularity when he set the troops to digging trenches and other fortifications to protect Richmond. The American soldier has never been noted in any era for his ability or eagerness to perform manual labor. It is only when shells begin to fall around him and he has learned from bitter experience that his life may depend on how rapidly and how well he may dig a trench for himself, that he will prepare fortifications with any degree of enthusiasm.

The Southern soldiers in front of Richmond were no exception. Battle experience had not yet taught them that trenches would save their lives. So their new general acquired another uncomplimentary name—"The King of Spades."

Simultaneously Lee undertook to persuade President Jefferson Davis to consent to bring troops from Georgia and the Carolinas to increase the strength of the Confederate army at

Richmond. General Johnston had advocated the same course of action with no success, but the President agreed readily enough when Lee suggested it be done. With the addition of these troops, plus Jackson's army from the Valley, when Lee launched his attack on McClellan, which resulted in the Battle of the Seven Days, he had a larger army than Johnston had commanded, although it was still outnumbered by McClellan's Union Army of the Potomac.

When the attack was launched, but not until then, did the Confederate soldiers who had grumbled at the digging understand why all that work had been done. General Lee had simply applied the fundamental military principle of constructing fortifications so that he could hold the line defending Richmond with a minimum number of troops. Thus he was able to mass a greater number against the flank of McClellan's army. There had been nothing particularly brilliant about his plan. McClellan's right flank, with one corps isolated north of the Chickahominy River, had been the obvious target. But it had taken courage of the sort that McClellan lacked, willingness to attack a larger army with a smaller one. Also Lee displayed an insight into the mind of his opponent. There was the chance that McClellan might have thrust straight against Richmond, despite the fortifications erected in his path, while Lee was engaged north of the Chickahominy. But Lee had read his opponent correctly in the last few months of campaigning and had based his plans on the assumption that McClellan would not do the obvious. All Lee had to do to keep his enemy from even thinking along such a line of endeavor was to make a few demonstrations near Richmond while the main battle was fought elsewhere.

The Seven Days' Battle had relieved the pressure on Richmond, but by far the most important result of the action was its effect on the Confederate army, which Lee had christened the Army of Northern Virginia. The soldiers had no way of knowing that in the next three years they would make that name famous in the annals of history.

However, they did know, and could keenly appreciate, the obvious fact that, although outnumbered, they had continuously maintained the offensive, driving their better-equipped, more numerous opponents away from Richmond. In one month after taking command, General Lee had relieved the Confederate capital from the pressure of a siege; the besieged had become the victors. Furthermore, although their losses had been severe and greater than those of the enemy, the Confederate army had captured fifty-two guns and more than thirty thousand small arms while driving their enemy for more than fifteen miles, from battlefield to battlefield, from Mechanicsville to Malvern Hill. When the commander of an army gives his men so obvious a victory as the Seven Days' had been, their confidence in his ability as a leader and their eagerness to follow him on to the next venture can hardly be expressed in words.

There were perhaps a few men who were not surprised at the turn events had taken so quickly. One of these was certainly Winfield Scott, who had thought so highly of Lee for so many years. Another was certainly Jefferson Davis, who, despite the poor record of the West Virginia campaign, had retained confidence in Lee's abilities. Davis had subsequently appointed him as his chief military adviser and then had chosen him to command the army when General Johnston had been wounded.

Although the Southern people and the army may have been satisfied by the results of the Seven Days' Battle, General Lee certainly was not. How could he not be satisfied with such a victory? Simply because he had the vision to see what the average Southerner did not. The population of the North was about 22,500,000. The Southern people numbered only 9,000,000, but 3,500,000 of these were colored and the South did not employ colored troops. Thus the odds were apparently about four to one in favor of the North. In actual fact, however, the odds were about three to one because there was a very large peace party in the North which actively opposed the war.

Facing three to one odds, General Lee, as a trained soldier, knew that he could not afford just to win battles. He must win them so decisively that in every instance a large portion of the enemy army was destroyed in the process. Furthermore, he must do this as soon as possible before the Northern naval blockade became effective and the far greater industrial potential of the North made the odds even worse than three to one. It is a well-known fact, proven time and again in history, that a smaller nation with a limited industry must, if it is to defeat a larger nation with much greater industrial potential, win the war in a hurry—or the smaller nation will surely lose, so long as the larger one is willing to keep on fighting.

This meant just one of two things. The smaller nation, the South, must win so many battles, each so destructive of enemy manpower and combat ability, that the South would appear to have the capability of actually defeating the North, and with this would come foreign intervention. The other alternative would be to make the task of conquest appear so long and difficult that the larger nation, the North in this case, would decide that the war was too costly and settle for a peace.

Of these two alternatives, Lee, in July, 1862, naturally preferred the first choice. However, battles like the Seven Days', wherein the South lost more manpower than the North, simply would not do. It may be noted here that his first battle was the only instance throughout the war when Lee was on the field in command of the army that Southern losses were greater than Northern in a major battle.

General Lee was also well aware of the fact that his chances of destroying the entire Union army in a pitched battle were slim indeed, when that army heavily outnumbered his own. He might well be able to defeat that army on a battlefield and possibly could do so again and again, but complete and utter victory resulting in destruction would probably never occur. Throughout his long and varied career, Robert E. Lee had come to know too many good Northern officers for whom he had genuine respect, and he also was thoroughly acquainted with the excellent fighting qualities of the Union soldier.

Southern politicians and orators might talk at great length about the poor quality of Northerners when compared to Southern fighting men, but Lee was not one to be misled. Furthermore, by this time the soldiers on both sides were veterans and such troops are not inclined to retreat or to surrender if there is any chance of holding their ground. Lee knew full well how stubborn and persistent trained Union soldiers could be, even when defeat was staring them in the face.

The South could never win in a slugging match, even if Confederate losses were always smaller than Union losses. The South could not win in a series of pitched battles with one army pitted against the other, even though again and again Confederate losses were less than Union losses, because the stronger Northern army would probably not be destroyed but would simply return to fight another day. The South must win by maneuver and strategy, with the Confederates falling upon large portions of the Union army when they might be separated from their comrades. If this could be arranged, decisive battles could be fought and won. If one or more large portions of the Union forces could be effectively destroyed, then perhaps the two armies could finally meet on equal terms.

After the Seven Days' Battle was over, McClellan remained at Harrison's Landing. The presence of the Union Army of the Potomac constituted a threat, but as long as McClellan remained in command, it was safe to assume that nothing would be done. If, however, another commander were appointed, one who might be more eager to fight, then Lee would have to pay more attention to the Union army.

Lee withdrew his army nearer Richmond, where he could conveniently rest, refit and reorganize it for further action. He left only a brigade of cavalry in position to observe McClellan. It would be difficult to find in military history a greater or more justly deserved insult than this gesture toward the commander of a powerful enemy army.

Now while the Confederates had been making preparations

for the Battle of the Seven Days, President Abraham Lincoln had come to realize that the system of trying to coordinate, from the office of the Secretary of War, the operations of Frémont, Banks and McDowell had ingloriously failed. It was apparent that Mr. Stanton was not the proper man to attempt the coordination of several armies in the field. Therefore, when the Army of Virginia was created by Presidential order on June 26, Major General John Pope was appointed commander. To it were assigned the troops commanded by Frémont, Banks, and McDowell. All three of these generals were senior to Pope, but only one objected. Frémont resigned in a huff; Major General Franz Sigel was appointed to succeed him.

President Lincoln's choice of John Pope to command the new Army of Virginia was logical enough in view of that officer's record of successes in the Western theater. Pope had been in command of the troops that had forced the evacuation of New Madrid, Missouri, in March, 1862, then in April had captured Island No. 10 in Tennessee. The seizure of these two Confederate strongholds on the Mississippi River had marked the first great step taken by the North toward obtaining control of the Mississippi and dividing the Confederacy in two. Furthermore, while in command of the land forces attacking Island No. 10, General Pope had exercised unusual ingenuity, vigor and initiative. The transports required to move his troops across the river could not pass the Confederate guns. To enable them to join him, a navigable canal had been cut by his engineers through the flooded swampland above the island. The work, performed under cold, wet, miserable conditions, had taken nineteen days, but then four riverboats were moved safely through this remarkable bypass. With the aid of two gunboats, which could pass the Confederate batteries, General Pope then crossed the river, seized his objective, and captured nearly 7,000 of the Confederate defenders.

There was, however, one element of Pope's personality which Lincoln could not have known or foreseen. Less than three weeks after assuming command, Pope wrote an address to his new army which must have caused the President to shudder. In part, it read:

> Let us understand each other. I have come to you from the West, where we have always seen the backs of our enemies; from an army whose business it has been to seek the adversary and to beat him when he was found; whose policy has been attack and not defense. In but one instance has the enemy been able to place our Western armies in defensive attitude. I presume that I have been called here to pursue the same system and to lead you against the enemy. It is my purpose to do so, and that speedily. I am sure you long for an opportunity to win the distinction you are capable of achieving. That opportunity I shall endeavor to give you. Meantime I desire you to dismiss from your minds certain phrases, which I am sorry to find so much in vogue amongst you. I hear constantly of "taking strong positions and holding them," of "lines of retreat," and "bases of supplies." Let us discard such ideas. The strongest position a soldier should desire to occupy is one from which he can most easily advance against the enemy. Let us study the probable lines of retreat of our opponents, and leave our own to take care of themselves.

In view of what was soon to happen in the coming campaign, the last sentence quoted appears rather remarkable, for one month later he was, very wisely, retreating to save his army—and his greatest mistake was in not continuing that retreat.

General Pope has been severely criticized for many years by numerous writers for issuing this extraordinary address comparing the fighting qualities of Eastern and Western soldiers. It was in terribly poor taste, and the principal result was to arouse a feeling of hot resentment on the part of the troops composing his new command. At this point, most historians also mention Pope's announcement that his headquarters would be in the saddle. This proclamation, designed to indicate that he would wage an aggressive campaign, was immediately seized upon by the Confederates, who were quick to note that most people put their "hindquarters" in the saddle.

Although his pronouncements were ill-advised, in all fairness it should be noted that on the very day following the issuance of this address he received a dispatch from a brigadier general at Winchester. It described an "engagement" in which a regiment had retreated after the loss of two men wounded and four missing. Pope's caustic reply was thoroughly justified:

> Your dispatch received. A regiment of infantry in such a country is more than a match for a dozen regiments of cavalry, and ought never to retreat before them. Neither do I quite understand your calling an affair in which 2 men were wounded a "sharp engagement." I hope you will infuse a much bolder spirit in your men. The idea of retreating before a cavalry force with only 2 men wounded is hardly up to the standard of soldiership. In such a country no cavalry force is able to make your infantry give back a foot if they will only fight. How is it known that these cavalry columns are supported by infantry; who saw the infantry, and, if there were any, were they not dismounted cavalry? Please investigate the matter thoroughly. I do not like the idea of an infantry regiment of this army retreating without more loss and better reasons than are set forth in your dispatch.

This approach, applied where needed, singling out for censure those officers and units who were not doing their duty, would have been much more appropriate than a general condemnation of his entire new command. For there were, in that new Army of Virginia, many excellent officers and several fine units who resented their new general's announcement yet, despite it, would prove their worth in the campaign which had already begun.

On July 11 President Lincoln had called another officer from the West, Major General Henry W. Halleck, to whom he assigned what turned out to be a rather anomalous position, partly as commander of the land forces of the United States and partly military adviser. Pending his arrival, the President had retained Pope in Washington to advise on military matters. While awaiting Halleck's arrival, Pope had been trying to concentrate his army, which he had found scattered from the Valley all the way east to Fredericksburg, with some troops under his jurisdiction even located many miles away in the mountains of West Virginia.

By early July the majority of Pope's army had been moved out of the Valley to east of the Blue Ridge. Thus it occupied a central location in northern Virginia in the vicinity of Warrenton, and to the south and west of that town. There was one exception. A division of his army was still left at Fredericksburg. He wanted to move it also to the Warrenton area in order that his troops would be more thoroughly concentrated, but the authorities would not permit him to do so. Too many wharves, depots and warehouses had been built at Aquia Creek to risk their being captured by the Confederacy.

Nevertheless in mid-July General Pope moved forward and occupied Culpeper. He planned to advance farther, but his cavalry was slow to move and General Lee forestalled him by sending Stonewall Jackson with his own and Ewell's division to stop the Union advance.

On July 22 Halleck arrived in Washington and took over his new duties as general-in-chief on the following day. He then left Washington to confer with McClellan on the Peninsula. The principal purpose of his visit was to decide whether the Army of the Potomac should advance on Richmond from Harrison's Landing or, if not, to form some plan of uniting the armies of McClellan and Pope at some other point. McClellan of course told Halleck that the enemy was 200,000 strong and that he had only 90,000 men, but with 30,000 more he could attack Richmond with a good chance of success. Naturally this reasoning made no sense to Halleck, for, if Lee really had 200,000 men, how could McClellan hope to take Richmond with only 30,000 added to his 90,000? In any event Halleck could not promise more than 20,000. Therefore orders were issued, over McClellan's protest, withdrawing the army from the Peninsula.

In addition to McClellan's reported 90,000 men at Harrison's Landing, the other Union forces in the field consisted of Pope's army with an effective strength of some 47,000 (including the division still at Fredericksburg) and a force of about 14,000 men near Fortress Monroe commanded by General Ambrose E. Burnside. The latter had been brought from the Carolinas with the intention of reinforcing McClellan, but Halleck now decided that Burnside should be sent to Fredericksburg, releasing the division at that point to join Pope.

To oppose this aggregrate of more than 150,000 men, Lee had only 70,000 effectives, which included two brigades en route to Richmond from South Carolina. It would seem that, until McClellan moved away from the Richmond area, there was little the Confederates could do except remain near Richmond to guard the capital against an advance on the part of McClellan and his 90,000 men.

If General Lee had accepted this strategy, there could have been little criticism aimed at him, for he would have been adopting the careful, studied, cautious way of making war. Then, once McClellan had departed, Lee would be free to move against Pope, hoping to attack him before he and McClellan joined forces. Thus the Confederates would be taking advantage of their central position in between the two Union armies, and Lee would probably have been praised by historians for proper use of his interior lines. He would have been commended for continuing to ensure the safety of the Confederate capital until the threat posed by McClellan had dissolved. Then his advance against Pope, which would surely have caused the latter to retreat, would also have been cited as a fine example of good sound strategy.

However, as General Lee undoubtedly reasoned, if he waited too long, the probabilities of catching Pope's army would be very slim indeed. The net result would be nothing more than a stern chase, the regaining of some Virginia territory, praise in the newspapers for doing so, but no decisive battle, no destruction of Pope's army. For a sound, cautious, careful general, the regaining of territory could well have seemed an adequate goal. It would have put the Union armies right back where they had started from in March, 1862, four months before. But such an achievement would have been totally unsatisfactory. Lee's goal was the annihilation of Pope and his army—immediately—before they could join forces with McClellan. Here were Pope and McClellan widely separated. Destruction of Pope's army would cut down the size of the forces facing him by about one-third, a consummation devoutly to be wished. Annihilation of Pope's army would then make Lee's and McClellan's forces more nearly the same size so they could meet on equal terms. Almost any risk would be worth achieving that result.

The vast majority of historians and students have completely failed to grasp Robert E. Lee's instincts as a general. Anyone having any knowledge whatsoever of General Lee immediately thinks of him as the symbol of a truly noble Christian gentleman, calm and serene of purpose, possessed of infinite tact and patience. In the history of the United States of America there have been only two officers, George Washington and Robert E. Lee, who inspired such great trust and devotion in the troops under their command that their men willingly undertook and almost blindly accepted ordeals that, in retrospect, seem impossible for human beings ever to have attempted.

Yet Washington succeeded in leading his army to victory in the Revolutionary War, while Lee was defeated, although he was the better general. Lee's battles and campaigns have been studied again and again by military men, students, historians and armchair strategists with admiration and acclaim, but all too often without full understanding, and the reasons are not far to seek. It is difficult to erase the mental image created by his portraits and the word descriptions of his nobility of character in order to invoke the daring forty-year-old captain of engineers of the Mexican War, alone, far behind the enemy lines, hiding behind a log on which the Mexicans sat and talked, just inches above him. Then the very next day, un-shaken by his narrow escape, Lee was out again pushing his re-connaissance still farther behind the enemy lines.

To understand Lee's generalship, picture this same captain carrying vital dispatches across miles of torn lava in a drench-ing rainstorm, his way lighted only by intermittent flashes of lightning in the night. This was the Lee whom General Scott knew and admired. This is the Lee whom the student should see, a daring, resourceful man who would take remarkable chances to win this war. Furthermore, the risks that he would run would not be heedless but calculated, fortified with knowl-edge. For Lee, like Jackson, was a student of the great Napo-leon. Small wonder that Lee recognized in Jackson a kindred spirit, determined to win no matter what the odds.

So long as Jackson was alive, there was never any doubt in Lee's mind to whom he should entrust the most daring ven-tures. With Jackson, he could plan and undertake campaigns that scholars in later years would universally and categorically decree were far too risky to have been attempted, despite the fact that they were almost universally successful.

Would a daring, resourceful general, a student of Napoleon, have been content to wait for McClellan to leave Richmond be-fore moving to attack Pope's army? The question hardly needs an answer, for to Lee, as to Jackson, heavy Northern odds called for extreme measures. Lee must grasp any chance that presented itself.

Jackson, with only two small divisions, was facing Pope. Send him another division; Jackson would know what to do with it. The result was the Confederate victory of Cedar Mountain, Au-gust 9, 1862, where Jackson defeated one of Pope's corps com-manded by his old Valley opponent, General Banks. This was a good start, but Jackson still had only 24,000 men with whom to combat Pope's Army of Virginia.

Lee's decision would have been difficult for a lesser man to reach. Although McClellan might soon depart the Richmond area, there was no assurance that he would do so immediately with all his army. Robert E. Lee turned his back on the main Union army, ignoring that threat, leaving Richmond only lightly guarded, and marched away to join Jackson. When Lee joined Jackson, their combined forces numbered 54,000 men. In the meantime Pope's division from Fredericksburg had finally been returned to him. Thus Pope's troops were fairly well concentrated north of the Rapidan. The odds were about five to four. If Lee could strike, now was the time. He issued orders for an attack on Pope's left flank. His plan could have resulted in a decisive battle and the elimination of Pope from the campaign. That the Union forces escaped destruction was due partially to a premonition of danger on Pope's part, plus an element of chance that worked greatly in his favor. A small Union cavalry unit almost captured Jeb Stuart. They did get his cloak and the famous plumed hat, interesting but unimportant trophies of war. However, of great value was the capture of letters giving information of Lee's battle plans. With these to warn him, Pope escaped in time and retreated across the Rappahannock, placing that river between himself and his enemy.

After this narrow escape, John Pope should have continued his retreat toward Washington instead of halting behind the Rappahannock. One may assume that he was disinclined to retreat too far too fast, especially after telling his army that he had come from the West, where they had always seen the backs of their enemies. Yet discretion in this instance would have been the better part of valor. Reinforcements from McClellan's army were being rushed to him. Some were en route from the Fredericksburg area, having been landed at Aquia Creek. But the great majority were being brought by water to Alexandria, from which point they were being hurried to his aid. If Pope had continued his retreat to a point where his and McClellan's troops could have united, their combined armies would have greatly outnumbered the Confederates.

At this point General Lee's prime concern had been that Pope might not stop at the Rappahannock, but when he did so, Lee felt he had been given another opportunity, although it was growing less attractive with the passage of every fleeting day. There Stuart again entered the picture. On a raid into the rear of the Union lines his men made off with General Pope's uniform coat, hat and military cloak. This campaign seems to have contributed to a great amount of swapping of uniforms, but again the papers captured were of far greater value, for they included Pope's dispatch book and numerous letters. From these it was learned how rapidly reinforcements from McClellan's army were coming and that Pope's army would soon far outnumber the Confederates. Even troops from as far away as West Virginia had been ordered to join. Already Pope's numbers equaled Lee's; in two days he would have 70,000 and soon thereafter more than 100,000 men.

No time was to be lost. The opportunity of completely destroying Pope's Army of Virginia was probably gone forever, but there was still the chance of at least engaging it in battle and defeating it before it became too strong for the Confederates to attack at all. Lee's approach to the problems presented in this campaign illustrate one of his greatest characteristics as a general—flexibility. He was perfectly willing to change or alter his plans and ideas in order to accomplish a second, though less desirable, objective, in other words seek a different kind of victory, even though it would not be the smashing one he had originally intended. In order to attain this lesser objective General Lee calmly, in the face of the enemy, did an amazing thing. He took the enormous risk of dividing his army into two parts, sending Jackson with Stuart's cavalry, almost half the army, on a long march way beyond the Union right flank, then around to strike the railroad deep in Pope's rear.

To separate his army thus into two totally distinct parts, each completely unable to support or even communicate with the other, was a perilous violation of the principles of war. By doing so, General Lee could be sure of only one thing—that Pope would retreat. But would he then turn and destroy first Jackson, then Lee? Even if Lee were to escape, the annihilation of Jackson's 24,000 men would mean the end of the Confederacy. Furthermore, although completely out of contact with each other, both Lee and Jackson would have to coordinate and direct their movements so as to force Pope into a battle under circumstances favorable to the Confederacy, no matter what the Union forces might do.

But Lee had already taken Jackson's measure and had complete confidence in him. If he had not, Lee would never have taken the chance that he did in this campaign. Acting separately, each was to be guided in everything by his own discretion. From the morning of Jackson's departure on August 25 until Lee joined him on August 29 each had complete control of his own movements, yet so much were their actions in accord that, when the battle was fought, the plan had worked to perfection. Pope was brought to bay and forced to fight their combined forces.

One cannot help but marvel at Lee's ability to judge both his subordinates and his opponents. In very short order he seemed to know just how much he could risk against McClellan, against Pope, or any other of the generals who faced him. He never took the hazardous chances against Grant that he took with the others. And, on very short acquaintance with Jackson, he knew that this was the one man to whom he dared confide such a hazardous operation. Though his other generals were loyal and valiant, Lee recognized, as Jackson's great biographer Colonel G. F. R. Henderson wrote, ". . . in possessing one such general he [was] more fortunate than Napoleon."

Jackson started on his famous march as dawn was breaking on the morning of August 25. Lee followed on the afternoon of the next day with General James Longstreet's troops, leaving one division in place under Major General Richard H. Anderson to continue to attract the enemy's attention toward the Rappahannock crossings. By evening of August 26 Jackson's men had seized Bristoe Station and in the hours of darkness had gone forward to capture Manassas with its immense quantity of supplies stored for the use of the Union army.

On August 27 General Pope began moving to intercept

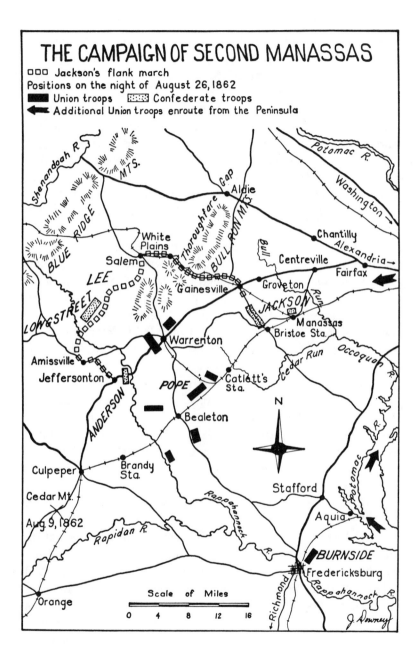

THE CAMPAIGN OF SECOND MANASSAS

□□□ Jackson's flank march
Positions on the night of August 26, 1862
■■■ Union troops ▦▦▦ Confederate troops
◀ Additional Union troops enroute from the Peninsula

Shenandoah R.
MTS.
Potomac R.
Washington
BLUE RIDGE
Thoroughfare Gap
Aldie
Chantilly
Alexandria →
White Plains
BULL RUN MTS.
Bull Run
Centreville
Fairfax
Salem
LEE
Gainesville
Groveton
LONGSTREET
JACKSON
Manassas
Bristoe Sta.
Warrenton
Occoquan R.
Amissville
Cedar Run
Jeffersonton
ANDERSON
POPE
Catlett's Sta.
N
Bealeton
Culpeper
Brandy Sta.
Stafford
Potomac R.
Cedar Mt.
Aug. 9, 1862
Rappahannock R.
Aquia
Rapidan R.
BURNSIDE
Fredericksburg
Orange
Scale of Miles
0   4   8   12   16
Richmond
Rappahannock R.
J. Downey

Jackson's command. His initial dispositions were excellent, but then he became confused by Jackson's movements. Some of Pope's troops were sent to Manassas, others to Centreville, where some Confederates had been seen, while simultaneously Jackson moved to a position near Groveton. Union troops marching and countermarching grew weary as Pope hunted in vain for Jackson and his men. Finally in the early evening of August 28 Jackson revealed his position to attack a Union division passing in front of him on the turnpike through Groveton. His action produced the desired effect of precipitating the Second Battle of Manassas, which was fought the next two days, August 29 and 30.

The battle resulted in a decisive Confederate victory, for, by the twenty-ninth, Lee and Longstreet were also on the scene; even Anderson's Division reached the field by August 30. Lee's army of 54,000 was thus fully employed, while Pope only used some 63,000 of his force of more than 70,000 men. Union casualties totaled about 14,000; Confederate casualties were fewer than 10,000 and the victors captured thirty guns and thousands of small arms.

It was not, however, as destructive a battle as Lee had hoped for back on the banks of the Rapidan when he had planned to annihilate his enemy. By the time the armies had reached Manassas too many reinforcements had been brought to Pope's aid. Lee would have to try again to create a situation wherein he could effect the destruction of some large portion of the Union army.

With this hope in mind he undertook his first invasion of the North.

Second Manassas had been a fine victory, worth celebrating; the enemy had been forced back into the Defenses of Washington; but the issue must be pushed further. Fortunately McClellan was back in command of the Union forces; this was good news for the South. People talk about Gettysburg in July, 1863, as being "the high-water mark of the Confederacy." It is a beautiful, dramatic phrase but it is not accurate. In the late summer of 1862, the Southern armies were on the march in both the Eastern and Western theaters. In mid-August General Kirby Smith had moved north and by the end of the month had won a victory in Kentucky. General Braxton Bragg was also on his way into Kentucky. In the first days of September, Lee's army crossed into Maryland. Concurrently, a small force invaded western Virginia and captured Charleston, which was someday to become the capital of the state of West Virginia. This month, September, 1862, was the true high tide, the real high-water mark of the Confederacy when its armies were advancing victoriously in both the East and the West.

When he invaded the North for the first time, Lee's army numbered, at the start, about 55,000 men. His troops were in the best possible state of morale after their recent victory, but as Lee wrote to Davis: "The army is not properly equipped for an invasion of the enemy's territory. It lacks much of the material of war, is feeble in transportation, the animals being much reduced, and the men are poorly provided with clothes, and in thousands of instances, are destitute of shoes." We read of all sorts of objectives, all sorts of things that various writers have claimed that Lee intended to do. For example, it has been said that, if successful in Maryland, he would destroy the Baltimore and Ohio Railroad, then push into Pennsylvania and destroy the Pennsylvania Railroad. He could then turn his attention to Philadelphia, Baltimore and Washington.

His marching orders might give these destinations as directional guides, but they were not his true objectives. The Union troops in and around Washington, even after their defeat at Second Manassas, far outnumbered Lee's, and there were several thousand more Union troops elsewhere. Furthermore, the Defenses of Washington were extremely strong. The Confederates could not have afforded to settle down to a siege. And Lee was certainly not going to get his army involved in an attempt to capture a large city. What was he trying to accomplish? He had high hopes that he would find recruits in Maryland, but he also had his eyes set on foreign intervention. A successful campaign in the North would be far more impressive to a foreign power than simply defeating another invasion of Virginia, which the Union army would surely try again if the Confederates just sat still after Second Manassas.

From a military point of view, the word "invasion" is, strictly speaking, a misnomer. It implies coming to conquer, or at least to seize and hold certain parts of the enemy territory, and this was the farthest thought from Lee's mind. On the other hand, to call it a raid is also a misnomer because that implies a hit-and-run affair. Actually Lee was looking for a fight on his own terms, hoping that an opportunity might present itself whereby he might catch a part of the Union army off by itself. Perhaps another situation would arise wherein he could maneuver and get between parts of the Union army as he had partially gotten between Pope and McClellan. Knowing the caution of McClellan, there was a good chance that one, two, or possibly three corps would be cut off and destroyed. That great cavalryman Jeb Stuart was with him to keep him well posted at all times on the movements of the Union troops in a far more efficient way than his opponent would be served by his cavalry. This time he might be successful. Certainly he was *not* initially after the whole Union army. Later it would be his target when it was reduced in size.

The campaign started out beautifully from Lee's point of view. When the Confederate Army of Northern Virginia crossed the Potomac and advanced to Frederick, Maryland, it had been assumed that the Union garrisons at Martinsburg and Harpers Ferry would be evacuated. McClellan had wanted to abandon the posts, but Halleck would not permit him to do so. Here was a perfect target, a large garrison at Harpers Ferry held in place in an absolutely indefensible position, just waiting to be captured. This was the sort of thing that Lee had hoped to find in Maryland. Also, the removal of this garrison would enable the army to use the natural supply route of the Shenandoah Valley. The capture of several thousand Union soldiers would make an excellent beginning for the campaign.

Then the Confederate army could go on from there to bigger and better goals.

The order was issued to divide the army into four parts. Stonewall Jackson was sent with three divisions westward, to circle around from that direction. General Lafayette McLaws with two divisions was ordered to the Maryland side, while General J. G. Walker was to go to the Virginia side, thus encircling Harpers Ferry from all directions. The rest of the army was to march westward across South Mountain in the direction of Boonsboro and Hagerstown.

The plan was executed to perfection. Stonewall Jackson herded the garrison of Martinsburg into the trap at Harpers Ferry. A total of more than 12,500 Union soliders, nearly one-fourth the size of Lee's entire army, surrendered to the Confederacy on September 15, 1862.

This division of his army into four parts, in the face of the enemy, has always seemed a bit incredible to most students of the war. To have done so when facing a vigorous, aggressive opponent would have been the height of folly, but the opposing general's name was George B. McClellan. If Lee could divide his army in front of Pope into two parts, why not divide it in front of McClellan into four parts? Both Lee and Jackson considered it a safe thing to do, and it would have been, if a copy of Lee's orders had not fallen into the enemy's hands.

Lee's order for the march had been issued September 9, 1862, to take effect early the following day. This order turned out to be probably the most important order ever written in the annals of American military history. For shortly after noon on September 13 a copy of Lee's Special Orders No. 191 containing all the details of his plans was delivered to McClellan. It had been found in an abandoned Confederate campsite wrapped around three cigars, and there was no doubt that it was a genuine document. Was ever a general handed such a piece of good fortune?

Yet even then McClellan was slow to act. Lee's army should have been, at the very least, hustled back across the river in an

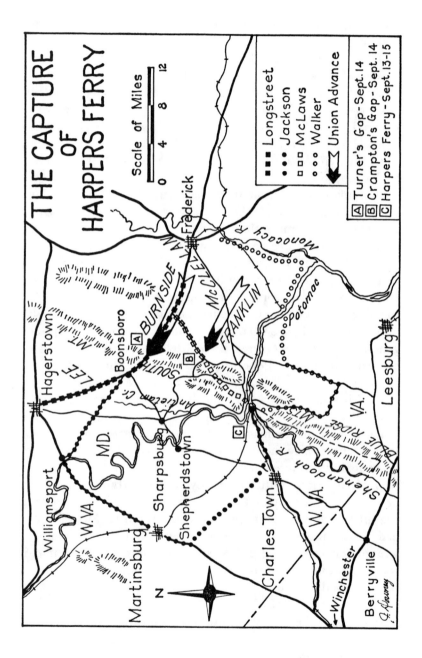

THE CAPTURE OF HARPERS FERRY

Scale of Miles

0   4   8   12

Legend:
- ▪▪▪ Longstreet
- ••• Jackson
- □□□ McLaws
- ∘∘∘ Walker
- ◁ Union Advance

Ⓐ Turner's Gap - Sept. 14
Ⓑ Crampton's Gap - Sept. 14
Ⓒ Harpers Ferry - Sept. 13-15

Frederick

Monocacy R.

Potomac

BURNSIDE

McCLELLAN

FRANKLIN

Hagerstown

Boonsboro

Ⓐ

Ⓑ

SOUTH MT.

LEE

Antietam Cr.

MD.

Williamsport

W. VA.

Sharpsburg

Shepherdstown

Ⓒ

Shenandoah R.

BLUE RIDGE MT.

VA.

Leesburg

Martinsburg

Charles Town

W. VA.

Winchester

Berryville

N

J. Downy

undignified way. If Lee had been in command of the Union Army of the Potomac, the war would have ended right there. After obtaining possession of the all-important order, McClellan waited sixteen hours before getting his men on the move. He should have marched that very night, but even then he surprised Lee by moving faster than he usually did, until the latter learned of the loss of Special Orders No. 191.

Then Lee hurried men back to South Mountain and started Longstreet back from Hagerstown. As a result there was a brisk fight at Turner's Gap and another at Crampton's Gap before McClellan's columns broke through the passes of South Mountain. Lee then did the only thing he could do; he retreated toward Sharpsburg intending to recross the Potomac, for he had only 19,000 men against McClellan's more than 70,000 men with 20,000 more available.

When he reached that town, a message came from Stonewall Jackson that Harpers Ferry had been captured with almost its entire garrison. Immediately Lee turned the army about to form line of battle at Antietam Creek. This was September 15, but McClellan following in a leisurely manner did not begin the battle for two more days.

Of course Lee was taking a tremendous risk to stand against such odds, but he knew his army. He knew they would make every effort to reach the battlefield at the fastest possible marching speed. Three Confederate divisions arrived on the sixteenth. Two more came on the morning of the seventeenth; they arrived exhausted after an all-night march, were allowed one hour's rest, then flung into battle. The last division, commanded by Major General A. P. Hill, had been left to arrange for the surrender of Harpers Ferry. But even these men arrived in time, marching furiously to fall upon the Union flank at the crucial moment and drive it back to Antietam Creek.

Lee's army had marched and fought as magnificently as he knew it would, and his opposite number, George B. McClellan, had played his role to perfection. Lee knew McClellan was much worse as a general than John Pope when it came to directing a battle. At Antietam, as in the Seven Days', McClellan let his division and corps commanders fight by themselves without supervision, while two Union corps took no part in the battle at all. The losses on both sides on this September 17, known as "the bloodiest day of the Civil War," were staggering. The Confederate casualties were about 10,000, one-fourth of those engaged. The Union losses were more than 12,000, again one-fourth of those engaged. Yet the next day General Lee, against the advice of all his officers, stood his ground and dared his opponent to attack, confident that he never would, even with his two fresh corps. Not until the night of September 18 did the Confederates retreat across the river. Lee knew the value of morale. He was determined to prove to the Army of Northern Virginia that it could not, and never would be, driven from any battlefield; and, under Lee's command, it never was.

The Battle of Antietam would never have been fought had it not been for the discovery of the famous "Lost Order." In his report of the campaign Lee gave a very prosaic account of his reasons for capturing Harpers Ferry. It would have been unusual if he had done otherwise when the real object of his campaign had been thwarted; and he could certainly expect to come this way again with high hopes of accomplishing his true purpose, of outmaneuvering his opponent and defeating him in detail.

If it had not been for the finding of the "Lost Order," the campaign into Maryland would have gotten off to a flying start, and there is no telling how it might have ended. With Lee pitted against McClellan it seems almost certain that a Southern victory would have ensued. The Army of the Potomac might then have been whittled down to a size where the Confederate Army of Northern Virginia could have had its decisive victory.

Only two criticisms have ever been successfully leveled at General Lee. First, in the field of grand strategy, he was lacking in one respect. He was inclined to think too much in terms of his beloved state of Virginia and pay too little attention to the battles and campaigns of the war being fought elsewhere.

The second criticism makes a distinction between leadership ability and command ability. He was just a bit too polite and courteous and therefore inclined to issue discretionary or vague orders when clear, peremptory orders were required. In the latter respect he differed widely from his great lieutenant, Stonewall Jackson, who expected and required instant obedience, or his great opponent, Ulysses S. Grant. Both of these officers possessed the maximum in command ability, while Lee was the sublime leader.

At fifty-five years of age, General Lee had proved himself greatly daring, possessed of the supreme audacity required to be the successful leader of a smaller nation if it hopes to defeat a larger. A successful campaign in Maryland in 1862 would have gone down in history as an extraordinary exploit and might have changed the course of the war. We must alter our concept of Robert E. Lee from the sublime, kind, sympathetic, inspiring leader, which he was, to include the greatly daring, bold, unorthodox general, willing to take great risks against superior forces which should have produced the results he sought.

4

James Longstreet

In the Confederate Army of Northern Virginia there was another corps commander whose name appears more often in the records than that of Stonewall Jackson. He is the man whom General Lee fondly referred to as "my war horse." The occasion was the evening of Antietam, "the bloodiest day of the Civil War," when Lee greeted him with: "Here comes my war horse from the field he has done so much to save." The praise was well deserved. James Longstreet's conduct on that battlefield near Sharpsburg, in Maryland, had been magnificent. When, following that bloody day, the army was organized into corps, Longstreet was one of the two major generals promoted, senior to Jackson. He was, in fact, the senior lieutenant general in the entire Confederate Army.

It has been claimed that General Lee was too partial to Virginians. The outstanding exception was James Longstreet, who was born in 1821 in South Carolina but reared in Augusta, Georgia, until he was twelve years old, when his father died and he moved with his mother to north Alabama. Longstreet was graduated in 1842 from the United States Military Academy at West Point, number 54 in a graduating class of 56—2 had died as cadets, and 41 others had failed to graduate.

His first duty assignment was with the 4th Infantry at Jefferson Barracks, St. Louis, Missouri. There he was joined in the following year by a new graduate of West Point named Ulysses

S. Grant, who, in May, 1844, became engaged to Longstreet's cousin, Miss Julia Dent. In describing the events surrounding his courtship of Miss Dent, General Grant wrote in his *Memoirs*: "If the 4th Infantry had remained at Jefferson Barracks it is possible, even probable, that this life might have continued for some years without my finding out that there was anything serious the matter with me. . . ." They were married four years later. There is a persistent rumor that Longstreet was best man at the wedding. Whether this is true or not, it is certainly a fact that Longstreet and Grant were the very best of friends. Their lasting friendship was due to have a profound effect on Longstreet's postwar career.

During the Mexican War, Lieutenant Longstreet served both in General Zachary Taylor's army and with Winfield Scott in his campaign to Mexico City, participated in eight battles, was severely wounded at Chapultepec, and won the brevets of captain and major. Four years after the war he was promoted to captain and in 1858 to major to serve as paymaster and was stationed at Albuquerque, New Mexico.

When war broke out in April, 1861, Longstreet, unlike the great majority of his countrymen, was slow to move, cautious in deciding what to do. He did not arrive in Richmond until late in June and then merely asked for an appointment in the pay department. The South, however, in contrast to the North, where many generals were political appointees with little or no military experience, had the much wiser policy of giving high command only to trained soldiers. This was undoubtedly due primarily to the influence of West Point graduate President Jefferson Davis. As a result Longstreet was given a commission as a brigadier general and ordered to report to Manassas, where he was placed in command of an infantry brigade.

On July 18, three days before the First Battle of Manassas, or Bull Run, it was Longstreet's brigade that was primarily responsible for the repulse of a Union reconnaissance. It was only a small skirmish. The Union commander had orders not to bring on a general engagement, but it elated the Southern forces and had a correspondingly depressing effect on the Northern volunteers. In the battle itself, three days later, Longstreet's brigade took only a minor part.

In October, 1861, Longstreet was promoted to major general. Up to this period he had established a reputation as an individual who enjoyed a good party and being among friends. However one gets the impression that he contributed more by his presence than by his conversation. Many have attributed this to a slight deafness on his part, but a study of his life, his personality, and his generally impassive disposition, even under the most exciting battle conditions, indicates that he would have probably talked very little under any circumstances, whether slightly deaf or not. For he seems to have had a stolid, imperturbable personality that prevented him from responding outwardly to stimuli of any sort. But it was this ability never to appear anxious or worried that would, during the war years, cause his troops to hold steady in battle under the most trying conditions, reassured by his calm demeanor, excited neither by victory nor by defeat.

It has been frequently mentioned by various authors that in these early days Longstreet established quite a reputation as a poker player. It is easy to agree that such would be the case.

In January, 1862, there occurred a terrible personal tragedy that served to accentuate these qualities. Scarlet fever had been raging in Richmond. Summoned by his wife, he found three of his children dead or dying within a week. From that moment forward there was no more poker or parties. No conversationalist in any event, his subordinates now were often treated to nothing more than a rasping "yes" or "no." The business of fighting the war became the sum and substance of his life.

As a division commander in the Peninsular campaign his performance was above average. At the Battle of Williamsburg, he displayed a calm, professional attitude and a cool competence—his soldiers fought well. At Seven Pines the troops under his command again rendered a good account of themselves, but mistakes were made by Longstreet in understanding and executing the orders given him, which resulted in failure of the army plan of battle. However, in his report, Longstreet made it look as if Major General Benjamin Huger had been responsible. Since the facts were not known for many years afterward, Longstreet emerged with an untarnished reputation.

Then came the Seven Days' Battle. Since this was the one battle in his career when Stonewall Jackson appeared to falter (through sheer exhaustion), Longstreet then seemed the more competent because his performance was excellent. The effect was lasting. When the next promotions were made, to lieutenant general, Longstreet's name remained ahead of Jackson's.

After the Peninsular campaign came the great days of the Army of Northern Virginia: Second Manassas, Antietam, Fredericksburg, and Chancellorsville. In each instance, except the last, when Longstreet was away on a separate mission, the operations bear a marked resemblance to each other. The army was divided, for purposes of command, into two parts, with Longstreet commanding the larger, Jackson a somewhat smaller half. Invariably Lee stayed with Longstreet, while Jackson was given the more dangerous, independent assignments. One cannot help but feel that General Lee knew exactly what he was doing and had accurately judged his two subordinates. Jackson was by far the more resourceful and daring of the two, whereas Longstreet was more cautious and careful. He disliked taking chances and wanted to have everything ready and in its place before committing his troops. He knew well how to fight a battle but was less likely to seize an opportunity when it was presented. Lee once said: "Longstreet is a good fighter but he is very slow to move."

In the Battle of Second Manassas, when Longstreet and Lee arrived on August 29, 1862, a prompt attack should have been made. Almost all authorities today agree that the Confederate victory would have been far more decisive if the Southern attack had been launched on the twenty-ninth as Lee wanted to do, instead of waiting until the following day, August 30. The commanding general should not have let himself be dissuaded by Longstreet's worries about his right flank, nor by his asking for more time to reconnoiter. In letting himself be persuaded, Lee perhaps remembered that Longstreet had been right when he had suggested that Jackson should be allowed an extra day to get into position for the opening battle of the Seven Days'. In the first instance Longstreet's advice should have been followed, but at Second Manassas Longstreet's advice should have been rejected.

By the time the invasion of Maryland was undertaken General Lee must certainly have known that Longstreet's voice would always be the voice of caution and deliberation. Unlike Jackson, he never agreed with any of Lee's bold schemes. Lee and Jackson fought an entirely different kind of war than Longstreet. They complemented each other magnificently, whereas Longstreet believed in fighting "by the book." It could have come as no surprise to Lee, in the Antietam campaign, to find Longstreet earnestly objecting to the division of the Confederate army into four parts in front of a much stronger Union army. Longstreet would never willingly sanction such a violation of the rules of war as to divide the army in the face of a superior foe.

When the "Lost Order" was discovered by the enemy and the Confederates found themselves fighting with their backs to the wall against superior numbers, Longstreet felt this was proof positive Lee had been in error when he had discarded the good advice offered him against undertaking such a rash maneuver. To his dying day Longstreet, in common with all "book" tacticians who have studied it since, considered the Antietam campaign badly mismanaged and never understood Lee's objectives.

Yet, the day of battle, Longstreet's performance was superb beyond measure. He commanded the right half of the line, Jackson the left. It would be impossible to say which of the two rendered the more conspicuous service. Both were magnificent. Although suffering from an injured heel so that he had to wear carpet slippers, Longstreet kept ranging up and down his line, riding or limping as best he could. At one point, when a gun section was being furiously cannonaded, his staff helped man the gun while he held the horses and directed the fire. It is small wonder that after this desperate battle General Lee referred to him as "my war horse" who did so much to save the field.

The name "War Horse" became well known through the army, and, in a sense, it appears appropriate if one visualizes a steady, dependable rugged individual who can endure the rigors of battle—rather than a dashing, gallant leader. His troops generally preferred their favorite nickname for him of Old Pete, probably derived from his Dutch ancestry. He had other nicknames too—Bull of the Woods and Bulldog. These names tend to indicate that his veterans were good judges of their commander's character. He held, and never lost, the confidence of his men, who trusted him. Wherever "Old Pete" led, they followed willingly, though not with the blind devotion accorded "Marse Robert." In short, Longstreet's men knew him to be a good general and a hard fighter, who would be difficult to replace if anything were to happen to him.

During the operations following Antietam, preceding the Battle of Fredericksburg, General Lee followed his customary practice of remaining with Longstreet. This custom was to continue, almost as a routine. Some writers have contended, or implied, that this arrangement indicates that Lee leaned heavily on Longstreet for his opinion. This is doubtful, to say the least, for it would be difficult to find two senior generals in the armies of the Confederacy whose concepts of war were so totally different in so many ways.

Nor would it be fair to say that Lee did not trust Longstreet to be left alone. In reality, the practice of Lee's staying with Longstreet can be compared more accurately to General Grant's decision, when he was given command of all the armies of the United States, to go with General George Meade's Army of the Potomac.

In offensive situations, Longstreet lacked the quick insight of

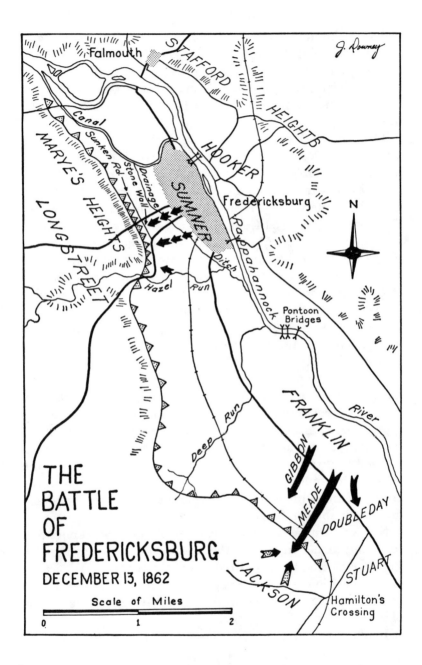

J. Downey

Falmouth

STAFFORD HEIGHTS

HOOKER

Canal

Sunken Rd.

Drainage

Stone Wall

MARYE'S HEIGHTS

LONGSTREET

SUMNER

Fredericksburg

Rappahannock

Ditch

N

Hazel Run

Pontoon Bridges

FRANKLIN

River

Deep Run

GIBBON

MEADE

DOUBLEDAY

THE
BATTLE
OF
FREDERICKSBURG
DECEMBER 13, 1862

JACKSON

STUART

Hamilton's Crossing

Scale of Miles

0   1   2

Jackson, his intuitive genius to probe his opponent's mind, his understanding of the effect that a quick, daring, perhaps unorthodox move might have. In an attack Longstreet was too inclined toward delay in an effort to ensure success, but in a defensive situation Longstreet had scarcely a peer. This had been conclusively demonstrated at Antietam. It was to be proven again at Fredericksburg.

For Longstreet, Fredericksburg was the great, the perfect, battle of the war. The Union losses in killed, wounded, captured and missing totaled more than 12,600 men while the Confederates had some 5,300 casualties, a ratio of well over two to one in favor of the Confederacy.

Whereas at Antietam the issue had often been in doubt, and the possibility, even probability, of defeat had stared the Confederates in the face, Fredericksburg, for Longstreet, was a totally different story. On his half of the line there was never at any moment a question as to the outcome. In the center of his position, where the Union forces made their main assault, the casualties inflicted were appalling. There, with a loss of only 1,450 casualties, Longstreet's men inflicted upon the enemy a loss of more than 7,300 men, a proportion of five to one.

The prelude to the Battle of Fredericksburg is comparatively simple. There was no long involved campaign with the armies maneuvering for position. Antietam had been fought on September 17, 1862, but it was not until the night of September 18 that the Confederates began their retreat. By the next morning the last units were safely across the Potomac. On the following night, the nineteenth, and again on the day of the twentieth, McClellan made a halfhearted attempt to follow but was firmly repulsed. This ended operations for both armies for a period of more than a month.

The latter part of September and the month of October, 1862, were probably one of the most pleasant periods of the whole war for the contending armies in the East. This was fine for the spirits of the men in the ranks, but the people of the North were becoming impatient. McClellan, after a great deal of prodding from the White House, finally began to cross the Potomac on October 26, but he took his time about it, and the last troops were not across until November 2. By November 7 McClellan's army was assembled around Warrenton. Longstreet and Lee were at Culpeper, Jackson was with his corps in the Valley.

On the evening of this date a special messenger from the War Department appeared in McClellan's tent to relieve him of command. Major General Ambrose E. Burnside was appointed in his place. For the last hundred years there has been a great deal of criticism of President Lincoln for this choice, but somebody had to be appointed to relieve McClellan, who had now twice proved himself incapable of bringing the war to a successful conclusion. Lincoln had tried McDowell, then McClellan, then Pope, then McClellan again. Someone else was obviously needed. Burnside was one of the senior corps commanders, and he was the only one, with the Army of the Potomac, who had successfully conducted an independent operation, the seizure of a large part of the coast of North Carolina earlier in the year. Although this had been a simple task, it was felt that Burnside just might be the general the North needed so badly. It is true that Burnside tried to refuse the appointment, saying he did not feel qualified, but how could the President know whether this effort at refusal was a real confession of inadequacy or simple modesty?

Burnside evolved a plan to march straight forward toward Fredericksburg, cross the Rappahannock River, then advance on Richmond. The success of the scheme depended on marching rapidly, crossing the Rappahannock, and seizing the heights behind the city before Lee's army arrived. Since all the bridges crossing the Rappahannock at Fredericksburg, including the railroad bridge, had been destroyed, pontoon bridging equipment was ordered. Burnside did move rapidly, far faster than McClellan had ever moved. When the first Union troops arrived on the scene, there was practically no one to oppose their crossing, but the pontoons had not arrived. The river was fordable at the time, but Burnside would not permit the leading troops to cross, for fear that the water would rise and they would become isolated from the rest of the army. Then, despite the fact that almost all his army reached the scene before the Confederates appeared, he still waited for the pontoons. By the time these reached the area Lee with Longstreet's corps was present to oppose the crossing.

The leading Union troops in this case had been the Right Grand Division commanded by General Edwin V. Sumner. When Burnside assumed command, he had organized his army into three "Grand Divisions," each composed of two corps of three divisions. The Right Grand Division was commanded by Sumner, the Left Grand Division by General William B. Franklin, and the Center Grand Division by General "Fighting Joe" Hooker. It is a peculiar thing that no other Union commander ever organized the Army of the Potomac in such a manner. It was a good idea, for it simplified Burnside's command problems, but the idea did not last.

By December 1 Jackson's corps reached the Fredericksburg area. Both armies were now united on the scene, 120,000 Union troops on the north bank of the Rappahannock facing about 78,000 Confederates. However crossing operations did not begin until the night of December 10, 1862. These were discovered by the Confederates before dawn on the eleventh.

Lee's army was not drawn up along the water's edge. There is an open plain along the south bank, and an army posted there would have been utterly exposed to artillery fire from the hills across the river. Major General Henry J. Hunt, the Union chief of artillery, had concentrated 147 of his 312 guns at Falmouth, and on Stafford Heights opposite Fredericksburg, to dominate the area around the city.

Lee had placed only one brigade in the city itself to delay the crossing. The bulk of the Southern army was drawn up in battle array beyond the range of the Union artillery generally parallel to the river. At the northern end of the line the plain between the river and the plateau was only some 600 yards wide.

In the center it extended to a width of nearly 2 miles, then near the southern end at the right of the Confederate line the plain narrowed again to about a mile in width.

Burnside's orders required Sumner's Right Grand Division to cross on three pontoon bridges at Fredericksburg while Franklin's Left Grand Division was to cross on other pontoon bridges farther downstream. Hooker's Center Grand Division was to hold itself in readiness to support either column.

On the Union left the Confederates were too far from the river to oppose the crossing of Franklin's Grand Division. The bridges there were quickly laid, in spite of the fact that the ice in the river was half an inch thick.

At Fredericksburg, however, the first attempts to construct pontoon bridges were complete failures. No troops had been sent across the river to protect the bridge builders while they worked. Again and again, General William Barksdale's Mississippi brigade posted in the city shot the engineers off their pontoons every time they tried to work. General Sumner made no effort whatever to seize the opposite shore to provide protection. About midmorning the Union artillery started to bombard the city; thousands of shells were fired, doing tremendous damage to the houses but not much harm to the Confederate brigade. As soon as the bridge builders started back to work, the Confederate sharpshooters sprang into action again. Finally infantry was ferried across in the pontoons, whereupon Barksdale retired to the heights beyond. By then it was almost dark. Burnside suspended operations, and the crossing was not completed until the next day, December 12, under cover of a heavy fog. By evening all the Union troops were in position, ready to attack at daybreak.

Late that same afternoon Burnside approved a plan of attack prepared by Franklin proposing that the Union main effort be an assault by the Left Grand Division against Jackson's corps. This was certainly the correct plan, for, if an attack had to be made, that part of the line held by Jackson with four divisions was much harder to defend and therefore much easier for an attacking force to penetrate. There were no natural obstacles other than a slight rise in the ground. The position had been hastily strengthened but was not nearly as formidable as the hills behind Fredericksburg on the Confederate left, where Longstreet's five divisions occupied the ground north of Deep Run, and particularly the steep slope known as Marye's Heights. In front of this position were a wide canal that limited movement to the north and a drainage ditch, which the Union troops attacking Marye's Heights would have to cross. Behind the ditch, at the base of the hill, there was also an old sunken road with an old stone wall just the right height to protect the defending troops while they shot over it.

Early in the morning of December 13 General Burnside changed his mind. Instead of General Franklin launching an attack with his entire Left Grand Division, only a part of it was to be used, while General Sumner was directed to advance against Marye's Heights with a part of his Right Grand Division. Hooker, in command of the Center Grand Division, was directed to put four of his six divisions in position behind Sumner, ready to cross. His other two divisions were to be placed behind Franklin.

Franklin selected General Meade's division to make the prescribed attack, supported by John Gibbon on his right and Abner Doubleday on his left. Meade's division crossed the road about 10:00 A.M. and advanced slowly forward under cover of a dense fog. Suddenly the fog lifted and then occurred the extraordinary exploit of Major John Pelham of Stuart's horse artillery. With only two guns, one of which was soon disabled, he galloped to the Confederate right flank in front of the lines and with one gun halted the entire Union advance. For more than half an hour he and his men fought four Union batteries until their ammunition was almost gone and then galloped back to safety.

The Union artillery then shelled the woods as Meade again advanced, with Gibbon echeloned to his right rear. Doubleday did not move forward again, but remained facing to his left toward the point where Pelham had appeared, to guard against attack from that direction.

Meade's columns kept moving until they were within 800 yards of the Confederate batteries. When these batteries opened fire on the Union troops, the advance was halted for a second time. Then for an hour and a half the Union artillery shelled the Confederate batteries. After that bombardment Meade's lines made their third move forward.

Throughout this period the woods had remained ominously silent. Not a musket shot had been fired. As Meade's lines came closer to the woods, the Confederates held their fire until the enemy was at point-blank range, then opened with a blast of musketry, canister and grape. Meade's men, however, found a gap in a swampy wooded area and pushed straight through, to the complete surprise of the Confederate troops immediately in rear of the position. Some of Jackson's reserves were rushed forward, checked Meade's advance, then drove the Union troops out of the woods. For all practical purposes this ended the battle on Jackson's front. About midafternoon Franklin received a request from Burnside to make another attack, but wisely refrained. Jackson considered a counterattack but found that the Union artillery could inflict too many losses upon his men to make the attempt worthwhile.

On the Union right, the initial attack had been delayed until 11:00 A.M., principally because of the fog. When it lifted and disclosed the streets of Fredericksburg crowded with Union soldiers, the Confederate artillery began to shell the town. Union artillery on Stafford Heights could not engage in counterbattery fire because the range was too great.

The advance had to be made across an open plain about 800 yards wide, cut by a drainage ditch with steep banks. The ditch was 30 feet wide and 6 feet deep. There were only two bridges over this obstacle, and they had been damaged. A large proportion of the Union troops was thus forced to remain in column until across, presenting massed targets to the Confederate artillery. Then beyond the ditch at the foot of the hill was the sunken road with its stone retaining wall.

The slaughter began. First came French's division followed by Winfield Hancock's, charging forward with incredible bravery, straight for the stone wall, brigade after brigade in column, to be met by a withering fire that cut men down by the hundreds. Yet they kept coming while the Confederates reinforced their line at the stone wall until there were four lines firing as fast as they could aim, fire, change places, and reload. Some of Hancock's men actually got within 30 to 40 yards of the wall before they fell.

Next Oliver Howard's division was sent into the charge, over the wounded, dead and dying bodies of its predecessors. It also was hurled back. General Couch's entire Second Corps had now been sacrificed, but then Sturgis' division of the Ninth Corps was ordered forward to meet the same dreadful fate.

General Hooker was ordered to continue the hopeless assault with troops from his Center Grand Division. Under protest, he did so, with two divisions of his Fifth Corps. Finally, as darkness came early on this cold winter day, still another division from the Ninth Corps went forward, again to be cut down in its tracks. In all, seven divisions made a total of fourteen assaults on this utterly impregnable position without any hope of success whatever. It is sometimes difficult to understand how any soldiers survived unhurt, yet Burnside issued orders to renew the attack the next day, and it was only with difficulty that he was persuaded to cancel those orders.

Those who lived through the battle and saw the dreadful slaughter wrought by the Confederates at the foot of Marye's Heights never forgot it. Certainly one who was most impressed by what happened there was James Longstreet, who commanded the defending troops. If he had not already convinced himself that a defensive battle was the only way to fight a stronger enemy, he was now a firm believer. Indeed he now felt that it was the only way the Confederacy could win the war.

From then on it was his continual hope that every great battle might somehow be made to resemble another Fredericksburg.

At first glance, this idea of always fighting on the defensive against a stronger enemy might sound attractive. How the enemy was to be induced to attack was another question. Even if the army were somehow placed in the enemy's rear, across his lines of communications and supply, there could be no assurance that the opposing commander would feel forced to make an assault. To expect another enemy general to repeat the performance at Fredericksburg was asking a great deal.

On the other hand, Generals Lee and Jackson were not at all satisfied with the results of the battle. For, after Fredericksburg, there was no opportunity for the victorious Confederates to inflict further damage upon the Union army as it retreated from the field. No great general of history would have willingly chosen to engage in a battle where there was no hope of pursuing a defeated enemy. Prior to the battle Jackson had advocated retreating thirty-six miles to the North Anna River where there would have been a chance to engage in a pursuit after victory, but Lee felt that he could not abandon Fredericksburg without a struggle, although he fully recognized the merit of Jackson's proposal. Battles can be won by staying on the defensive, but wars are not won that way unless the people of the enemy country are not willing to continue to fight for what they believe, and the people of the North were firmly resolved to preserve the Union.

When the next great battle was fought at Chancellorsville on May 1-4, 1863, Longstreet was not present. He had been sent with two of his divisions on a detached mission to the area southeast of Richmond and Petersburg, and therefore took no part in the campaign. With Longstreet absent, General Lee could not have asked for his advice, but it is certain that Longstreet would have strongly objected to the way that the battle was fought, by dividing the army into two parts, although it resulted in the greatest Southern victory of the entire war against an army outnumbering the Confederates by odds of over two to one.

After the death of Stonewall Jackson, eight days after his being wounded at Chancellorsville, it might have been expected that Longstreet, being the senior corps commander, would have been selected to lead the advance to Gettysburg, but such proved not to be the case. In that campaign it was Lieutenant General Richard S. Ewell who was chosen. Lee's judgment was superbly vindicated. Ewell's performance was outstanding. The clearing of the Shenandoah Valley, the capture of 4,000 Union soldiers, the rapid advance across Maryland, and on into Pennsylvania was reminiscent of Jackson at his best.

In the summer of 1864, when a corps was sent to save the Shenandoah Valley from destruction, it was Lieutenant General Jubal A. Early who was selected. Of course on this occasion Longstreet could not have been appointed. He had just been badly wounded at the Battle of the Wilderness. By a very odd coincidence it had occurred close to the same location where, one year and four days before, Jackson had been wounded, also by accident by his own men. If Longstreet had been capable of undertaking the assignment and had been asked to do so, he would almost certainly have been as successful as Early in defeating the Union army there. However, after clearing the enemy out of the Valley, he would surely have returned to the Richmond-Petersburg area. The daring demonstration conducted by Jubal Early leading to the very gates of Washington would never have occurred. Such a risky enterprise would have run directly counter to Longstreet's cautious nature. The pressure by Grant's armies upon Petersburg and Richmond would then have continued unabated and been increased, whereas Early's demonstration proved so highly successful that an entire corps from Grant's army was hurried back to Washington, and a second Union corps diverted to the Valley to face Early's little army.

The chances are, though, that Longstreet, even if he had not been wounded, would never have been chosen by Lee to go to the Shenandoah Valley instead of Early. When action was impending or in progress, Lee was accustomed to having Longstreet close at hand. He obviously trusted and respected him, had great affection for him, and enjoyed his serene, unruffled presence. A meticulous, conservative and thoroughly dependable officer was good to have around. Longstreet's objections to Lee's plans could always be overridden whenever Lee chose to do so, but it does not seem too far-fetched to say that it was a comfort to Lee to have Longstreet by his side. This must have been particularly true during the Gettysburg campaign while Lee inwardly fretted over Jeb Stuart's continued absence on a misguided raid around the Union army that was wrecking all Lee's hopes and plans on this second invasion of the North.

Throughout the years when Lee commanded the Army of Northern Virginia there were only three extensive periods of time when Longstreet was not by his side, riding with him, or close to him, fighting the campaigns together. There was, of course, the nearly six months' period when Longstreet was recovering from his wound received at the Wilderness, and two occasions when he was given a chance at independent command.

The first of these has already been mentioned, when Longstreet was sent with two divisions on a detached mission to the Suffolk area southeast of Richmond to guard against an advance from that direction, while foraging for supplies badly needed by the army. Nothing much was expected of him on this mission, and nothing much was accomplished.

In the lull following Gettysburg, he was sent with two divisions of his corps to fight under the command of General Braxton Bragg. At the Battle of Chickamauga, Longstreet achieved spectacular results.

After that battle, while the Siege of Chattanooga was in progress, General Bragg ordered Longstreet into east Tennessee to fight against his old opponent, Burnside, who had occupied

Knoxville at the beginning of the Chickamauga campaign. This gave Longstreet his second chance at independent command. The results were disappointing. His efforts to capture Knoxville failed, and eventually he rejoined Lee in Virginia.

It seems only fair to conclude that Longstreet lacked the imagination and the initiative required for independent command of an army in the field, but under the guidance of another he proved an excellent corps commander.

In one respect, however, Longstreet surpassed his chief. When General Lee decided to fight for the South, he wrote: "Save in the defense of my native State, I never desire again to draw my sword." Surely no one at the time, or later, ever accepted this statement as literally true. Certainly he must have meant that he was going to fight for the Southern cause as a whole, not just for Virginia. However, during the entire four years of war Lee seems to have paid little attention to what was happening in the West. Even during the short period from the middle of March to the first day of June, 1862, when he served as Jefferson Davis's military adviser, his energies were devoted for the most part to affairs in, or concerning, Virginia. In his defense it may be said that, as commander of the Army of Northern Virginia, he may not have considered it proper to offer advice to President Davis concerning the war in the West, especially during the eleven-month period when Braxton Bragg was serving as the President's military adviser. It was only at the very last, in February, 1865, when it was too late to save the Confederacy, that he was appointed general in chief of all the armies.

On the other hand, many senior generals of the South were intensely worried about the Western theater, where the war was going steadily against the South. They did not hesitate to write or talk to the President concerning their fears. Yet Lee seems not to have looked beyond Virginia and the Eastern theater. It would seem that he, of all people, whom Jefferson Davis trusted so greatly, should have discussed the subject with the President at great length.

It was Longstreet who suggested the movement of his troops westward to help Bragg, and it was his corps that made the breakthrough at Chickamauga to decide the day and produce the only great victory won by the South during the entire war in the West. The inescapable conclusion is that Longstreet, although he was not good at operating on his own, surpassed Lee in his grasp of the essentials of grand strategy and the importance of making use of the South's interior lines.

After the war Longstreet's military and personal reputation suffered a violent eclipse. First he made the political mistake of becoming a Republican and advocating that the people of the South accept the fact that the Reconstruction period must be endured as an inevitable result of the war. His friends promptly began to snub him. His New Orleans cotton brokerage business was ruined. He turned for help to his old friend President Grant, who gave him the post of surveyor of customs at the port of New Orleans. Other federal appointments followed. He was not the only Confederate officer who accepted a government appointment after the war, but in his case, because he had been such a senior officer in the Army and because he was the first to accept such an appointment, his actions were considered outrageous, equivalent to treason.

His former military colleagues then began attacking his war record. Specifically they accused him of having lost the Battle of Gettysburg on the second day. It was a well-known fact that he had opposed making an attack on the second day. He was now accused of being slow and dilatory when ordered to do so. In the war of words Longstreet was badly worsted. Instead of a Confederate hero he was cast in the role of a villain. The publication of his memoirs in 1896, entitled *From Manassas to Appomattox*, did nothing to help his cause, for his book was obviously not written by the Longstreet of 1861-65 but was the work of a tired, embittered man who had been the target of too many enemies for too many years.

This criticism of Longstreet in the postwar years was totally unfair. It completely ignored the outstanding service he had rendered the Southern cause. On many a hard-fought battle-field he had been a tower of strength to General Lee and the Army of Northern Virginia. The Longstreet to remember is not the man who lost the postwar battle of words but the stead-fast corps commander who held that position longer than any other in the Army of Northern Virginia, who stayed until the very bitter end, never once even suggesting that surrender be considered. On the morning of Palm Sunday, April 9, 1865, Appomattox Day, General James Longstreet rang down a fitting curtain upon his military career when that arrogant, obnoxious upstart George Armstrong Custer came riding into his lines under a flag of truce to demand surrender. "Old Pete" told him in a few precise, well-chosen words to go back where he came from and stay there, while his betters made the decision.

5

---◀◉▶---

Ulysses S. Grant

OF all the leaders of the Civil War the most successful began his wartime career with the smallest apparent hope, or chance, of acquiring distinction, fame, or even recognition. He was known as a person addicted to alcohol, who had resigned from the service, and whose every business venture had failed miserably. About a month after the war began, he wrote The Adjutant General of the Army tendering his services, expressing the opinion that he was competent to command a regiment. No reply was ever received. Years later his letter was discovered. No action whatever had been taken. It had not even been filed. The letter had simply been mislaid.

Eventually in June, 1861, this man, who had served for fifteen years in the Regular Army, including four years at West Point, was appointed a colonel by the governor of Illinois to command a regiment of infantry. By this time, however, so many others had been appointed ahead of him that he was far down the list of colonels and could not have entertained much hope of rapid advancement. However, one of his most outstanding qualities was an innate, quiet modesty. He probably never expected to do more than serve his country to the best of his ability in whatever position his superiors might choose to employ him. It therefore came as a distinct surprise when he was promoted to be a brigadier general of volunteers. His commission was issued August 7, 1861, to date from May 17.

He had done nothing whatever to seek promotion, nor was he well acquainted with any politicians. It can truthfully be said that the appointment was a fortunate political accident. President Abraham Lincoln needed generals to command the large army that was being created, and he had called upon the Congressional delegations of each state to submit nominations. Thus each state would have its quota of generals. One of the most prominent and influential Congressmen from Illinois was Elihu B. Washburne, and he was determined to have on the list someone from his hometown of Galena so that he could show his constituents that their Congressman was working for them. The fact that Washburne and the man he nominated were of opposite political parties was of no consequence so long as Galena, Illinois, could boast of a brigadier general.

That Washburne's nominee was first on the Illinois list may have been due to Washburne's insistence, but it may also have been due to another factor. By this time every Congressman must have been heartily sick of the many hungry office seekers coming to them for jobs, and particularly for appointments relating to the Army or Navy. To discover a soldier who had not sought in any way for a favor of any sort and who would not even know his name was being submitted for promotion was a welcome change. It is easy to imagine that the Illinois delegation took pleasure in putting a non-office seeker at the head of its list of nominees. Thus, by accident, Ulysses S. Grant was placed in approximately the proper position that he should have occupied if appointments in the Northern armies had been made in an orderly, responsible fashion.

Born April 27, 1822, at Point Pleasant, Clermont County, Ohio, the new general was thirty-nine years old. He had been graduated from the United States Military Academy at West Point in 1843, twenty-first in a class of 39, and commissioned in the infantry. When the Mexican War came, although he considered that the war had been unjustly provoked by the United States, Second Lieutenant Grant placed his duty to his country ahead of his personal feelings. He served first under the command of General Zachary Taylor, taking part in three of the four major battles of his campaign, then with his regiment went to participate in General Winfield Scott's campaign that led to the capture of Mexico City. In this second campaign, Grant was present at every major battle except one and received two brevet promotions for gallantry in action at Molino del Rey and again at Chapultepec. During most of the war, and for a time thereafter, he was also regimental quartermaster and commissary officer, so he emerged from the conflict better acquainted, at first hand, with the practical problems of supplying troops than most of his contemporaries who served as strictly line officers in the infantry, cavalry, or artillery.

After the war and his marriage in August, 1848, to Miss Julia Dent of St. Louis, Missouri, Grant was stationed in upper New York State and in Michigan. In 1852 the 4th Infantry was ordered to California. Separated from his wife and family, it was there that his troubles began. In 1854 he resigned and left the Pacific coast, eventually settling in Galena, Illinois, in May, 1860.

At the beginning and throughout the first year of the war, the name Ulysses S. Grant would have meant practically nothing to the man on the street. Early in September, 1861, the average reader of the daily newspapers might have mentally noted the name in connection with the seizure of a part of Kentucky to keep it from falling into Confederate hands, but there would have been no reason for the man on the street to have done more than that unless he had been present on the scene. Since General Grant never sought publicity, the headlines of the day were far more likely to be filled with the names of other generals seeking prominence or getting themselves embroiled in politics. However, anyone who had been in western Kentucky in the opening days of September would have discovered just how fast men could be made to move when an emergency arose.

Confederate troops had marched without warning into Kentucky, which had been trying to achieve the impossible goal of remaining neutral in this war between the Northern and

Southern states. Their advance northward, along the Missis-sippi, happened to coincide almost exactly with Grant's ap-pearance on the scene. With a crisis thrust upon him before he had even become acquainted with his new command, his reaction was so vigorous and prompt that within twenty-four hours his troops had countered the enemy thrust. In the face of Confederate action and Grant's counterthrust the vision of Kentucky remaining neutral vanished.

Then, with little fighting in that first year, Grant's name ap-peared briefly again in the press in connection with a battle in November at a place called Belmont in Missouri. An attentive observer of the war might then have concluded that the name Grant meant action not talk, as was unfortunately so often true of many others. Suddenly in February, 1862, the name became a household word when U. S. Grant became "Unconditional Surrender" Grant because of his ultimatum to the Confederate garrison of Fort Donelson, Tennessee. At Forts Henry and Don-elson, 11,500 men and forty guns were captured. A giant step had been taken, and this unknown soldier had been the one to take it.

Thereafter the name Major General Grant appeared again, but now people were watching for it, and this time they learned with an awful sense of shock that, whether they wanted to admit it or not, the war was going to be long, costly and bloody. The Battle of Shiloh, fought on April 6-7, 1862, cost the North more than 13,000 casualties and the South about 10,700 killed, wounded, captured or missing. Grant and his commanders were accused in the newspapers of being unprepared, of being taken by surprise, of failing to entrench their position, and the old charge of drinking was brought against him.

If the public expected a flood of denials or explanations by General Grant, they were disappointed. On this one occasion he did write a letter for publication, and it seems to have been the only time that, as a general in the field, he ever responded to criticism in the public press. The attacks made on him must have hurt deeply, but his friends, including Congressman

Washburne, rallied to his support. Thereafter General Grant seems to have concluded that it was far better to proceed with the work at hand than to take time to indulge in replies to his critics.

Throughout the war this was his attitude. His correspondence with higher headquarters is not filled with continued requests for reinforcements or with promises of what he could do if only he had more men. Nor did he indulge in speculation as to what might be accomplished if the circumstances were different. Grant just went ahead with what had been assigned him to do with a businesslike, realistic approach toward defeating his enemies by whatever means he could.

Lest this description bring the wrong image to mind, let it be said that the greatest injustice that can be done is to evaluate the generalship of Ulysses S. Grant strictly in terms of his own words, that he would "fight it out on this line if it takes all summer." This dispatch so often quoted as typical of General Grant's bulldog tenacity, stubbornness, and determination gives a false picture of the man. It was written on May 11, 1864, while the Union Army was engaged in that long bitter struggle known to history as the Battle of Spotsylvania. The message was intended to convey hope to the administration that victory would be won; that there would be no turning back until the war was over.

Many of his predecessors opposing the Confederate army in Virginia had talked this way before battle had been joined, but Grant was the first one to keep on fighting; the others had all retreated. Yet Grant has been censured for pursuing an unimaginative policy of hammering away at Lee's army, taking tremendous losses, as if this was the only way he knew to fight. Overlooked entirely in this criticism is the fact that he undertook a series of successive turning movements aimed at the Confederate right flank. Each effort when made had the positive hope that it might succeed in cutting the enemy's communications and possibly get between the Confederate army and Richmond. That these successive efforts failed can be blamed not on Grant but on the wisdom and foresight of his great opponent, Robert E. Lee. Yet with all Grant's losses the principal Union objective was slowly being gained: Lee's army was being brought to battle and was taking its losses too. Furthermore, the Northern army was doing something it had never done before in Virginia; it was advancing, fighting, and advancing again; and at one point it did effect a surprise when it crossed the James River to make a stab at Petersburg, which almost succeeded. The long siege that followed, lasting nearly ten months, fixed in the public mind the legend of General Grant as a determined, stubborn, tenacious man who would not quit until he had won. And since there is nothing that quite succeeds like success, the North, though bemoaning its heavy casualty lists, was content to accept this analysis of their great leader. This concept is the one that is generally accepted today, although it is a completely one-sided picture of Grant as a general.

A study of either the Chattanooga campaign or the Vicksburg campaign would show a different leader who fought in many other ways to win victories without relying on a constant hammering policy. These campaigns would show a general quick to seize the initiative, eager to grasp an opportunity when presented.

During the long campaign to Petersburg and throughout the siege there were very few opportunities presented by General Lee, who knew full well that the days when he could take daring risks against such opponents as McClellan, Pope, and Hooker had long since passed.

One such occasion, however, did arise at the beginning of July, 1864. No one but Grant seems to have seen it. No one but Grant made any effort to take advantage of the situation. His subordinates failed him completely and were acclaimed as heroes. As a result, Grant quietly let the matter drop, although, for a similar offense, General Philip H. Sheridan relieved a corps commander on the eve of the victory of Five Forks, April

1, 1865, nine months later. In this latter instance, with the end so near in sight, Sheridan's action was unduly harsh. The lesson should have been taught earlier.

The occasion that presented itself early in July, 1864, was the demonstration against the capital city of Washington by Lieutenant General Jubal A. Early. There were very few events in the history of the War Between the States that caused so much excitement. It was the only time in the war that a Confederate army ever got that close to Washington, and it was the only time in the history of the United States that a President was under fire while in office.

When General Early started down the Shenandoah Valley, he had with him only a small force of about 14,000 men, but reports concerning its size were greatly exaggerated and many feared for the safety of the capital. That this fear was unfounded has been proven for more than a century, yet to this day the idea still persists that Jubal Early was trying to capture Washington.

An experienced, capable soldier like Early knew full well that with such a small force he had no chance whatever of seizing Washington. Furthermore, by the time he reached Fort Stevens on the outskirts of the northern side of Washington, where President Lincoln came out to watch the fighting, he could not have had with him much more than about 11,000 men. Perhaps Early might have captured one or two of the sixty-eight forts and batteries surrounding the city and created even greater consternation than he actually did, but his real purpose was to relieve the pressure that Grant's armies were exerting on Richmond and Petersburg. In this, he succeeded admirably. The entire Sixth Corps was sent north to Baltimore and Washington and a part of the Nineteenth Corps coming from Louisiana was also diverted to Washington. Eventually many more troops were brought against him.

The question immediately arises: Why did General Grant, in command of all the armies of the United States, permit the diversion of so many troops from the main operations against

Petersburg unless he also was worried about the safety of the capital? A careful study of General Grant's messages during this crisis makes it abundantly clear that he was not in the least disturbed concerning the loss of Washington. Grant knew as well as Early did that the capital needed no saving. On the contrary, he saw the raid as a great chance to cut off, capture, and destroy Early's force before it could cross back over the Potomac into Virginia. Yet he seems to have been the only one who saw the possibility and was mentally prepared to take advantage of it. Everyone on the scene in Washington appears to have been completely satisfied with the halfway measures taken that resulted in Early's escaping with ease. There can be no doubt that a grand opportunity was missed to inflict damage on the retreating Confederates, but all that anyone, other than Grant, could think of was that the capital had been saved.

Almost to the end of its days the Army of the Potomac was to suffer from the legacy left it by McClellan of being satisfied with halfway measures. Perhaps it was the memory of this lost opportunity, and many others like it over the years, that caused President Lincoln to write General Grant about one month later:

> I have seen your despatch in which you say, "I want Sheridan put in command of all the troops in the field, with instructions to put himself south of the enemy, and follow him to the death. Wherever the enemy goes, let our troops go also." This, I think, is exactly right, as to how our forces should move. But please look over the despatches you may have received from here, even since you made that order, and discover, if you can, that there is any idea in the head of anyone here, of "putting our army *south* of the enemy," or of "following him to the *death*" in any direction. I repeat to you it will neither be done nor attempted unless you watch it every day, and hour, and force it.

Lincoln was fed to the teeth with halfway measures. The Early demonstration had been just one more illustration of the lack of offensive spirit that had for three long years prevailed in Washington and among a number of the leaders of the armies in the East. Also Major General Henry W. Halleck, whom he had brought from the West in 1862, had, to Lincoln's sorrow, proved to be as bad as any of them. From 1862 until 1864, when Grant was made commander of all the armies of the United States, Halleck had acted as general-in-chief and adviser to the President. As an administrator he had been capable, but his advice had always been on the side of excessive caution. Now, with Grant in command, Halleck had been retained in Washington to act as a coordinator and liaison between the President, General Grant and his army commanders.

When Early advanced down the Shenandoah Valley and crossed the Potomac into Maryland, Halleck had become obsessed with fear for the safety of Washington, had magnified the size of Early's force out of all proportion, and had gotten the President upset about the danger of the situation. Too late, after Early had departed, Lincoln had become aware of how badly he had been misled. Also, by this time, he had figured out that Major General Horatio G. Wright, the commander of the Sixth Corps, whom Grant had sent to Washington to capture Early, had not done at all what Grant had expected him to do. A grand parade up the streets and avenues of Washington to stop Early at Fort Stevens may have cheered the people of the city, but it had done nothing toward capturing the Confederates. Lincoln now knew that the Sixth Corps had not been handled properly at all. Wright should have moved promptly upon landing toward the upper reaches of the Potomac to block Early's escape route, not have followed around behind as the Confederates withdrew in their own good time. The President was convinced that this would always be the way things would be done unless Grant watched every day and hour and forced those generals to action.

Perhaps this is too strong an indictment, but by this time Lincoln had learned a bit about how the Vicksburg campaign had been fought, and now the victor of that campaign was in command of all the armies. Surely he could inject into the leaders of the Eastern armies some of the spirit with which that long struggle had been fought and won.

In 1863 the objective of Vicksburg had appeared just as unobtainable as Richmond in 1864. Not only was there a Confederate army to protect Vicksburg, but the approaches to the city presented tremendous obstacles in themselves. To the north, between the Yazoo and Mississippi rivers, there was a vast bottomland known as the Yazoo Delta, 60 miles wide and reaching northward for 175 miles. Westward across the Mississippi was another expanse of bottomland. It was not as wide as the Yazoo Delta, but it stretched for many miles north and south of the city.

The only firm ground where an army could operate was to the south and east of Vicksburg. Thus the problem confronting General Grant was to reach somehow this high ground where he could engage the enemy. In late November and December, 1862, he had attempted a long march overland from the northeast, while simultaneously sending a part of his army in boats down the Mississippi River. This combined land and water movement had failed. The whole army had subsequently been brought down the river. After effecting a concentration north of the city, his problem was now to find a way to get behind it: either by going across the Mississippi to the west, then crossing back again; or by effecting a passage through the maze of swampland, bayous, and little rivers comprising the Yazoo Delta.

Prior to Grant's arrival, work had been begun on a project to cut a canal across the neck of land where the Mississippi made its great bend directly under the frowning guns of the great Confederate stronghold. It was hoped that the canal would divert the course of the river so that ships could pass safely by the batteries. General Grant did not have much faith in the idea, but because he had been told that the President attached importance to it, he kept the men steadily at work. Even when

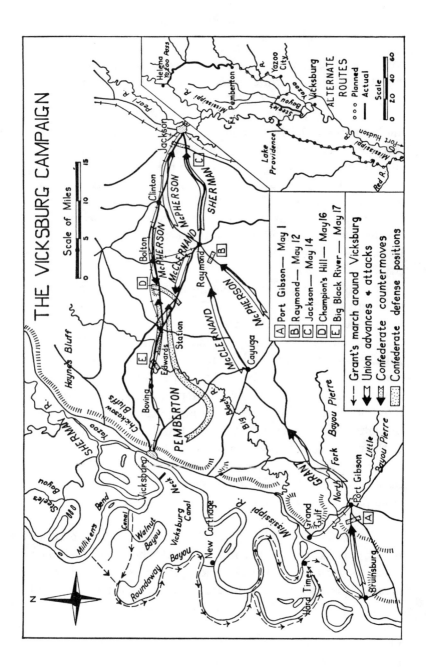

THE VICKSBURG CAMPAIGN

Scale of Miles

0   5   10   15

A   Port Gibson — May 1
B   Raymond — May 12
C   Jackson — May 14
D   Champion's Hill — May 16
E   Big Black River — May 17

Grant's march around Vicksburg
Union advances + attacks
Confederate countermoves
Confederate defense positions

ALTERNATE ROUTES
ooo Planned
—— Actual
Scale
0   20   40   60

the levee broke and water flooded the entire Vicksburg Neck, the work kept on until Confederate artillery forced its abandonment.

Another attempt to bypass Vicksburg by cutting a canal to the westward was also tried. It became known as the Lake Providence Route because the canal was to connect the Mississippi River with that lake, then follow a winding series of bayous and rivers for 200 miles southward to the Red River. Although this would have meant a detour of nearly 400 miles before reaching Vicksburg from the south, General Grant believed that this project might be successful. After nearly two months of hard work in chilly, wet and dreary weather a channel was cut that would carry boats of light draft, but a special type of underwater saw was needed to cut down the larger trees before gunboats could make the passage. This special machine had not arrived, and since the season of the year would soon be approaching when the waters would begin to recede, this project was reluctantly abandoned.

Since he was not the type of man to be content with putting all his eggs in one or even two baskets, Grant concurrently undertook operations to try to cross the Yazoo Delta. There also two efforts were made, both of which involved cooperation with the United States Navy. In fact, neither attempt could have been undertaken at all without the help of the Navy. Rear Admiral David D. Porter, an extremely energetic, enthusiastic and capable naval officer, eagerly entered into the spirit of things. Gunboats and ironclads were brought into places where their designers never dreamed they would be required to operate. Incredible difficulties were encountered. Tree stumps and floating logs stove in housings and fouled wheels; overhanging vines and willows snared and held on smokestacks; passages were blocked by felled trees. Although unsuccessful, the story of the Yazoo Pass Expedition and the Steele's Bayou Route, which was attempted as a diversion to help the former, is fascinating, especially when it came time to back the ships out stern first, around bends in the streambeds, with Confederate sharpshooters swarming on all sides, so no one dared show himself on deck.

After four unsuccessful attempts, not counting the land and water movement that had failed in November and December of 1862, one cannot help but wonder how General Grant must have felt. Fortunately, for the record, he has told us in his *Memoirs,* which he just barely managed to complete in an awful race against coming death. It was his final and surely his most heroic battle. He knew that he was dying of throat cancer. At times he could not speak but still continued to write, for he had to complete his work to give his family an income after he passed on. The book was finished just one week before he died on July 23, 1885.

General Grant turned out to be almost as good a writer as he was a soldier. His book is by far the best autobiography of any written covering the Civil War. It is honest, sincere, and as accurate as he could make it. His writing is clear, concise, and as forceful as his orders were. No officer could ever complain that he did not understand what Grant had told him to do, nor try to justify failure by saying that the orders he had received had not been clear. A reading of Grant's orders today makes the careful military student wonder if the Army field manuals of today on the subject of how to write orders were not prepared after studying Grant's written directives as models.

Yet, withal, Grant's autobiography is an interesting, human document. Nothing could better describe his difficulties in the early spring of 1863 than an excerpt from his own *Memoirs*:

> This long, dreary and, for heavy and continuous rains and high water, unprecedented winter was one of great hardship to all engaged about Vicksburg. The river was higher than its natural banks from December, 1862, to the following April. The war had suspended peaceful pursuits in the South, further than the production of army supplies, and in consequence the levees were neglected and broken in many places and the whole country was covered with water. Troops could scarcely find dry ground on which to pitch

their tents. Malarial fevers broke out among the men. Measles and small-pox also attacked them. The hospital arrangements and medical attendance were so perfect, however, that the loss of life was much less than might have been expected. Visitors to the camps went home with dismal stories to relate; Northern papers came back to the soldiers with these stories exaggerated. Because I would not divulge my ultimate plans to visitors, they pronounced me idle, incompetent and unfit to command men in an emergency, and clamored for my removal. . . . I took no steps to answer these complaints, but continued to do my duty, as I understood it, to the best of my ability. Every one has his superstitions. One of mine is that in positions of great responsibility every one should do his duty to the best of his ability where assigned by competent authority, without application or the use of influence to change his position. . . .

In time of war the President, being by the Constitution Commander-in-chief of the Army and Navy, is responsible for the selection of commanders. He should not be embarrassed in making his selections. I having been selected, my responsibility ended with my doing the best I knew how. If I had sought the place, or obtained it through personal or political influence, my belief is that I would have feared to undertake any plan of my own conception, and would probably have awaited direct orders from my distant superiors. Persons obtaining important commands by application or political influence are apt to keep a written record of complaints and predictions of defeat, which are shown in case of disaster. Somebody must be responsible for their failures.

With all the pressure brought to bear upon them, both President Lincoln and General Halleck stood by me to the end of the campaign. I had never met Mr. Lincoln, but his support was constant.

There have not been many instances in history where support of a general in the field by the Chief Executive of his country have paid such tremendously rich dividends. Mr. Lincoln could not possibly have known beforehand that the most remarkable Union campaign of the entire Civil War was about to begin.

At the end of March, 1863, the final advance against Vicksburg was made. If this fifth and last attempt did not succeed, it would surely have marked the end of General Grant's career. Certainly he must have known and recognized this as a fact, and, with the average general, such knowledge would almost certainly have led to caution. The opposite proved to be the case. Grant's final plan was not reckless, but it certainly was bold, unorthodox, and hazardous both for himself and his army, as well as for the naval force that was to operate with him.

The route chosen this time wound through a circuitous series of bayous west of Vicksburg on the opposite side of the Mississippi River. It was manifestly impossible for the entire army to advance rapidly through this treacherous bottomland, and the march would require a long time to complete. It did, in fact, take almost a month, using small boats collected from the surrounding bayous, building others from material at hand, constructing countless bridges as the men advanced over roads that soon became seas of mud. Under these conditions General Grant could hardly expect his move to take the enemy by surprise.

The Army of the Tennessee at Milliken's Bend consisted of the 13th, 15th, and 17th Army Corps commanded by Major Generals John A. McClernand, William Tecumseh Sherman, and James B. McPherson, respectively. Grant decided to employ McClernand's and McPherson's corps in the advance, leaving his most trusted general, Sherman, in the vicinity of Vicksburg. When these first two corps reached the Mississippi below Vicksburg, they would have to depend on the fleet to provide most of their supplies, and this meant that the fleet would have to undertake the passage of the guns of Vicksburg. If Admiral Porter was unwilling to try this extremely dangerous undertaking, Grant's plan would have no chance of success at all, but, when the idea was proposed to Porter, that officer enthusiastically agreed and immediately began preparations. Hay, cotton, and grain were piled high against the sides of his transports, while even the sides of the ironclads were strengthened with logs.

On the night of April 16-17, 1863, the first part of the fleet began the run past the Confederate guns. It was truly a dramatic event, almost certainly the most dramatic of the entire war. The defenders of Vicksburg were fully prepared and on the alert. Huge barrels of tar had been placed across the river on the opposite shore. These were immediately lighted and buildings also set afire to give the gunners the best possible chance to see their targets. For two and a half hours the guns thundered; smoke and sheets of flame enveloped the river; numerous hits were scored, but only one transport was sunk. Six nights later the remainder of the fleet ran the batteries, again with the loss of one transport; but only half the barges they were towing, filled with rations and supplies, got through.

The fleet was now in position below Vicksburg ready to ferry the first two corps across the river to the eastern shore. From the beginning General Grant had recognized that this crossing and the first few hours on shore would be hazardous. The fleet could not move all the troops across at one time, and even when all the men of his first two corps had been landed, General Grant believed that he would be outnumbered by the enemy.

Circumstances had forced him to divide his army. Therefore he had done everything in his power to try to confuse his enemy and make him divide his army. About the first of April a division of Sherman's corps had gone up the Mississippi and then made a demonstration in the Yazoo Delta as if another attempt were to be made in that direction. Then, with perfect timing, on the very morning following Admiral Porter's dash past Vicksburg, a cavalry force was sent down through Mississippi to confuse the enemy further. This cavalry raid, led by Colonel Benjamin H. Grierson, succeeded beyond anyone's wildest expectations. Starting with only 1,800 men, dropping off detachments to divert the enemy's attention, Grierson then dashed through the entire state of Mississippi with 1,000 cavalrymen to join the Union troops to the south at Baton Rouge, Louisiana.

Nor were these all the diversions planned by Grant. While preparations were being made to get the first two corps across the river below Vicksburg, Sherman was to make a strong demonstration at Vicksburg itself. On April 29, while Admiral Porter bombarded Grand Gulf to the south with a view toward possibly landing there, Sherman moved against Vicksburg. Since the batteries at Grand Gulf proved to be too strong, the landing was begun the next day, April 30, farther south at Bruinsburg, while Sherman continued his operations against Vicksburg. Again the timing had been perfect.

At the beginning of the campaign, Lieutenant General John C. Pemberton, the Confederate commander at Vicksburg, had been provided by his superiors with an adequate force of infantry and artillery, but with very few cavalry. Early in April he had received orders to send reinforcements to east Tennessee if they could be spared. Misled by the movement upriver of one of Sherman's divisions, he had sent three infantry brigades. Although these troops were subsequently ordered to return, this action weakened the forces protecting Vicksburg. Then, because he had practically no cavalry to oppose Colonel Grierson's raid and wild reports greatly exaggerated its size, Pemberton further spread his infantry over the state to try to catch the Union cavalry. Finally, Sherman's diversions at Vicksburg helped confuse the Confederate command. Thus when Admiral Porter ferried Grant's troops across to Bruinsburg, the landing was entirely unopposed, and there were too few troops at hand to stop the Union advance at Port Gibson on the following day, May 1, when the first of the five battles of the Vicksburg Campaign was fought.

Then came the crisis for General Grant. The War Department had expected him to cooperate with Major General Nathaniel P. Banks, who was supposed to have been advancing up the Mississippi from the south against Port Hudson. But now came a letter from Banks saying that he would be delayed and could bring only some 15,000 men.

A less courageous man than Grant would probably have turned back, halted in place, or almost certainly consulted the War Department. To turn back was to admit to another defeat. To wait for Banks would mean the loss of days, or possibly weeks, during which time he not only would lose the initiative but would be giving the enemy the opportunity to concentrate and bring great numbers of reinforcements against him, probably many more than Banks could bring. At this moment General Grant made the most momentous decision of his career. He decided to cut loose entirely from his base of supplies, abandon his line of communications, and, taking with him only what he could carry (primarily ammunition), advance resolutely forward. He certainly did not notify the War Department until he was on his way, for he knew that the ever-cautious Halleck would surely stop him in his tracks. Even the redoubtable General Sherman advised against taking this gamble which ran counter to all the generally accepted rules of war, but Grant moved forward and the audacity of his decision worked in his favor, for it was the very last thing that his opponent Pemberton expected him to do.

The result was a brilliant and, to the Confederates, almost a bewildering series of victories. First came the defeat of a Confederate brigade at Raymond on May 12. On the following evening General Joseph E. Johnston, the senior Confederate general in the West, arrived at Jackson, Mississippi, to find but two brigades, one of them the brigade that had been driven back from Raymond. Although two other brigades were expected to arrive soon, such a small force was totally inadequate to hold the city against a Union attack launched on the following day, May 14.

After the capture of Jackson, General Grant immediately turned toward Vicksburg. If Pemberton had not throughout the campaign held back the greater part of two Confederate divisions to guard Vicksburg, he might then have had a reasonable chance of stopping the Northern advance. But with these troops absent from the field, idly garrisoning Vicksburg, the battles of Champion's Hill and the Big Black River were almost foregone conclusions. The Confederates were driven from both fields into the defenses of Vicksburg. In a campaign lasting just eighteen days Grant had won five separate battlefield victories and bottled up the Confederate defenders in their stronghold from which there was no chance whatever of escape. In all the campaigns of this war there is but one other that can compare with Grant's Vicksburg campaign and that is Stonewall Jackson's campaign in the Shenandoah Valley in 1862.

When Congress revived the grade of lieutenant general, the only possible choice was Ulysses S. Grant. He arrived in Washington on the afternoon of March 8, 1864. As the result of someone's error no one met him at the railroad station, which was probably as he would have wished, for he generally felt embarrassed by public receptions. Accompanied only by his thirteen-year-old son Fred, he arrived at the Willard Hotel, where, until the clerk noticed his name on the register, he and his son were almost put on the top floor instead of in the suite that had been reserved in his name.

On the next day, March 9, he was given his commission. Then, by executive order, he was assigned to command all the armies of the United States. Thereafter, for the first time since the beginning of the war, a coordinated, concerted plan of action was evolved for the Union forces.

As soon as possible Grant left Washington to take the field and get out of the political atmosphere of the capital city. Recognizing that the principal campaign would be that between the Army of the Potomac and Lee's Army of Northern Virginia, he established his headquarters with the Army of the Potomac. As previously noted, he left Halleck to act as his chief of staff in Washington, thus making him in effect a coordinator and liaison officer between Grant and the other army commanders, as well as between Grant and the President.

Until they met at the White House in March, 1864, President Lincoln and General Grant had never seen each other before, but from that moment the homespun President and the new lieutenant general seemed to understand each other very well. Each was a product of the new frontier America and there developed rapidly a mutual respect and admiration for each other. As a team, no two men could possibly have worked better together. Each recognized in the other a kindred spirit who would wholeheartedly devote his entire energies toward one common end, the winning of this terrible war as soon as it could possibly be done.

Yet for a long, long time the Army of the Potomac never seemed to understand this fellow Grant. He didn't look like their idea of a general and he didn't act like any they had ever seen before, but since his arrival there had been a difference. War had become a very grim affair. Fighting had become a business to be conducted with maximum efficiency and aggressiveness, never giving themselves or the enemy a rest.

In May, 1864, their march southward had begun (coordinated for the first time with the advances of the Union armies to the west and south). There had been the Battle of the Wilderness, which would have stopped the advance of any general who had previously commanded them. Then they had fought the long twelve-day Battle of Spotsylvania and again advanced to fight three more battles in rapid succession, crossed the James River, and begun the Siege of Petersburg. Under his command they had persisted, although some said their casualties had been greater than the total number of men Lee had in his entire army. Nor would their commander relax his vigilance after the siege had begun. Even after the failure of the explosion of the underground mine on the morning of July 30, 1864, known as the Battle of the Crater, active operations continued both northward near Richmond and south of Petersburg in August, September, and on until the very end of October. After winter weather set in and the muddy roads became almost impassable for wagons and guns, troops were still set to work destroying the Confederate railroads for 40 miles to the south to aggravate the Confederate supply difficulties. Then in February, 1865, in the dead of winter, another expedition was dispatched to operate against Lee's supply routes and the Union siege lines were further extended so that General Lee was forced to hold a line of trenches from north of Richmond to south of Petersburg 53 miles long, one-ninth as long as the western front in Europe in 1918, with barely 1,000 men per mile.

Historians and students who think of General Grant during this period only in terms of conducting a war of attrition and a policy of nothing but "constant hammering" seem not only to forget these constant efforts of his to extend beyond Lee's lines and break Confederate resistance, but also ignore the fact that he was simultaneously supervising and directing the movements of all the other armies of the Union throughout every one of the other Southern states with extraordinarily excellent results. In the field of grand strategy General Grant stands head and shoulders above any other officer during the Civil War, although General Lee might have proved his equal if he had been given the opportunity to exercise his talents.

It was not until the spring of 1865 that Grant was again given a chance to demonstrate the lightning sort of campaign that had gained him such fame at Vicksburg.

The Confederate military leaders long had known that eventually they would have to evacuate Richmond and Petersburg, since President Jefferson Davis refused to negotiate. He would rather go down in defeat than accept terms that did not recognize Southern independence. Therefore a retreat ultimately would become necessary, but the Confederate army could not simply march away any time it chose. Not only were the men half-starved, but so were the horses. The animals did not have the strength to haul the artillery and wagon trains over the muddy winter roads.

Slowly March passed. The roads were still not in good condition. Then on March 29 the Union armies began their last turning movement to their left (south) flank. It ended in a

Major General and
Mrs. George B. McClellan

Lieutenant General Thomas
J. ("Stonewall") Jackson

Left: General Robert E. Lee as superintendent, United States Military Academy, West Point, New York. Photo of the painting in Washington Hall by E. L. Ipsen. *Below:* Lieutenant General James Longstreet. *Right:* Lieutenant General Ulysses S. Grant.

Major General George G. Meade

General Joseph E. Johnston

Major General William Tecumseh Sherman. Photo taken in May, 1865, showing him wearing a badge of mourning for President Lincoln.

General John B. Hood

Major General George H. Thomas

victory at Five Forks on April 1. Grant immediately launched a general assault on the Petersburg lines at dawn of April 2, which broke through the Confederate right.

That night the Army of Northern Virginia left their trenches at Petersburg and evacuated Richmond. Rarely in history, and never before or since on this continent, has a large army been asked to undertake such a superhuman task as Lee now urged his army to attempt. He had already warned Jefferson Davis, on several occasions, of the odds that his men would have to face if forced to retreat. All through the perishing cold of the last winter, Lee's soldiers had barely escaped starvation. Half-rations were a luxury; sometimes they had one-sixth rations. Scurvy, infections of all sorts, attacked men whose starving bodies, clad only in rags in bitterly cold weather, had no powers of resistance. Nevertheless, simply because their beloved commander asked them to try, the devoted soldiers of that great Confederate army left Richmond and turned westward to make a last supreme effort.

The plan was to try to join forces with General Johnston in North Carolina, crush Sherman, who was pushing Johnston's army northward, then turn back to fight Grant again. There was scarcely a chance to succeed; a tremendous amount of extraordinary good fortune would be necessary—but all the luck ran the other way. Through a delay in transmission of orders, the food supposed to be collected for the march did not arrive. A day was lost vainly scouring the countryside for supplies which did not exist. That day was never regained, for, on April 6, 1865, the swiftly pursuing Union troops caught up with the retreating army at Sayler's Creek, eight miles east of Farmville. Douglas Southall Freeman has labeled this "The Black Day of the Army." The proud victors of Manassas, the Seven Days', Fredericksburg, and Chancellorsville, who had never been driven from a battlefield, not even bloody Antietam, or Gettysburg, the Wilderness or Spotsylvania, were finally reaching the limits of human endurance. There, at Sayler's Creek, General Ewell was faced with a terrible choice. As a gallant soldier, Dick Ewell followed the path of honor. He sacrificed himself and his command to let the rest of the army escape.

That Grant's troops were able to close so rapidly with the retreating Confederates is proof of how hard and fast they also had been marching. Instead of sending his armies along the roads used by Lee's soldiers, he moved to intercept. After four long years of war, sensing victory at last, the Northern soldiers responded eagerly.

On the next day the people of the little town of Farmville, Virginia, on the Appomattox River, a place that had not yet been touched by the sights and sounds of battle, saw, for the first time, their world-famous Army of Northern Virginia and received a stunning shock. This was Longstreet's corps (all that was left of it) composed now of only a few thousand emaciated, footsore, starving men who, even at this last moment, strove onward with that same indomitable spirit which had won so many brilliant victories on hard-fought battlefields. As they wound down into the streets, many of the troops passed close to Longwood, the splendid mansion that was the birthplace of Joseph E. Johnston, the very man they were trying to join. In later years, an old lady, who saw that army come into Farmville, described them as "ghosts walking." Shocked though the townspeople were, they hurried forth to distribute food to the worn and weary column dragging its slow length through the streets.

Shortly after noon, General Grant rode into Farmville. He rode straight to the hotel known as The Randolph House and there established his headquarters. In the afternoon a small battle developed near Cumberland Church, three and a half miles up the road from Farmville. The Sixth Corps was ordered to cross the Appomattox and move to the support of the troops engaged.

It was a routine order for a routine march. The same sort of thing had been going on for four long years. Many, many times before, these veterans had trudged along the roads of Virginia, been halted, and then summoned again to move toward a distant battlefield. Sometimes, on arrival, they had been victorious, but far more often the Army of the Potomac had been defeated or met bloody repulse. Sometimes they wondered why they kept trying to win against an enemy who inflicted such enormous losses upon them. Again and again they had marched south toward Richmond and repeatedly been forced to turn back defeated, retracing the same steps they had taken, along the same roads.

Yet somehow, despite the losses and the misery of trench warfare, they had persisted; Petersburg was at last behind them. At this moment they were being urged forward in pursuit. The army had been marching night and day. The men were weary and footsore, but there was a different spirit in the air. With the instinct of the veteran soldier they knew that there would be no more dreary retreats back along the same trace. Every step taken now was leading toward the victory that had so long eluded them.

The people of Farmville watched silently as the long, superbly equipped, disciplined column composing the Sixth Corps marched onward in the gathering darkness. In that long column, 17,000 strong, flowing steadily forward, there were three divisions of eight brigades of infantry and an artillery brigade with eight batteries. One was the Vermont Brigade of the 2nd Division, another a brigade composed entirely of New Jersey units. Two-thirds of the remainder came from Pennsylvania and New York. There was a regiment each from Connecticut, Massachusetts, Wisconsin, Rhode Island, Maine, one from Maryland, and three regiments from Ohio.

As the Union soldiers strode along Main Street, they spied their general-in-chief watching them with evident pride from the broad piazza of the hotel. All at once they realized that this quiet, unassuming man, who never made bids for popularity, was the one individual directly responsible for their success and for guiding them straight and true along the right road at last. None could know that future generations of soldiers would be told to study Grant's pursuit as a model of its kind. But every man in blue suddenly felt that he owed his commander far more than the complaints and the grudging respect that he had previously given him.

A wave of enthusiasm gripped the leading brigade. Cheers arose in the darkness. Men broke ranks to light bonfires along both sides of the street. Seizing straw and pine knots, they hastened back to march past, waving their improvised torches. Onward they came in ever-increasing numbers, eager to shout their tribute to their leader.

There have been many organized victory parades in the history of warfare. Usually they are planned at the end of the war when the troops return home. Sometimes they take place in the enemy's capital or in the capitals of countries freed from the enemy's grasp. Veterans of the 28th Division will long remember the tumultuous welcome given them on August 29, 1944, in Paris when they marched down the Champs-Elysées, then through the city, on toward further combat.

On the night of April 7, 1865, the Sixth Corps was also en route to further combat, but no one had organized their parade. Yet they had their own marching music as they swung by with banners waving, torches blazing, and muskets raised— some even throwing their weapons into the air and catching them as they came down. Hearing the music of "John Brown's Body," an entire regiment began to sing. In dignified Army parades the men passing in review are not supposed to sing, but soon a whole division was roaring out the chorus. That modest man General Grant did not record his emotions on this occasion, but his aide, General Horace Porter, called it "one of the most inspiring scenes of the campaign," noting that: "The night march had become a grand review, with Grant as the reviewing officer."

When they staged their spontaneous torchlight parade, the men of the Sixth Corps had no way of knowing that, on that same afternoon, their commander had begun the exchange of letters with General Lee which was to lead to Appomattox only two days later.

6

George G. Meade

In the Presidential campaign of 1864 the voters were urged that it was "no time to swap horses in the middle of the stream." The slogan came from a remark made by President Lincoln when the Republican national convention met in Baltimore and nominated him to run for a second term.

The advice was sound, and the voters of the country must have agreed with it when they reelected Abraham Lincoln. Yet during the Gettysburg campaign the President was guilty of doing exactly that while the campaign was in progress. Just four days before battle was joined, he "swapped" commanding generals of the Army of the Potomac. His nominee did not receive the news that he had been chosen until 3:00 A.M. of the following morning, June 28, 1863, when a colonel from General Halleck's staff handed him the order from Washington. The President's decision had been made late on the fourth day before the battle, but this gave the new general just three days to prepare himself and the army to engage in the largest battle ever fought on the American continent. Few men in the military history of this nation have had thrust upon them greater responsibility suddenly, without warning.

It was Major General George G. Meade, the forty-seven-year-old commander of the Union Fifth Corps, upon whom this awful responsibility descended at such an ungodly hour in the morning. Up to that moment his career had been a successful one, eventful but not startling. He had served with distinction and had proved his competence and skill on several occasions, but there was nothing in his record to indicate that he was slated to become a hero to the people of his country.

George Gordon Meade was born December 31, 1815, at Cadiz, Spain, where his father had established a business and was acting as naval agent of the United States. Young Meade received his preparatory education in Philadelphia and in Washington, D.C., where he attended the school run by Salmon P. Chase, later Secretary of the Treasury in President Lincoln's Cabinet. He was then appointed to the United States Military Academy at West Point and in 1835 was graduated number 19 in a class of 56. Commissioned in the artillery, his first post was in Florida, where he took a brief part in the Second Seminole War that had just begun, but he was stricken with fever and reassigned to Watertown Arsenal, Massachusetts. After only a year and a half's service he resigned from the Army to become a civil engineer. For the next five and one-half years he was engaged first in railway construction, then, under the War Department, aided in conducting surveys of the Mississippi and in the establishment of the country's international boundaries. In 1842 Meade applied to be reinstated in the Army and was commissioned a second lieutenant of topographic engineers. He had lost seven years' seniority in the Army.

In the war with Mexico, Lieutenant Meade served as a topographic engineer on General Zachary Taylor's staff. He took part in the battles of Palo Alto and Resaca de la Palma and received a brevet promotion to first lieutenant for daring reconnaissance work performed at Monterey. Transferred to General Winfield Scott's staff, he was present at the Siege of Vera Cruz, where he and Captain Robert E. Lee became acquainted, but this ended his active combat service. Until the outbreak of the Civil War he was successively engaged in various engineering works: first in designing and constructing lighthouses in Delaware Bay; then as a first lieutenant in related work on the Florida Keys. Promoted to captain, he was transferred to undertake the geodetic survey of the Great Lakes.

It has often been surmised by many writers that Meade's service as a topographic engineer was of great benefit to him during the war years because it gave him a knowledge and appreciation of terrain. This may be so, but very little of his service could have equipped him for duty with troops. It was not until August 31, 1861, four and one-half months after the Civil War began, that he was commissioned a brigadier general of volunteers and given command of a Pennsylvania brigade. His unit saw little action until the end of the Peninsular campaign, being held back from joining McClellan because of Stonewall Jackson's activities in the Shenandoah Valley. Finally it was released in time to take part in the Seven Days' Battle. The brigade was heavily engaged at Mechanicsville, Gaines' Mill, and then Glendale (Frayser's Farm), where Meade was seriously wounded.

He returned to duty in time to take part in the Second Battle of Bull Run. From this point onward his rise was steadily upward. He commanded a division in the Antietam campaign at Turner's Gap and, at the Battle of Antietam, was appointed temporary commander of the First Corps when "Fighting Joe" Hooker was wounded and carried off the field. Later, in November, he was made a major general of volunteers, and at Fredericksburg his division was the only one to penetrate the Confederate lines. This achievement was certainly a persuasive factor in his favor when he was chosen soon thereafter to command the Fifth Corps, which he led in the Chancellorsville campaign. Then came the crisis in his life, at Gettysburg.

When he took command of the Army of the Potomac, General Meade wrote Halleck that the order had been "totally unexpected" and that he was "in ignorance of the exact condition of the troops and position of the enemy. . . ." This statement was probably accurate because Meade had a high regard for the truth, whether it might hurt himself or others, and it would seem that his predecessor had not kept his corps commanders informed. However, within a very short time Meade must have learned, at army headquarters, all that was known of the enemy and certainly the location of his own troops. Yet this information was only the beginning of a solution to the problems pressing upon him. He had little time in which to make new decisions for the army and practically no background for making those decisions because he had not been present at army headquarters as the campaign had progressed. Now, for the first time, he had the authority and the responsibilities of the commander of the most important army in the nation.

The campaign had begun nearly a month before with the two armies facing each other across the Rappahannock River at Fredericksburg in the positions they had occupied prior to the Battle of Chancellorsville, May 1-4, 1863, and to which they had returned after that battle.

The Confederate army was more than 70,000 strong. After the death of Stonewall Jackson it had been reorganized into three corps. Lieutenant General James Longstreet remained as the commander of the First Corps. Richard S. Ewell, back on duty with the Army after the loss of a leg at the Battle of Groveton (the day preceding Second Manassas), commanded the Second Corps. The newly formed Third Corps was commanded by General A. P. Hill. Both Ewell and Hill were newly appointed lieutenant generals.

This organization of the army into three corps of approximately equal size was a better arrangement than the former division of the army into two larger corps (under Jackson and Longstreet) and far superior to the unwieldy Union army. The latter was composed of seven corps of varying sizes and strengths. The Sixth Corps, for example, had more than 15,500 men while the Twelfth Corps had fewer than 10,000. The average strength of the Union corps and divisions was about half those of the Confederate army. Furthermore, as always, the Army of the Potomac was suffering from the federal government's peculiar replacement system. Instead of keeping the old and tried units up to strength as much as possible, letting the new recruits learn from the veteran soldiers the way the Confederates did, and as our Army does today, the Northern government permitted the formation of new untrained regiments of recruits. The old veteran regiments with experience were as capable, efficient and aggressive as any in Lee's army, but they were allowed to fight battle after battle, continually losing men by death and wounds, exhausting themselves but only occasionally receiving new men. No Union commander could simply count his regiments. He had to stop to remember which ones were trained, which were not, how large each was, and what kind of a record it had before he could decide how far to trust it in battle.

Man for man, the Confederate army that General Lee led on its second invasion of the North was thus unquestionably superior to that of his enemy. The men had been actively campaigning for two years. They had almost always defeated their more numerous opponents. They were thoroughly trained, had experienced every type of combat, and were completely inured to hard field service. It can truthfully be said that the Confederate Army of Northern Virginia constituted as fine a unit as ever marched to battle on this continent. Flushed with victory, full of confidence in their great leader, the men were again ready to engage and defeat the Northern army. No matter how much they might be outnumbered, they felt equal to any undertaking.

General Lee would probably have been greatly surprised if, at the beginning of the campaign, he had been told that for once the army of his enemies would not far outnumber his own. Throughout the campaign he assumed that he was facing the usual great disparity in numbers and acted accordingly. In fact, the Army of the Potomac numbered not much more than 100,000 men. The casualties suffered at Chancellorsville accounted for only a part of the loss in numerical strength. The ill-conceived recruitment policies of the Northern government, permitting enlistments varying from nine months to two years, accounted for the rest. If General Lee had known this fact, he might have set about the campaign entirely differently. He might have crossed the Potomac and marched into Maryland and Pennsylvania eager for battle with the Union army instead of waging the same sort of campaign of maneuver that he had the preceding year.

The campaign began on June 3, when Lee started to move some of his troops from Fredericksburg northwestward toward Culpeper. By June 8 two of his three corps were concentrated there. General A. P. Hill was left temporarily in position at Fredericksburg with the Third Corps.

General "Fighting Joe" Hooker, who had been the Union army commander at Chancellorsville, was still in command. Discovering that there were fewer troops at Fredericksburg, he proposed to President Lincoln an attack on A. P. Hill's position. When this idea was rejected, Hooker sent a large cavalry force with infantry support to attack the Confederates at Culpeper. The result was the Battle of Brandy Station, fought on June 9, 1863, the largest and most important cavalry battle of the entire war. There for the first time the Northern cavalry was able to hold its own in battle against the Confederates. Prior to this engagement the superiority of the Southern horsemen had been universally recognized. Brandy Station gave the Union cavalry that much needed confidence in its ability which was essential to proper performance of its duties. From this point onward the cavalry of the North and the South met and fought on more equal terms.

Also as a result of Brandy Station General Hooker proposed an advance on Richmond, which the President promptly rejected as he had Hooker's previous proposal. Thereupon Hooker withdrew from Fredericksburg. From then on his movements simply paralleled those of Lee, although at a much slower pace. The Union army fell far behind the Confederates, who were moving rapidly.

General Ewell with the Second Corps led the van, followed by Longstreet, then by A. P. Hill, who had left Fredericksburg when Hooker had departed. By June 13 Ewell had reached

[138]

Winchester. At the Second Battle of Winchester on June 14–15 Ewell captured nearly 4,000 prisoners, large quantities of small arms and ammunition, and more than twenty cannon. The Second Corps pressed vigorously forward across the Potomac into Maryland.

For the next two weeks the Confederate army, with Ewell's corps in the lead, ranged at will over the countryside. One of Ewell's columns captured Carlisle and threatened Harrisburg, the capital of the state of Pennsylvania. The other column passed through Gettysburg, captured York, and reached the Susquehanna River at Wrightsville. There the local militia almost burned down the town when they set fire to the bridge over the river to keep the Confederates from crossing. By working feverishly a Confederate brigade saved Wrightsville from destruction.

By June 28, when General Meade received orders to assume command, the situation must have looked confusing to him. His predecessor, General Hooker, had been very slow to move. He had been reluctant to accept the obvious, that Lee's army had crossed the Potomac and embarked on a second invasion of the North. As a result it wasn't until June 24 that a few of Hooker's units followed northward over the river. The bulk of the army crossed in the next two days, and by June 28 occupied positions in the general vicinity of Frederick, Maryland, to the west and to the south of the city.

The Northern army was now in the peculiar position of being due south of the Confederate army, which was stretched in a wide fan from Chambersburg to Wrightsville, a distance of more than 60 miles. At this point "book" tacticians enjoy criticizing General Lee for having "scattered" his army, yet all are in agreement that Lee was a great general. Conceding the fact that Lee was exceptionally able, perhaps a genius in the art of war, it is ridiculous to imply that he permitted his troops to be "scattered" in a careless manner over the countryside. He must have had a good reason for doing so. The only proper assumption that can be made is that he had purposely spread his army over a wide area. His report submitted at the end of the campaign does not explain why, nor should we expect it to do so. Reports submitted to higher authority after a campaign or battle are not the proper vehicle for a discussion of strategy or tactics. A study, even a hasty one, of Lee's other campaigns preceding Gettysburg provides a ready, proper explanation. He thought he was facing, as always before, an enemy army much larger than his own. The way to defeat that army was to fight it in detail until it had been reduced to a strength he could combat on fairly equal terms. His troops, all of them well north of the Union army, spread across the lower part of Pennsylvania, should attract the enemy. The people of the North were excited and alarmed, fearful for the safety of Harrisburg, Washington and Baltimore. General Lee's hope was that his opponents would react to this state of affairs and give him the opportunity of engaging them corps by corps, before turning on the entire army.

At this moment, however, Lee was not in the enviable situation he had hoped and planned to be. His three infantry corps had done splendidly, particularly the leading corps commanded by Ewell, who had been setting an example for the army of rapidity of movement, precision, and efficiency. The problem was the fatal mistake that had been made by his cavalry commander Jeb Stuart. In the first invasion of the North the performance of the cavalry under his command had been flawless. He was a splendid officer, highly respected and greatly admired. Today he is considered one of the greatest cavalry leaders in American history, but in this campaign he committed a terrible blunder.

Lee had given Stuart orders to guard the right flank of the advancing army, with particular attention to Ewell's Second Corps. There is no doubt what Lee wanted him to do, but the orders were vaguely worded and left much to Stuart's discretion. Unfortunately at this moment "Jeb" was still smarting under the effects of the Battle of Brandy Station. His pride had been deeply hurt, and the fact that the engagement had followed directly on the heels of a grand review that he had staged to show off his cavalry made matters far worse. Undeniably, Stuart felt that his prestige had suffered greatly and that something must be done to recover it. Lee's orders appeared to offer a solution. When he read them, Stuart undoubtedly remembered the great acclaim with which he had been received upon his return from the great ride around McClellan's army near Richmond the year before. Now here was a chance for him to ride again around the Union army. Another exploit of the same nature would wipe out the stain of Brandy Station and forever reestablish his own and his cavalry's reputation.

When Stuart made the decision to go around the Union army and then join Ewell to the northward, he expected to be absent only a short time, for he assumed that the Union army would remain in place. He did not take into account the tremendous difference that prevailed between June, 1862, and June, 1863. In the first instance when he had circled McClellan's army, the situation had been static. But on this march northward, in a moving situation, such a raid was not only utterly impractical but inexcusable. In a campaign of maneuver, the cavalry is more important than at any other time to find out what the enemy is doing and prevent him from discovering your own movements. Although Stuart did not take all his men with him, he took enough so that the remainder, without Stuart to lead them personally, were no match for the Union cavalry. General Lee was left without "the eyes and ears of the army," almost totally ignorant of what the enemy was doing. As far as he was concerned, Stuart had disappeared without a trace, and the Union army was moving. Every time it changed position Stuart had farther to go to get around it. He and his cavalry did not rejoin until July 2, the second day of the battle, and his cavalry was so exhausted that it could not be put into action until the third day.

June 28, the day General Meade assumed command, turned out to be a crucial day for General Lee also. Late that night he learned from a spy named James Harrison, who had been hired by General Longstreet, that the Union army had crossed the

Potomac River two or three days before and that Meade was its new commander. If Stuart had been with him, this would have been just the news that Lee had been waiting to hear. With Stuart to watch the movements of the Union forces and keep him informed at all times, the campaign would then have begun in earnest with every hope that his better-trained army, under his guidance, could defeat portions of the enemy in detail, then force a decisive victory on Northern soil.

Without Stuart, from whom he had not heard a word, the campaign of maneuver that he had planned was wrecked. There was only one proper course to take now. Orders were issued to concentrate the army in the vicinity of Cashtown, midway between Gettysburg and Chambersburg. This meant turning Ewell's Second Corps around and bringing it back to join the rest of the army. No battle was planned at this stage. The concentration was purely a safety measure until the situation developed, and possibly Stuart would return.

Meanwhile Meade, earlier on this same day, had issued orders to the Army of the Potomac to concentrate at Frederick preparatory to a move northward toward the Susquehanna in order to cover Baltimore and Washington more effectively than he could if the army were to remain at Frederick. This was certainly the correct move. The army under Hooker had fallen so far behind Lee's troops that, when Meade inherited it, the army was completely out of position. Meade's directive from the War Department required him to "keep in view the important fact that the Army of the Potomac is the covering army of Washington as well as the army of operation against the invading force of the rebels." He was "to cover the capital and also Baltimore. . . ." The only possible way that this could be done was to move to the northeast. Meade's first day was very busy, but very successful. He accomplished a rapid concentration, then got his troops off to an early start on the following morning, June 29. On that second day they averaged a good twenty miles, a far better pace than normal. Then on the next day, June 30, knowing that battle was probably imminent, he shortened the marches prescribed in order not to wear out the troops.

He was now in the position that he had wanted to reach, covering both Washington and Baltimore, and could begin to think about places he might choose to offer battle. In addition, completely contrary to Hooker's method of operation, he kept his corps commanders well informed of the location of all elements of the army and told them what he knew of the enemy's movements. In his first days as an army commander General Meade was obviously getting off to a very good start.

There was one arrangement made by Hooker that Meade wisely continued in effect. Of his seven corps commanders there were three exceptionally capable officers: Major General John F. Reynolds, commander of the First Corps; Major General Winfield Scott Hancock, who commanded the Second Corps; and Major General John Sedgwick, commander of the Sixth Corps. Hooker had assigned General Reynolds command of the left wing of the army, since this was the post of greatest danger. Meade also foresaw the need for having an officer whom he could trust on that flank where action was most likely to occur. As events were to prove, this was a wise delegation of authority. Later when Reynolds was killed, Meade sent General Hancock forward to take command. As for Sedgwick, his Sixth Corps was off on the right flank by itself to protect against possible attack in that direction. It is doubtful that Meade expected such an attack, but it seemed necessary to him to guard against it. There was one objection. If the battle developed on the opposite (left) flank, the Sixth Corps would have an exceedingly long march to reach the field. As it happened, this is exactly what occurred. One cannot help but feel that Meade was counting on Sedgwick to make that march, just as, at Antietam, Lee and Jackson counted on A. P. Hill to reach the field in time. Sedgwick did get there after a terrific march of thirty-four miles. Meade, it would seem, had the ability to pick the right men for the right job, a good quality in any commander.

As a precautionary measure, he had his engineers select a defensive position to the rear behind a stream called Pipe Creek. His commanders all were notified of the location of this position to which they could retreat or withdraw if the occasion should arise. General Meade has been criticized for being slow and cautious and for taking a defensive attitude when he assumed command. Certainly he did not begin by planning to attack the Confederate army. His was a defensive strategy to cover the cities he had been ordered to protect, and in the event of an enemy attack he appeared to be planning to fight a defensive battle. It is difficult to see how any intelligent officer would have acted otherwise on the first three days of his new command when he suddenly found himself pitted against the now famous Confederate Army of Northern Virginia commanded by its equally famous leader, Robert E. Lee.

Thus neither Meade nor Lee was planning to fight a battle at Gettysburg. Neither one of them knew anything at all about the terrain in that area. The selection of the site for the largest battle ever fought in America was purely an accident. On June 30 a Confederate brigade moved toward Gettysburg looking for some shoes which they hoped to find stored there. Upon discovering Union cavalry in possession of the town, the Confederates withdrew to return in greater strength the next day.

It is doubtful if any battle in American history has evoked so much discussion, argument, and disagreement among historians, students, and the public. The battle will not be described in detail here, but there are certain aspects of it involving particular actions by individual leaders that cannot be overlooked in this study.

On the morning of the first day, July 1, 1863, the Confederates approaching Gettysburg were repulsed, but they were arriving on the field in greater numbers. In the afternoon they drove the Union troops pell-mell through the town of Gettysburg and into the hills beyond. This was exactly the sort of battle that Lee had hoped to fight when he marched north into Pennsylvania. His men outnumbered the Union forces three to two. The victory should have been completed, and the

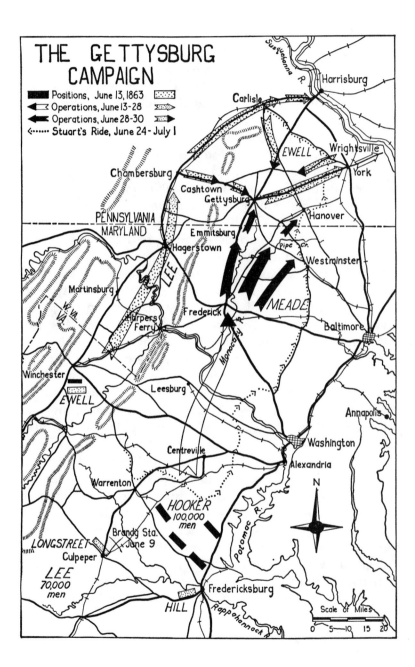

THE GETTYSBURG CAMPAIGN

Positions, June 13, 1863
Operations, June 13-28
Operations, June 28-30
Stuart's Ride, June 24 - July 1

Susquehanna R.

Harrisburg

Carlisle

EWELL

Wrightsville

York

Chambersburg

Cashtown

Gettysburg

Hanover

PENNSYLVANIA

MARYLAND

Emmitsburg

Hagerstown

Pipe Cr.

Westminster

Martinsburg

W. VA.

Frederick

MEADE

Harpers Ferry

Monocacy R.

Baltimore

LEE

Winchester

EWELL

Leesburg

Annapolis

Centreville

Washington

Alexandria

N

Warrenton

HOOKER
100,000
men

Potomac R.

Brandy Sta.
June 9

LONGSTREET

Culpeper

LEE
70,000
men

HILL

Fredericksburg

Rappahannock R.

Scale of Miles

0   5—10   15   20

defeated Union troops driven and pursued. The Battle of Gettysburg would have ended as a Southern victory. Meade would undoubtedly have retreated to the Pipe Creek area, where the principal battle of the campaign might then have been fought. It is conceivable that General Lee after his initial victory would then, a few days later, have had the decisive victory he so keenly desired on Northern soil.

When General Reynolds had been killed in the morning, Meade had sent Hancock to take command. His commanding presence on the field, as always, had inspired the troops to greater confidence and renewed resistance. The positions on Cemetery Hill, Culp's Hill, and the north end of Cemetery Ridge were hastily consolidated and prepared against a renewed attack, but it never came.

General Ewell's failure to launch a final vigorous attack, which most historians now agree would probably have succeeded despite Hancock's best efforts, must rest on the shoulders of General Lee rather than on Ewell. The order Lee sent to Ewell was to capture those hills, if practicable. This was Lee's second fatal discretionary order of the campaign (the first had been to Stuart, resulting in the misguided ride around the Union army). Ewell, who was not as well acquainted with the overall situation as Lee, exercised the discretion given him and decided not to make the attempt. If Lee had definitely wanted the attack made, he should have issued a clear, peremptory order which Ewell would have promptly obeyed. If Lee had been doubtful of success, he should have ridden over to look at the ground and then made the decision himself. At this stage the important place to be was with Ewell and nowhere else.

For several generations it has been standard practice to accuse Longstreet of losing the battle on the second day. Recently students have restudied the facts, paced off the ground, made a tremendous number of calculations of marching speed, distance and so forth, and now are inclined to exonerate Longstreet. It is not necessary to enter into an involved discussion of routes, distances, or time factors in order to comment on what happened. First, it is a well-known fact that Longstreet was opposed to making the attack. In later years he claimed that Lee had promised him before they left Virginia that he would conduct a campaign of maneuver involving an offensive strategy but, if forced to fight a large-scale battle, would stand on the defensive.

Lee categorically denied having made any such promise, and it is impossible to believe that he could have done so. In the first place, it would have been entirely impractical to make such a promise before the campaign had even started. Second, General Lee hoped to conduct the campaign in such a way that he would not have to fight the entire Union army until after portions of it had been defeated and destroyed. After that had happened, it would have been completely contrary to his nature to have stood passively on the defensive against an army of about his own strength that he could fairly expect to defeat and destroy. The very worst that could possibly occur would be to have to fight the entire enemy army without any preliminary victorious engagements, and it was this eventuality that Lee had in mind when he wrote in his final report: "It had not been intended to deliver a general battle so far from our base unless attacked. . . ." Of course Lee had hoped this would not happen, and on the morning of the second day at Gettysburg such was not yet the case. All but one Confederate division was on the field, while Meade had only some three-fourths of his army present.

Longstreet did obey the orders given him, but it cannot be said that he did so with any alacrity. In spite of this his troops almost captured Little Round Top. Regardless of all the mathematical calculations done by students and historians, one cannot help but feel that if Longstreet's heart had been in it, the attack would have been a success. The time differential was so slight that if he had moved forward with the enthusiasm, aggressiveness and speed usually exhibited by the Army of Northern Virginia enroute to battle, Little Round Top would have been captured. Then, if his attack had been properly supported, it could have swept onward along Cemetery Ridge. At Gettysburg, however, the usual verve and élan of some of the leaders of the army was missing.

It seems hardly necessary to say that if Stonewall Jackson had been alive and in command of the attack on the first day, Gettysburg would have been a Southern victory. Certainly if the attack of the second day had been made by Jackson, it would have succeeded gloriously.

There is no question today that "Pickett's Charge" at the center of the Union line should not have been made. Yet some of the reasons why the attack was launched have not been sufficiently emphasized. The first day's battle had been very favorable to the Confederates; victory should have been won on that day. Again, on the second day, the army had come close to victory. General Lee was very reluctant to return to Virginia with nothing gained, after having come within such a narrow margin of winning. It was too late to continue the campaign; supplies, particularly ammunition, were too short; the time for maneuver had passed. Lee had no choice but to retreat and admit failure, or try one more assault.

As for Meade's conduct of the battle it was practically flawless from a strictly defensive point of view. There has never been any really valid criticism of anything he did or failed to do. Some have contended that he should have hurried immediately to the battlefield instead of sending Hancock, or that he should have ridden with him, or gone forward as soon thereafter as possible. On the other hand, Meade's guiding hand was needed at army headquarters to ensure that proper orders were issued for all the army to reach the field as soon as possible, whereas Hancock was perfectly capable of taking charge on that first afternoon at Gettysburg. Also, bluntly speaking, Meade's personal presence would have added little. In appearance he was not prepossessing—a tall, slim, gaunt man who wore an old slouched hat and looked somewhat ungainly. His arrival on the scene would not have produced the electrifying effect, the resurgence of confidence, the renewed will to resist that the appearance of Hancock "the Superb" almost instantly created. Meade did well to select Hancock as the man whose presence on the field would be the most effective toward inspiring the men to renewed efforts.

On the second day it has been suggested that if Meade had personally ridden again over the field toward the left flank, he might have been in time to prevent the Third Corps from moving forward to occupy the advanced positions of the Peach Orchard and the Wheatfield. There is some validity to this criticism, for General Daniel E. Sickles would not have dared move forward if Meade had specifically told him not to do so. There was no reason, on the other hand, for Meade to suspect that such a move was being contemplated directly contrary to his orders. When Meade did inspect the position and saw the radical change that had been made in his plans, he instantly recognized the possibility that the battle could be lost at this point but that it was too late to undo the damage. Adopting the only practical course, he left Sickles where he was, in the wrong place, and reinforced the Third Corps as rapidly and as often as he could.

General Meade has been unfairly criticized for not launching an immediate counterattack as soon as "Pickett's Charge" was repulsed. Ideally, this would have been the perfect time to have mounted an assault while the Confederate army was reorganizing, but he had no troops readily available. It is claimed that the Sixth Corps should have been kept well in hand for just this purpose, but that Meade failed to do so and thus threw away his opportunity to inflict a decisive blow. This claim overlooks completely the cumulative effects of Sickles' nearly fatal error of advancing his Third Corps forward way beyond its assigned position. In order to support Sickles, who could not be withdrawn at the very last hour in the face of the approaching Confederate attack, Meade had to feed in his troops piecemeal as they arrived, using up far too many men of the Fifth and then the Sixth Corps.

As a result, Sedgwick's Sixth Corps was not readily available.

Its units, by necessity, were widely dispersed and there was no time to assemble them. If a counterattack were to be launched, it had to be done within, at most, one hour's time. If attempted later, it would surely have failed. General Lee's army was by no means shattered simply because its attacks had been repulsed. Any Union counterattack not launched immediately would have been thrown back with ease by the Confederate army.

General Meade was 100 percent correct in not attempting a counterattack that would have met with a bloody repulse. However, his failure to pursue Lee's army after the battle is another story. One gets the impression that he was happy to see Lee march away and gave little consideration to a pursuit of any sort. During the three days of battle some of the leaders of the opposing armies appear to have reversed their roles. During those three days it was the Southern leaders who seemed content with halfway measures while the Northern leaders were the ones who exhibited aggressiveness, vigor, and an eagerness to come to grips with the enemy. Perhaps the fact that the battle was being fought on Northern soil had its effect. But when Lee began his retreat, Meade and most of his army seemed content with simply driving the invader away. A vigorous pursuit probably would not have resulted in the destruction of Lee's army, but extensive losses could have been inflicted that the South could have ill afforded.

After the battle there were no more changes of commanders for the Army of the Potomac. Meade continued to lead it until the very end, although there was nothing brilliant or outstanding in his performance of his duties. During these last two years of the war he could not have been a very popular leader, for he had a rather violent temper that was liable to explode without warning at any indication of negligence or when he was operating under great pressure. Soldiers are always good at finding names for their officers; Meade was known to them as The Old Snapping Turtle. However, after an outburst of irritation he would always regret it and try to make amends if he had been in error.

George G. Meade

He had a strong dedication to duty; for him the cause was far more important than any individual. When General Grant was appointed to command all the armies, Meade offered to give up his place, thinking that Grant might prefer another, perhaps Sherman, who had served with Grant in the West. He begged Grant not to hesitate to make any change because he believed that the feelings or wishes of an individual should not be considered when it came to selecting the right man. Grant wrote later: "This incident gave me even a more favorable opinion of Meade than did his great victory at Gettysburg the July before. It is men who wait to be selected, and not those who seek, from whom we may always expect the most efficient service." That Meade gave such service throughout his career is well illustrated by his refusal to be left behind in the final pursuit. Although quite ill, so much so that, if he had not been the army commander, he might have been placed in a hospital, he insisted on continuing to do his duty all the way from Petersburg to Appomattox.

Gettysburg was General Meade's finest hour. There may have been two or three other officers in the Army of the Potomac who might have done as well as he, but there were several who could not have. From the moment when he was called in the hour of his country's need until the conclusion of the battle, practically no one could have improved on his performance. The decisive victory at Gettysburg occurring simultaneously with the surrender at Vicksburg marked the turning point of the war, when the North could at last see victory ahead.

7

William Tecumseh Sherman

It was a beautiful Sunday morning in April on the banks of the Tennessee River. In the woods and fields beside the river some 37,000 men of the Union Army were peacefully encamped. Reveille had sounded; the cooking of breakfast had just begun when there burst upon them 40,000 Confederate soldiers. The date was April 6, 1862, the first day of the battle to be known forever as "Shiloh, Bloody Shiloh."

Raw, green untrained troops fled by the thousands to cower in terror under the bluffs by the river; but somehow most of the men stayed to fight. If all had run away, it would not have surprised the few trained soldiers who were on the field that fearful day. Nor could they have held their positions at all if the attacking troops had been any better trained and disciplined. Hundreds of the Confederates stopped to loot the deserted Union camps. The first large battle in the West degenerated into the most confused, disorganized, killing melee ever seen in the Civil War. The fight continued from dawn to dusk. The Northern army was slowly driven backward, step by step, from position to position, until at the last the Southern forces could do no more.

On the next day, with 25,000 Union reinforcements on the field, the tide turned. Pressed back by the weight of numbers, the Confederate army was driven from the field. The Southern loss in the two-day battle was 10,700 casualties, while more than

13,000 Northern soldiers were killed, wounded, captured or missing.

On neither side was the reputation of any senior officer enhanced, with one lone exception. Amid the roar of cannon, the crack and rattle of musketry, in the heat of that embattled melee, one man found himself at last and for the first time faced his future with a new courage and conviction. Perhaps, for him, it was necessary to endure that awful killing, to be wounded, to have a shoulder strap shot off his uniform, his hat smashed by a cannon ball, to have four horses shot from under him in order to cleanse his mind and soul of his uncertainty, for prior to that day his had been a very checkered career.

Tecumseh Sherman, named by his father in honor of the great Indian chief, was born at Lancaster, Ohio, February 8, 1820, the sixth of eleven children. When "Cump," as he was called, was nine years old, his father suddenly died, leaving his mother with entirely inadequate means to support such a large family. Their great family friend, Thomas Ewing, who lived almost next door and would someday be a United States Senator and serve in the cabinets of three Presidents, raised a fund to help support the widow and then stepped in to ask permission to rear one of the children for her. Tecumseh was chosen and went to live with the Ewing family, although the houses were so close that, in a way, it was not too greatly different from living at his own home. When the Ewings learned that he had not been baptized, he was given the name William Tecumseh Sherman. Perhaps the Catholic priest objected to an Indian name without another first name to precede it.

Sherman was graduated from West Point in 1840, sixth in a class of 42. His was one of those classes where more cadets failed than passed. Among those who were graduated with him were two cadets from Virginia whose names would also become household words during the Civil War: George H. Thomas, who stood number 12; and Richard S. Ewell, who was graduated next in line as number 13.

Commissioned in the artillery, Sherman was sent to Florida,

where he saw practically no action against the Seminole Indians, but there began for him an association with the people of the South that lasted until the beginning of the Mexican War. After Florida, he was stationed at Fort Moultrie, Charleston, South Carolina, where he served under the command of Captain Robert Anderson. Sherman also traveled extensively in the South, made friends easily, and definitely became more Southern than Northern in his outlook.

When the war with Mexico began, he volunteered but, instead of being assigned to a combat unit, was sent to California and missed the war action completely. After the gold rush came to California, Sherman was ordered to Washington, where, to no one's surprise, he married his benefactor's daughter, Eleanor Ewing, always known as Ellen. He was stationed at St. Louis, then ordered to New Orleans, and from there went to San Francisco, where he resigned from the Army to become a banker. In this new career he proved highly successful. He personally saved the bank in a crisis in California, but he had lost some money invested for Army friends. Although he had been in no way responsible, Sherman insisted as a point of honor that he must repay every penny, although it left him with practically nothing. Returning to St. Louis at loose ends, he practiced law for a while at Leavenworth, Kansas. Finally in 1859 he applied for and, through the help of such friends as Braxton Bragg and Pierre G. T. Beauregard, was appointed the first superintendent of what later was to become Louisiana State University. He was back in his beloved South again and his future seemed assured, except that Sherman could see the clouds gathering on the horizon. He had always been gifted with a quick mind and a rare sense of intuition and recognized long before most people that a tremendous crisis was coming which could wreck the nation.

After the secession of South Carolina, when it became increasingly clear that the other Gulf States, including Louisiana, would secede, Sherman was terribly torn by conflicting emotions. By this time he had more personal friends in the South than in the North, certainly more in South Carolina than in his home state of Ohio. Duty to his country, however, must come first, although, as he expressed it to a friend, the war would cause him to fight "your people, whom I love best." In an almost brokenhearted manner he warned that the South had no chance of winning; that the Southern people must stop to think; in the end they would surely fail; the war was a totally unnecessary evil and would bring untold suffering to both sides and disaster to the South.

Sherman resigned as superintendent, telling the governor of Louisiana before he left the state: "I prefer to maintain my allegiance to the Constitution as long as a fragment of it survives." Yet after his former commanding officer, Major Robert Anderson, was forced to surrender Fort Sumter, Sherman held aloof. When his younger brother John, an influential United States Senator, tried to obtain a place for him in the War Department that could have led to his becoming Secretary of War, he refused the position. When John made arrangements for him that almost certainly would have given him a commission as a general of Ohio volunteers, he still held aloof; McClellan was chosen instead of Sherman.

Finally in May, 1861, when informed that he had been appointed colonel of the 13th Infantry (Regular Army), Sherman obeyed. His first battle was Bull Run, July 21, 1861, where he acquitted himself remarkably well. According to probably the best authority, and the officer most capable of making a balanced judgment, Major Matthew F. Steele, who taught the subject in later years at the Command and General Staff School at Fort Leavenworth, Kansas, there were only two brigade commanders on the field that day who really distinguished themselves in their first great battle: Stonewall Jackson and William Tecumseh Sherman.

Promoted to brigadier general, he was chosen by his former commander, Robert Anderson, as one of his senior officers to assist him in the defense of Kentucky. Sherman's classmate, George H. Thomas, was also selected, although Sherman had to practically guarantee the latter's loyalty to President Lincoln personally. People were very suspicious of Thomas because of his Virginia birth. It would not be long before suspicions of Sherman's loyalty would arise, for it was in Kentucky that he entered upon that peculiar period of his career that has never been satisfactorily explained. He became terribly despondent, nervous, irritable, and absent-minded. Constantly he magnified the numbers of his enemies beyond all reason and worried about the fate of the supposedly outnumbered troops under his command.

Early in October, 1861, Anderson retired for reasons of poor health. Sherman was appointed to succeed him as commander of the Department of the Cumberland. Before going to Kentucky, he had made the peculiar request that he not be assigned such an important command, and now he had inherited it. Things went from bad to worse, and he also ran afoul of the newspaper correspondents. Sherman was one of the few to understand the necessity for censorship but made no effort to explain his thoughts to the reporters, who in turn criticized him at every opportunity. On a visit by Secretary of War Simon Cameron (Stanton's predecessor) Sherman, when asked, said 200,000 men were needed by him. This figure was outrageous if, as Cameron understood it, that many were needed to save Kentucky. Probably Sherman meant that 200,000 soldiers would be required to clear the entire Mississippi Valley. In any event it was foolish to have talked in such terms so early in the war, even though before the war was ended, more than 200,000 men were needed to recapture control of the Mississippi. Perhaps Sherman was also one of the few who realized how desperately the Southern people would fight to save their land, but the word rapidly spread that because of his Southern associations he was not to be trusted, that he was erratic and probably out of his mind. The newspapers called him insane. Recognizing that he was at least approaching a nervous breakdown, General Halleck gave him an extended leave of absence.

When Sherman came back to duty, he appeared a changed

man but still was regarded with suspicion until he proved himself as a division commander on that fateful day at Shiloh. Despite the fact that his division was composed of the newest recruits in the army, almost everyone on the field that day universally acclaimed him as the one indispensable officer who saved the army. Those who observed him in action, from the lowliest private to the highest-ranking officer, felt that if Sherman had been killed, the battle could have been lost. Halleck, who was not present, after consulting with those who had been, immediately recommended Sherman for promotion to major general. The Congress and the President acted with unusual rapidity to appoint him.

On that first day at Shiloh, Grant and Sherman took each other's measure. Thenceforward Sherman was Grant's most trusted lieutenant, the one to whom Grant always assigned the most difficult, exacting tasks, while Sherman became Grant's most loyal, admiring follower. The two became the Northern equivalent of the South's immortal Lee-Jackson combination.

When, in November and December, 1862, General Grant undertook his first combined land and water movement against Vicksburg, he led the advance overland while entrusting to Sherman the move by boat down the Mississippi River. Again, in the final effort that succeeded against Vicksburg, it was Sherman whom Grant left in charge to act independently against the great Confederate stronghold while he advanced in command of the other two corps of the army. When the city was invested and the besieging army was being threatened with the possibility of an attack by General Joseph E. Johnston from the rear, it was Sherman's corps that was assigned to protect the army against that threat. On the evening of July 4, 1863, the day Vicksburg surrendered, Sherman was immediately sent with 50,000 men to attack Johnston, who prudently retreated.

In the battles around Chattanooga, Grant again gave Sherman the most difficult assignment. His troops, coming from the west, were to cross the Tennessee River, march completely around the north of the city of Chattanooga, cross the river a second time, and attack the northern end of Missionary Ridge. In this instance his assault was repulsed, while General Thomas' attack in the center succeeded. General Sherman's detractors, particularly those who are emotionally disturbed by false notions concerning the famous "March to the Sea," enjoy pointing to Sherman's unsuccessful assault at this point and fail to give credit where credit is due. Sherman's attack failed for one reason and one reason only. The position was held by the best division in the Confederate Army of Tennessee commanded by probably the most capable, intrepid division commander in the entire Confederate States Army, Major General Patrick R. Cleburne, who then, with his division, covered the retreat of the army and stopped the Union pursuit.

In March, 1864, when Grant was assigned to command all the armies of the United States, there was only one logical choice to succeed him as commanding general of the Military Division of the Mississippi, the same man who had succeeded him in command of the Army of the Tennessee, Major General William Tecumseh Sherman. This new assignment included the Departments of the Ohio, the Cumberland, and the Tennessee and command of the three armies bearing the same names.

The Army of the Cumberland was by far the largest; it numbered 60,000 men and was commanded by Sherman's West Point classmate, Major General George H. Thomas. The Army of the Tennessee, Grant's and Sherman's old army, was now led by Major General James B. McPherson, and it numbered 25,000 men. The Army of the Ohio contained only 13,500 men and was under the command of Major General John M. Schofield. The total combined strength of Sherman's force, including the cavalry, was about 110,000 men.

His opponent in the coming campaign was General Joseph E. Johnston, who had been appointed to command the Confederate Army of Tennessee after General Braxton Bragg's disastrous defeats at Lookout Mountain and Missionary Ridge. In the beginning General Johnston had only two corps commanded by Lieutenant Generals William J. Hardee and John B. Hood. A few days after the campaign began, they were joined by Lieutenant General Leonidas Polk's Army of Mississippi, which then became, for all practical purposes, a third, although somewhat smaller, corps. Johnston's total Confederate force, including his cavalry, numbered about 65,000 men.

It should be noted that Sherman's and Johnston's opposing armies were of almost exactly the same strength as the principal opposing armies in Virginia—Meade's Union Army of the Potomac that General Grant accompanied into battle and Lee's Confederate Army of Northern Virginia.

These were the two great campaigns planned by General Grant for the year 1864. All other operations were of a secondary nature, or subsidiary to these offensives, designed in one way or another to aid in the accomplishment of the objectives set forth for these two major campaigns. In each case the target was the same, the destruction of one of the two large remaining Confederate forces. In each case also there was a secondary objective, the capture of a great Southern city, railroad and manufacturing center.

It had taken a long, long time, but at last, the two greatest leaders of the North were commanding the North's two largest groups of armies, and they were facing the strongest of the Southern armies, commanded by the two most famous Southern leaders still alive. General Grant (working through General Meade) would now be confronting General Robert E. Lee for the first time, while his most trustworthy officer, Sherman, would be fighting against Joseph E. Johnston. The only other possible combination of commanding generals that could have produced greater interest for a student of the military history of this war would have been if Stonewall Jackson had been living. The student might also have wished that General Nathan Bedford Forrest, undoubtedly the greatest cavalryman in the history of this country, had also been scheduled to take a direct part in the coming campaign to Atlanta; but then, if Forrest had been present, his extraordinarily brilliant operations conducted simultaneously in Mississippi and Tennessee could not have taken place.

Shortly after midnight, May 3–4, 1864, Grant's campaign against Robert E. Lee's army began, with Richmond as its secondary objective. Only three days later, Sherman's campaign against Johnston's army began, with the city of Atlanta, Georgia, as its secondary objective. With so many points of similarity, the strengths of the opposing armies in each case about 110,000 against 65,000, the objectives the same, each led by the most capable leaders in the field, it might have been expected that the campaigns would have been fought in somewhat the same way.

For two principal reasons the similarity disappeared almost as soon as the campaigns began. In the contest between Grant and Lee all flank movements made by Grant were to his left because there was nothing to be gained by moving in the opposite direction into the central part of Virginia. Such a move would lead nowhere. It would greatly increase his supply problems and lead him away from any possibility of being supported by the Navy, which eventually was of great aid to him when he reached the Richmond-Petersburg area.

On the other hand, Sherman's campaign was conducted entirely inland, with no consideration given to naval support. Each group of armies, both Sherman's and Johnston's, would, in the long run, be supported logistically by one prime means, the railroad line running between Atlanta, Georgia, and Chattanooga, Tennessee. Therefore it made no difference from the logistical point of view whether Sherman moved by his right or by his left flank. He could do either, and he did both.

Yet the principal difference between the two campaigns is to be found, as always, not in the physical characteristics of the terrain, but in the personalities of the two commanding generals. Never has the old axiom that it is the man, the leader, who counts above all else been more thoroughly proven than here in a comparison between these two campaigns, in Virginia and in

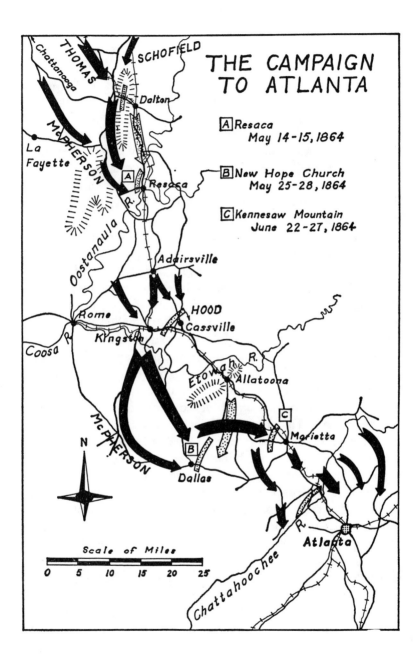

THE CAMPAIGN
TO ATLANTA

[A] Resaca
May 14-15, 1864

[B] New Hope Church
May 25-28, 1864

[C] Kennesaw Mountain
June 22-27, 1864

Scale of Miles

0   5   10   15   20   25

Georgia. Neither Sherman nor Johnston was afraid to fight, nor hesitated when battle was offered, but they were neither as audacious or as ready to engage in battle as Lee or Grant. The result was a campaign of skillful maneuvering, during which three significant battles were fought; but the principal memory that lingers is that it was a carefully waged campaign, with hardly a mistake or an error made on either side as the commanding generals of both armies proved they possessed extraordinary ability and capacity for intelligent leadership.

General Johnston's first position was on Rocky Face Ridge, a line of hills running north and south across the main railroad line about three and a half miles northwest of Dalton, Georgia. The position was far too strong and heavily fortified for General Sherman to attack. He therefore sent McPherson's army on a wide turning movement to the south, aiming toward a gap in the ridge line that led to Resaca, while Thomas with his larger army made a strong demonstration against the front of the Confederate position, and Schofield with his smaller force moved down from the north toward Johnston's right flank.

Upon reaching Resaca on the ninth of May, McPherson attacked but met unexpectedly strong resistance. According to Sherman's plan, McPherson was to have captured the town, seized the railroad line, and blocked Johnston's line of retreat toward Atlanta. His army was sufficiently strong to have accomplished this mission with ease. The Confederates had only a very small force at hand, but their resistance was so stout and vigorous that McPherson greatly overestimated their strength and halted. Thereupon Sherman moved almost all his troops southward toward Resaca. When Johnston learned of this, he also marched to Resaca, where he was joined by Polk's Army of Mississippi. The result was the two-day Battle of Resaca. On the first day, May 14, the Union forces made a partial attack, which was repulsed. On the second day the fighting was resumed, and again the attackers were repulsed until General Johnston was informed of a Union force crossing the Oostanaula River to the south, threatening his left flank and his line of retreat. This caused him to withdraw.

Most of the country between Chattanooga and Atlanta was generally wooded, rugged and hilly, except for the area between the Oostanaula River and the Etowah River, which both flow westward to join at Rome, Georgia, where they form the Coosa River. General Johnston hoped that he might find a good defensive position along his line of retreat somewhere in this area between the two rivers but was disappointed.

An opportunity did, however, arise where he planned to turn and attack a portion of Sherman's advancing army. The chances of success appeared excellent, but his plan was ruined by General John B. Hood, who was supposed to make the main attack. Somehow Hood conceived the notion that he was being outflanked and halted his corps to face it in the wrong direction. Johnston then reluctantly withdrew to Allatoona Pass.

When Sherman reached Allatoona Pass, no one needed to tell him how strong a position he faced. He had seen it before during those pleasant years after graduation from West Point when he had learned to like the Southern people so well. Sherman had ridden extensively on horseback over the area from Atlanta north to Marietta and beyond, westward as far as Rome, Georgia, and the terrain was firmly fixed in his memory. That rocky barrier to his front was practically impregnable and could easily be held against all assaults. Another wide turning movement would be necessary to outflank the Confederate army.

He therefore gave his troops three days to rest and refit, meanwhile filling all his wagons with supplies because he would have to leave the line of the railroad temporarily until he could get south of Allatoona Pass. For the second time in the campaign he moved westward, again with McPherson's army on the right flank. His target was Dallas, Georgia, but General Johnston had detected the move and foreseen the probable target. When the Union troops arrived, they found the Confederates waiting at a new position at New Hope Church, blocking their path.

The ground was wooded, rugged terrain, a tangle of deep ravines and ridges. It took three days of sharp skirmishing to develop the Confederate position, culminating in an unsuccessful assault launched on May 27 against Johnston's right flank that met a costly repulse. On the next day Sherman started to shift back to his left toward the railroad again, but a strong Confederate attack on May 28 delayed the move. It was not until June 6 that Union troops were again astride the railway line. Incessant rains beginning on June 1, as well as Confederate opposition, delayed all movements. The Union forward advance along the railroad line was slow and disheartening with frequent engagements occurring between portions of the two armies until the line of Kennesaw Mountain was reached.

There on June 22 all forward progress was completely stopped, and Sherman was confronted with one of the most difficult decisions of his entire career. There were only three possible choices. The first, to wait in place while daily skirmishing continued between the two hostile armies, was completely unacceptable. Next, he could continue to maneuver back and forth, from right to left, as he had done from the beginning, forcing Johnston slowly backward, but the conditions at the time were especially difficult. The roads were nothing but mud, every stream was overflowing its banks, fast marching would be impossible, and the chance of effecting a surprise move against his ever-alert opponent would be practically nil under such conditions.

His men were gradually showing a growing feeling of dissatisfaction and unrest at the constant maneuvering that had been taking place. They had advanced over three-fourths of the distance to Atlanta in seven weeks, had fought several skirmishes and engagements and two significant battles at Resaca and New Hope Church, but nothing that could compare with the great and famous battles of the war. They were fully aware of the fact that they heavily outnumbered the smaller enemy army, were confident of success, and felt assured of victory. The Union soldiers wanted to fight and end the campaign.

Sherman decided in favor of the troops. On June 27 the grand assault was made. It was a valiant effort, executed with great bravery and courage, but the position proved far too formidable, the defenders far too skillful, and fully determined to hold their positions. In a very short time the attack was repulsed with a loss of nearly 3,000; the Confederate casualties numbered only about 500 men. Most military authorities agree that the attack was a mistake, but there are many who think that Sherman acted correctly in at least making the effort.

After that failure there was nothing else to do but embark on another flank maneuver. However, the incessant rains had stopped and the roads were drying, so marching conditions were much improved. For the third time Sherman moved by his right flank. Two successive advances brought him to the line of the Chattahoochee River, where, to his surprise, he found Johnston entrenched with his back to the river in a strong position previously surveyed and prepared by his engineers, but with six bridges available to retreat across if necessary.

In his *Memoirs* Sherman wrote that these proved to be "one of the strongest pieces of field-fortification I ever saw." He therefore made no attack at that point. Feinting toward his right as if he were again going to outflank his enemy for the fourth time in the same direction, Sherman undertook to cross the river in the other direction, for the first time advancing by his left flank. Unable to prevent this crossing, Johnston withdrew to another position that was being prepared just north of Atlanta, where he could dispute an advance across Peachtree Creek. There on July 17 Johnston was relieved from command by order of President Jefferson Davis. He was replaced by John B. Hood, who was appointed a temporary full general.

This ended the adroit campaign of maneuver waged between Sherman and Johnston to reach Atlanta. The story of the battles that followed, the capture of the city, and the succeeding operations should more properly be told in connection with the study of the new Confederate commander, John Bell Hood.

It was during the period following the capture of Atlanta that General Sherman conceived the great strategic idea of making his celebrated "March to the Sea." It took a bit of persuasion on his part to obtain General Grant's approval, but once Grant had agreed, President Lincoln accepted the decision. They were certainly aware of the direct military advantages to be gained. (Today the concept of strategic air warfare, whose objective is the progressive destruction of the enemy's military, industrial and economic systems, is universally accepted.) However, it is doubtful that either Grant or Lincoln saw how much else was to be gained. Sherman appears to have been the only one to realize fully how stunned the South would be by his ability to march a great army wherever he wanted, with ease, through a vast expanse of Southern territory. He alone was perceptive enough to understand how damaging a blow would be dealt to Southern morale, as well as Southern resources. It was only after he had reached the sea at Savannah, Georgia, that Sherman received a personal letter from President Lincoln acknowledging how truly successful the march had been and admitting that actually all that Lincoln or anyone else had ever done was "to acquiesce" in Sherman's proposals.

Unfortunately it is still difficult for some people even today, more than one hundred years after the event, to think of the "March to the Sea" in a fair, impartial manner. Unfortunately, also, whenever the name General Sherman is mentioned, the first thought that leaps to many people's minds is the thought of destruction. He has been called everything from a "pyromaniac" to, more humorously, "the father of urban renewal."

Yet those who lived in the South during the decade immediately following the Civil War thought very highly of Sherman. Southerners thought of him as a friend in contrast to the Radicals. Few persons today know that it was not his march through Georgia that caused him to be hated down South. Nor was it uncommon for his men to be asked by Georgians to be sure to punish South Carolina when they got there. These sentiments agreed perfectly with those of his own men. The great majority were Westerners who thought very little about slavery one way or another. They fought for one idea, one purpose only, to preserve the Union. They would just as soon have marched on abolitionist Massachusetts as on South Carolina because they believed these two states to have been equally responsible for starting the whole bloody mess.

How many people who hate General Sherman have actually read his official orders to the troops issued three days before the march began? Here they are, in part:

4. The army will forage liberally on the country during the march. To this end, each brigade commander will organize a good and sufficient foraging party, under the command of one or more discreet officers, who will gather, near the route traveled, corn or forage of any kind, meat of any kind, vegetables, corn-meal, or whatever is needed by the command, aiming at all times to keep in the wagons at least ten days' provisions for his command, and three days' forage. Soldiers must not enter the dwellings of the inhabitants, or commit any trespass; but, during a halt or camp, they may be permitted to gather turnips, potatoes, and other vegetables, and to drive in stock in sight of their camp. To regular foraging-parties must be intrusted the gathering of provisions and forage, at any distance from the road traveled.

5. To corps commanders alone is intrusted the power to destroy mills, houses, cotton-gins, etc.; and for them this general principle is laid down: In districts and neighborhoods where the army is unmolested, no destruction of such property should be permitted; but should guerrillas or bushwhackers molest our march, or should the inhabitants burn bridges, obstruct roads, or otherwise manifest local hostility, then army commanders should order and enforce a devastation more or less relentless, according to the measure of such hostility.

6. As for horses, mules, wagons, etc., belonging to the inhabitants, the cavalry and artillery may appropriate freely and without limit; discriminating, however, between the rich, who are usually hostile, and the poor and industrious, usually neutral or friendly. Foraging-parties may also take mules or horses, to replace the jaded animals of their trains, or to serve as pack-mules for the regiments or brigades. In all foragings, of whatever kind, the parties engaged will refrain from abusive or threatening language, and may, where the officer in command thinks proper, give written certificates of the facts, but no receipts; and they will endeavor to leave with each family a reasonable portion for their maintenance.

These were the orders for the army in Georgia. Of course there were excesses. In an army that large there are bound to be lawless people who will do whatever they think they can get away with doing. And, in addition to natural-born looters, there were, for example, some Missouri regiments who had heard of atrocities committed by Southerners back in their hometowns. However, most of the men who felt duty-bound to punish saved their hatred for South Carolina. Through Georgia a great number of Sherman's soldiers converted the march into a wonderful Halloween picnic.

Then Sherman's soldiers learned that numerous civilian leaders had been calling on the people of the state (noncombatants) to bushwhack the invading army. They saw copies in the newspapers of hysterical exhortations to the people. No army can afford to stand for that sort of thing. The result was nothing but trouble when the people responded. Things got burned that never otherwise would have been touched. Fortunately most of the inhabitants had better sense than to listen or to pay attention to these ridiculous outbursts of emotion.

Sherman's orders deserve careful study. Regardless of excesses, these orders should be compared with the results inevitably obtained as a result of strategic air warfare or by naval blockade where the women, the children, the old, the defenseless, suffer equally—actually in greater measure. In fact, Sherman's army was far less destructive to innocent persons and nonmilitary property than air warfare, which is inhumane by its very nature, or naval bombardment of cities by hostile fleets.

The Southern people in the first decade following the war probably became acquainted with these orders, and many had personal knowledge of numerous instances where Sherman, his officers and his men showed kindness and consideration for people. A full and complete study of Sherman's march is not practicable here. But the Southern people also knew of another famous Union general who had mercilessly devastated the Shenandoah Valley of Virginia and seemed to take a grim pleasure in burning and destruction for the pure joy of it. There is absolutely no comparison between the total destruction wrought by Sheridan and the work done by Sherman. Once, after remarking that Sheridan just seemed to love destruction— the more he could burn, the happier he was—a noted historian said: "Sheridan was just a boy with matches and a .22 rifle who never grew up."

Immediately after the war was over, even the people of South Carolina respected Sherman, although, when his troops reached the borders of their state, his strict orders were relaxed, then put into effect again as soon as he reached North Carolina. So South Carolina was treated to a much more destructive march than either Georgia or North Carolina. The question then arises: Why is the march through Georgia so much more remembered and maligned than the later march through South Carolina, where greater destruction and devastation were permitted?

Until Sherman began his "March to the Sea," no one in the South would have believed it possible that a Northern army could simply march into one of the Southern states freely and at will, with ease and impunity, without being met by a Southern army that would throw it back into a headlong retreat. Until his march began, the South still held hopes of eventual victory. Nothing else could have demonstrated as effectively as Sherman's march the immense power of the North to win the war ultimately against the greatly outnumbered Confederacy. Prior to that time the Southern people, remembering great victories in the past, were still hopeful that their secession might yet succeed, if for no other reason than that the North might become weary of attempting to conquer them. But the "March to the Sea" practically obliterated all hope of success in their struggle for survival as a nation. The march through Georgia was more effective in ultimately destroying the Southern will to resist than the loss of a great battle would have been. If Sherman's army could do it, so could others. Georgia was only the first instance. What good did it do to have their men fighting at the front when such a thing as the "March to the Sea" could occur again at any time? The blow to Southern morale was far greater than the material destruction actually effected by Union troops in Georgia. It came as such a stunning shock that Sherman's later marches through South Carolina and into North Carolina were almost anticlimactic, even though the damage in South Carolina was greater.

In the years immediately following the War Between the States most of the Southern people slowly came to realize that, in the long run, the "March to the Sea" had been a way of ending the war comparatively quickly with little bloodshed. Few among them had any excessively harsh feelings toward Sherman. Instead they remembered clearly the extremely magnanimous terms extended by Sherman to Johnston and his army upon their surrender, even more generous than those given Lee by Grant at Appomattox, and they further remembered Sherman's attempt on that occasion to restore their state governments into the hands of the Southerners themselves. If President Lincoln had lived, Sherman's efforts might have been more successful, but instead his terms were repudiated and he was denounced by Secretary of War Stanton, all the Radicals in Congress, and a great number of the Northern newspapers, who had never liked him but until then, with his record of victories, had been unable to attack him successfully.

The Southern people, however, remembered what he had tried to do, and his trips down South after the war were agreeable and pleasant until the publication of his *Memoirs*. There have been very few books ever written that have produced such a remarkable effect on the people who read them.

General Joseph E. Johnston had been the first great military leader to write his own book about the war. His *Narrative of Military Operations* was published in 1874. In the following year Sherman's *Memoirs* appeared in print.

Overnight the book became a best seller. It was the first autobiography written by any of the famous Northern leaders, and the public read it avidly. They found it to be forceful, direct and blunt. They also recognized immediately that Sherman had written his book for his soldiers, more specifically the Army of the Tennessee. Of course by the end of the war he had become an Army group, or theater, commander, but his heart had always been with the Army of the Tennessee, in which he had commanded first a division at Shiloh, then a corps at Vicksburg, the army itself at Missionary Ridge; it had never left his command through Georgia, the Carolinas, and on to Washington, D.C., for the great victory parade.

For the Northern veterans it was a wonderful book. It was apparent from cover to cover that Sherman was proud of his army; and for a long time his army had been very proud of him. According to his son, he never aspired to any elective office except the presidency of the Society of the Army of the Tennessee, a position that he held for twenty-two years, from 1869 until his death in 1891.

His *Memoirs* met a totally different reception down South. The horrors of the Reconstruction period were not yet ended. Sherman could not have picked a worse time to give an account of what he had done. The *Memoirs* turned friendship into hatred. It is unfortunate that Sherman was not more tactful in his writing, and he omitted several things that would have helped the book's reception by Southerners. For example, he said practically nothing of how desperately unhappy he had felt when war came and he had been forced to leave Louisiana to fight against the Southern people.

Also, in his *Memoirs* the armistice he signed with General Joe Johnston, with whom he became such a good friend after the war, did not get proper treatment. If he had been writing for the Southern people as well as for his own soldiers, Sherman would have described this episode better, and the South would have been reminded again of what he had tried to do—in the spirit of Lincoln. But Sherman was writing for his Army of the Tennessee, who had so bitterly resented his treatment at the hands of Secretary of War Stanton when Sherman's terms with Johnston were so insultingly disapproved. Therefore he dwelt at greater length on this subject, rather than stressing his real purpose, which had been to deal kindly with the South.

In addition, the book began with an account of his being sent to California during the Mexican War. There was nothing in it at all about his early life or his Army service in the South for the six years following graduation from West Point. Ten years later he wrote a chapter concerning this period, and another entitled "After the War." Perhaps if this first chapter had been in his book from the beginning, it would have helped the book's reception down South. But because these two chapters were not issued until ten years later, the harm had already been done. His good reputation in the South was ruined.

Now let's turn to Sherman's concept of war. Expressed very simply his ideas were: first, crush the rebellion as rapidly as possible, then extend the olive branch with no thought of retribution afterward. No one can possibly argue against this philosophy.

In the American Revolution, General Sir William Howe, a capable general who knew very well how to fight and win a battle, lost the war because he failed to apply this principle. Rather than completely crush Washington's army, he let it escape, then tried to talk peace after a victory, on the theory that the colonists would (when the war was over) accept British rule more readily than if he completely crushed them in battle.

Sherman's brother, John, put it very well in a speech in 1892, one year after the death of the general:

> While the war lasted, General Sherman was a soldier intent upon putting down what he considered to be a causeless rebellion. He said that war was barbarism that could not be refined, and the speediest way to end it was to prosecute it with vigor to complete success. When this was done, and the Union was saved, he was for the most liberal terms of conciliation and kindness to the southern people. All enmities were forgotten; his old friendships were revived. Never since the close of the war have I heard him utter words of bitterness against the enemies he fought, nor of the men in the north who had reviled him.

Not everyone's friendship in the South was turned away from Sherman by the publication of his *Memoirs*. At the final service held for Sherman in New York City in February, 1891, his greatest battlefield opponent and one of his staunchest friends after the war, General Joseph E. Johnston, was present. The day was bitter and cold, windy and raw, with rain at times, but Joe Johnston was standing there with his hat off to do honor to Sherman. When a friend suggested that he was risking his own health (at eighty-four years of age) to stand bareheaded, Johnston replied: "If I were in his place and he were standing here in mine, he would not put on his hat."

Joe Johnston did die from pneumonia contracted at the funeral of his friend. His admiration and respect for Sherman should be given greater recognition in the South, for there was no one in the Confederacy more qualified to pass judgment on Sherman as a great leader, a loyal friend, and a courageous, intelligent soldier.

8

Joseph E. Johnston

WHEN the War Between the States was over, there remained but two full generals in the Confederacy who were absolute heroes to the men of their armies: Joseph E. Johnston and Robert E. Lee.

By way of illustration of how the veterans of the Army of Tennessee thought about "Old Joe," in the spring of 1890 he attended memorial exercises in Atlanta, riding in a carriage with the governor's Horse Guard as an escort. When the men recognized him, they pressed forward to shake his hand or just to touch him. The Horse Guard and the police were shoved aside. The only way the carriage could proceed was when the horses were taken out of the traces and the men pulled the carriage on.

During the war Johnston served successively as:

1. Commanding General of the Army of the Shenandoah
2. Commanding General of the Confederate Army of the Potomac
3. Commanding General of the Department of Northern Virginia
4. Commanding General of the Department of the West, embracing western North Carolina, Tennessee, northern Georgia, Alabama, Mississippi, and eastern Louisiana

[174]

5. Commanding General of the Army of Tennessee. He held this position twice. In the second instance he was also given command of all troops in South Carolina, Georgia and Florida; later he assumed command also of all troops in North Carolina.

Thus at one time or another he commanded all Confederate troops east of the Mississippi. Next to General Lee, Joseph E. Johnston was obviously the most prominent military leader in the Confederacy and, on more than one occasion, commanded more troops than General Lee.

Joseph Eggleston Johnston was born in Farmville, Virginia, on February 3, in the year 1807, exactly fifteen days after the birth of another great Virginian, Robert E. Lee. The careers of these two paralleled each other in many ways.

Both were graduated from West Point in the class of 1829. Lee stood number 2 in his class; Johnston was number 13. There were 46 graduated that year, and 53 nongraduates—a high percentage, well over 50 percent who failed to make the grade.

After graduation Johnston served in the Black Hawk War in 1832, also in the Seminole wars for a year, then left the Army in 1837 to become a civil engineer. However, one year later he was reappointed a first lieutenant in the Topographical Engineers, and on the same day, he was made a captain, having gained a brevet promotion in the Indian wars.

In the Mexican War both Lee and Johnston distinguished themselves. Each earned three brevet promotions, but Johnston, on the face of it, appears to have established a more impressive combat record. Counting his promotion in the Indian wars, he earned four brevet promotions against three for Lee, even though Lee had now become Winfield Scott's favorite young officer. Lee was wounded at Chapultepec. Johnston was wounded twice; at Cerro Gordo and in the assault on the city of Mexico. During his career Joseph E. Johnston was wounded *ten times* in battle.

Yet the people of his home state of Virginia seem to have done practically nothing to preserve his memory. A visitor en route to Farmville has a right to expect state historical markers along the roads and will find them.

PRINCE EDWARD COUNTY

AREA 356 SQUARE MILES

FORMED IN 1753 FROM AMELIA, AND NAMED FOR PRINCE ED-WARD, SON OF FREDERICK, PRINCE OF WALES, AND YOUNGER BROTHER OF KING GEORGE III. GENERAL JOSEPH E. JOHNSTON WAS BORN IN THIS COUNTY; HAMPDEN-SYDNEY COLLEGE IS IN IT.

The surprise will come at Farmville and at Longwood, the site of Johnston's birthplace. There the state of Virginia has erected nothing at all, although the birthplaces of other far less prominent persons are the subject of state historical markers.

There is a marker at Longwood. It talks of Johnston's ancestors, but there is not a word about the famous Joseph E. There is not a street, or a monument, a building or anything in Farmville named for Joseph E. Johnston. Longwood today is not even the original building. That burned down shortly after the family sold it and moved to southwest Virginia when Joseph E. was four and a half years old. The present building was erected on the same site a few years later and is now well known in Farmville because when it was restored the building was improved and the grounds beautified to form a recreation center for the women's state teachers school known as Longwood College.

If Farmville has done nothing for Joseph E. Johnston, Richmond certainly must have. Along the famous Monument Avenue we should surely find his statue. There is Jeb Stuart, Lee, Jefferson Davis, Stonewall Jackson, Matthew F. Maury, "the Pathfinder of the Seas"—but no Johnston. There is a bust of Johnston in the hall of the House of Delegates in the state capitol—along with many other less prominent persons.

[176]

Joseph E. Johnston

It would almost seem as if over the last one hundred years there had been a premeditated conspiracy to make Joseph E. Johnston somehow disappear from Virginia history. Perhaps if Johnston had become popularly known as a general who had won a great battle, he might have received proper commemoration. At least there would be a monument in his hometown or in Richmond.

Yet he did win his first battle. As Commanding General of the Army of the Shenandoah he slipped quietly away from the Valley and his opponent, General Robert Patterson, who did not even know Johnston had left, and brought his army to the battlefield of Bull Run on July 21, 1861, in time to win the First Battle of Manassas. In doing so Johnston demonstrated for the first time in the war on a large scale the proper use of railroads in concentrating troops rapidly. However, when he arrived on the scene, because he was not acquainted with the terrain, Johnston, although senior to Beauregard, sensibly let Beauregard go ahead with the plans he had already made for the coming battle. However, when those plans and orders proved unworkable and a Union attack developed against the Confederate left flank, Johnston was the first of the two to recognize the danger. Yet, when the battle was over, Beauregard received the credit in the Southern press rather than Johnston, although he, the senior, had done more to win the battle than Beauregard. So is history distorted. Johnston should be remembered as the victor of the First Battle of Manassas, but such is not the case.

Next comes another great distortion of history. After the First Battle of Manassas, when the first five full generals of the Confederacy were announced, Johnston found himself fourth on the list. The first five appointed ranked exactly according to their length of service and their standing at West Point:

> Samuel Cooper, Class of 1815
> Albert Sidney Johnston, Class of 1826

Robert E. Lee, Class of 1829 (2)
Joseph E. Johnston, Class of 1829 (13)
P. G. T. Beauregard, Class of 1838

This came as a shock to Johnston because in the intervening years since graduation he had passed all those ahead of him. In 1860 he had been promoted to brigadier general and assigned as Quartermaster General of the United States Army. Of the others on the list, Lee had been a colonel, as was Samuel Cooper, while Albert Sidney Johnston had been a brigadier general but only by brevet. The order deeply hurt Johnston's pride, and he made a vigorous protest in a personal letter to President Davis. Not intended to be made public, the letter provoked a caustic reply from Jefferson Davis. Then the matter was dropped.

It was dropped by Johnston and dropped by Jefferson Davis for the duration of the war. There was no mention of the subject again in an official message written by either man. Indeed, not long afterward, President Davis visited Johnston at Manassas and there were no ill feelings of any sort expressed; everything went well and smoothly.

The great distortion of history here has been the way historians have leaped upon this one exchange of letters, exaggerated the whole affair, and ballooned it out of all proportion. It has been claimed again and again that Johnston's complaint about rank touched off the feud between him and President Jefferson Davis. It would seem that the writers concerned are afraid to admit that Johnston was absolutely correct in his claim to relative rank for fear that, if they did so, it would hurt the reputation of their hero, Robert E. Lee.

One might assume that perhaps Lee and Johnston were bitter rivals. Quite the contrary is true. They were in fact the very best of friends and thought extremely highly of each other's ability. Johnston himself would have been the very last person to suggest that he was a greater general than Lee.

It was not rank at all that caused the trouble between John-

[178]

ston and Davis. It was the appointment in September, 1861, of Judah P. Benjamin as Secretary of War. Within a few weeks after his appointment, Benjamin, although he had no previous experience in military affairs, came to believe that he knew all there was to know about the art and science of war. The truth of the matter is that the famous statement made by Major Matthew F. Steele in his book *American Campaigns* concerning U. S. Secretary of War Stanton applied equally to his opposite number in the Confederacy: "[Stanton's] contempt for all sound principles and usages of war appears to have been exceeded only by his ignorance of them."

Judah Benjamin, instead of trying to cooperate and help solve difficulties with the generals in the field, fought every one of them as if they were personal adversaries. Stonewall Jackson tendered his resignation because of Mr. Benjamin.

Perhaps if Stonewall Jackson had known more about Benjamin, he might not have been so shocked and infuriated when the Secretary of War's order came to evacuate Romney. From past experience Jackson would have known that it was totally impossible to deal reasonably with the man. General Johnston, who had been suffering needless embarrassing harassment for a long time at the hands of the Secretary of War, could have told Jackson at great length what an infuriating meddlesome creature President Davis had installed in the War Office. Whenever Benjamin got into the act, trouble ensued. He acted as a catalyst producing sparks for Davis' worst moods. And of all the generals Johnston caught it the worst because he commanded the largest, most important army. With Benjamin in Richmond to encourage and inspire him, President Davis' letters became more critical, more acid with the passing of every week. The only way Johnston ever received any assistance in solving the multiple problems that confronted him in this trying period was when he was able to slip a letter past Benjamin to General Samuel Cooper, the Adjutant and Inspector General of the Army. Fortunately for the Confederacy, Benjamin, in the middle of March, 1862, was appointed Secretary of State. His place was taken by George W. Randolph, a person far better qualified both by training and by nature to fill that responsible position in the War Office. Johnston later wrote, in terse language eloquent because of its restraint, that the departure of Benjamin and the appointment of Randolph "enabled the military officers to reestablish the discipline of the army." But it was too late for Johnston and Davis; friendship was gone.

Joseph E. Johnston has been called vain, contentious, temperamental and extremely concerned that his prerogatives be respected. It seems odd that General Lee, who knew Joe Johnston as well, if not better, than any other man, never thought of him in these terms.

It has become popular to accuse Johnston of losing or burning great quantities of supplies in the retreat from Manassas in March, 1862, to keep them from falling into the hands of the Union troops. This completely ignores the fact that he had warned the Confederate government on numerous occasions that such would be the case if he were forced to keep supplies stored so close to the front lines and also that his army was overburdened with countless items of personal baggage. Unfounded criticism of this sort is apparently supposed to show that Johnston lacked administrative ability. It only proves his foresight.

Yet it was during this same retreat that he recognized some of the possibilities inherent in leaving Stonewall Jackson with a small force in the Shenandoah Valley. Johnston was responsible for making the initial dispositions which led to the undertaking of the first half of the famous Valley campaign. He also had the good common sense not to inquire as to the details of Jackson's plans. In any event, he must certainly have known how secretive Jackson was about committing his plans to paper. Johnston himself had learned through bitter experience the inadvisability of letting the authorities in Richmond know his plans in detail. Thus Johnston's orders were couched in general terms, leaving to Jackson the decisions as to how he might act. Although he had given Jackson freedom of movement and must have expected some action, the magnificent results achieved surely came as a delightful surprise, for Johnston was not by nature as bold and aggressive as his great subordinate.

"Gamecock" is the word most often used by writers to describe Johnston. Undoubtedly because of his appearance many people seem to think it apt. Short, stiffly erect, he always presented a neat appearance, wearing a carefully brushed and pressed gray uniform. Perhaps he did look like a gamecock. But no word could possibly be more inappropriate as a description of his generalship, since the word "gamecock" suggests fighting at the drop of a hat, regardless of the odds.

In the Peninsular campaign, nine days after General McClellan had come to a halt in front of "Prince John" Magruder's lightly defended works at Yorktown, a meeting was held in President Jefferson Davis' office attended by the President, Johnston, Lee, Secretary Randolph, General Longstreet, and General G. W. Smith. At this meeting Johnston urged a retreat to the area near Richmond, where the Confederate line could not be outflanked by an amphibious move up either one of the rivers and where the Union forces would also have to contend with the swampy Chickahominy. Johnston strongly urged the uniting at that point of all the available forces of the Confederacy in North Carolina, South Carolina and Georgia. With the army thus formed, he wanted then to fight near Richmond what might be the decisive battle of the war.

Johnston's advice was good and sound, but the bolder course advocated by General Lee was adopted. Johnston was overruled and told to march to Magruder's assistance to hold Yorktown as long as practicable, thus further delaying the Union advance and gaining more time. He would have to take a chance on being outflanked by an amphibious advance up one of the rivers and try to guard against that threat. It can be said that the plans proposed by Johnston and Lee were typical of the two. Both were excellent, but Johnston's was the more cautious; Lee's was more risky and promised somewhat greater rewards.

With a less capable officer than Johnston in command trouble could have ensued, but he executed his mission perfectly. McClellan was held in place for an excessively long time; then, just before the Union attack was launched, Johnston neatly executed his withdrawal. Furthermore, as he had predicted, McClellan did try an amphibious advance up the York River. Johnston had a division of his own all ready, at hand, to attack the landing force and hold it in place so that the Confederate retreat passed by, unhindered and uninterrupted, with no difficulty at all. Parenthetically, it is safe to say that General Lee would not have suggested his plan if he had not had complete confidence in Johnston's ability to execute it.

Then came the Battle of Seven Pines, or Fair Oaks. Johnston has been severely criticized for many years for drawing his orders carelessly, not circulating them promptly, and giving Longstreet a verbal order instead of a written one. In truth, Johnston's plan of attack was simple and should have succeeded. He had caught two Union corps south of the Chickahominy and they should have been badly beaten. Instead, Johnston was so severely wounded that there was considerable doubt that he would live. Lee assumed command on the next day.

One month later, with Lee in command, history repeated itself at the Seven Days' Battle. Again there was lack of coordination between units. Orders were confused, misleading or misunderstood. Units were slow in arriving, took the wrong roads, or never reached their destinations in time. This is not at all surprising; it takes far more training, experience, study, and years of application to produce an officer capable of leading large units in battle than it does to train enlisted men to perform their assigned duties. In those days there were no general staff schools or war colleges, and the general staff system had not yet been developed. As a result the division and brigade commanders were not well trained. They had to learn the hard way. Later on they knew their business very well indeed.

In comparing Seven Pines with the Seven Days', we are forced to deal with hero worship. Lee's orders were no better or clearer than Johnston's, nor was his supervision. Both battles were confused from start to finish. Both generals operated with inadequate staffs and both of them needed further experience themselves. Historians like to dwell on Johnston's mistakes at Seven Pines and generally pin most of the blame on him, whereas, at the Seven Days', Lee has escaped censure and most of the blame has fallen on his subordinates. Yet Johnston had the simpler, easier, more workable plan. That it failed was more Longstreet's fault than Johnston's. Furthermore, General Lee, having established a better relationship with the President than Johnston, had more troops in his army. He had managed to persuade Jefferson Davis to do what Johnston had recommended—*i.e.*, to bring to Richmond other available troops from Georgia and the Carolinas. Of course Lee had also brought Jackson's army from the Valley.

About six months later, in November, 1862, after he had sufficiently recovered from his wound to return to duty, Johnston was given command of the Department of the West. This huge command stretched eastward from the Mississippi to include a portion of North Carolina and Georgia, the states of Tennessee, Alabama, Mississippi, and eastern Louisiana. The principal troops under his command were, therefore, the armies of Generals Braxton Bragg in Tennessee and John C. Pemberton in Mississippi.

From then on, because of the great distances involved, his relations with President Jefferson Davis gradually worsened. On the occasions when they did meet face-to-face, there was no apparent ill feeling. This is not surprising, for everyone attributes a great deal of personal charm to Johnston. However these occasions were naturally very infrequent. For the next two and a half years almost everything between the two was handled by correspondence. Either Johnston was not facile at expressing himself on paper, or his manner of doing so was irritating to Jefferson Davis.

By far the most important action that occurred while Johnston was in command of the Department of the West was Vicksburg. Jefferson Davis expected Johnston to save Vicksburg. When Joe Johnston arrived at Jackson, Mississippi, he found just two brigades, with another expected possibly the next day, and perhaps a fourth brigade, a total strength of only 11,000 or 12,000 men. This force was totally inadequate, and there was no hope of enlarging it to a reasonable size rapidly.

There was only one chance of saving Pemberton's army from capture. Johnston ordered Pemberton to attack Grant in conjunction with Johnston's troops. When Pemberton failed to obey this order, Johnston gave him the order to evacuate Vicksburg and save the army. Again Pemberton disobeyed.

Lieutenant General John C. Pemberton was in a very awkward position in more ways than one. At the same time as he was receiving orders from Johnston to save the army, he was getting orders from Jefferson Davis to hold Vicksburg. Poor Pemberton was caught in the middle, and at the same time he had a personal problem of his own that somewhat restricted his freedom of action. He was a Northerner from Pennsylvania who had come to fight for the South, undoubtedly influenced by the fact that he had married a Southern girl.

If he had followed Johnston's orders and lost Vicksburg, even though he saved the army, his actions and motives might be severely criticized. It has been said that politically President Davis was right while militarily General Johnston was correct; but politics at this stage was meaningless. Only military matters counted. The one hope of saving Vicksburg was first to save the army, then try to defeat Grant with the combined forces of Johnston and Pemberton. If that could be done, then Vicksburg could be reoccupied. If not, at least the army, which was more important than the city, would have been saved instead of both being lost.

There is one criticism of Johnston in this campaign which is valid. Instead of stopping at Jackson, Mississippi, he should have hurried into Vicksburg and taken command in person. That is the sort of thing that Stonewall Jackson, Nathan Bedford Forrest, Grant, or Sherman would have done. Johnston's forte was not impetuosity.

[184]

Joseph E. Johnston

This was not the first time in American history that a general had tried to save a city and thereby lost his army in the process. The worst previous example had occurred in the Revolution. General Benjamin Lincoln, pressured by the civilian authorities at Charleston, South Carolina, had tried to save that city and thereby lost his army. And with it went the Virginia and North Carolina veteran Continental soldiers who had crossed the Delaware with Washington, had fought at the battles of Trenton, Princeton, Brandywine, Germantown, and had endured the grim winter of Valley Forge—only to meet the fate of being made prisoners of war at Charleston.

An even better example, because it more closely resembles the actual situation at Vicksburg, occurred in World War II. In the Battle of Stalingrad, Adolf Hitler would not permit the German Sixth Army to leave the city. He insisted that Field Marshal Friedrich von Paulus must continue to hold it at all costs. Field Marshal Erich von Manstein made a valiant effort to break through to save the Sixth Army, simultaneously ordering von Paulus to attempt to cut his way out. This was the only possible way that the Sixth Army could be saved. Von Paulus failed to move because Hitler's permission had not been granted. Pemberton failed to move because Jefferson Davis had not given his approval.

The next major episode in Joseph E. Johnston's military career began when he was appointed to succeed General Braxton Bragg in command of the Army of Tennessee after the latter's disastrous defeats at Lookout Mountain and Missionary Ridge. Johnston inherited an army that had fought many times brilliantly and well, although its record under the command of Braxton Bragg had consisted of more defeats than victories. The officers and men had just endured the most disheartening experience that can happen to an army in war. After winning the Battle of Chickamauga, the greatest Confederate victory of the war in the West, they had seen all the fruits of that victory frittered away by the inept leadership of General Bragg until they themselves had then suffered worse defeats in battle than they had ever thought could have been possible. For the first time in its history the army was truly disheartened, its morale badly shaken, and it was beginning to wonder seriously just how much hope there was of winning their war for Southern independence.

The prospect facing Johnston upon arrival at his new headquarters was discouraging in the extreme. He surely must have felt tremendous misgivings at the grim prospect that faced him, but he never let it affect his attitude toward his new command. Tirelessly, with unflagging energy, he visited every camp, talking cheerfully with the men, listening to their opinions, weighing their views, but missing nothing as he went his rounds. His chief concerns in the beginning were morale, discipline, and somehow providing supplies, food, clothing, and shoes for the thousands who were ragged, barefoot and hungry.

Previously, furloughs had been only rarely granted. Johnston initiated a generous system whereby every man had his chance to take leave. When a general amnesty was announced, deserters began flocking back to the colors. Morale rose and, with it, discipline. In a remarkably short time the army's pride and confidence rose to a higher level than it had ever reached before. The Army of Tennessee had at last found a commander worthy of it, and the army responded as it never had in its history by giving to that commander the same trust and devotion that the Army of Northern Virginia gave to its commander, General Lee.

The astounding results achieved cast grave doubts on the impartiality of the adverse comments leveled against Johnston by those who have criticized his administrative ability during the period of his command in Virginia.

Yet during this period when Johnston was accomplishing so much with the troops under his command, Jefferson Davis expected and ordered him to advance against the much more numerous army that had just defeated Bragg. In fact it was practically an ultimatum, and Bragg, now Davis' military adviser, had the temerity to agree that it should be done. Naturally Johnston had better sense than to try.

When the campaign to Atlanta did begin, Johnston may be said to have had three objectives in mind. The first was, as always, the defeat of the Union armies. Being so heavily outnumbered, the only way Johnston could accomplish this would be to catch his opponent in a mistake, meanwhile preserving his armies intact so that they would be able to take advantage of the opportunity when it arose. The second objective was the defense of Atlanta, where, as in the Peninsular campaign two years before, it was probable the decisive battle would be fought. The third was to prolong the campaign as much as possible, so that the war might appear to the people of the North to be too costly to continue. The 1864 elections were to be held in November. If Lincoln were not reelected, the South could win the war.

Prior to the capture of Atlanta, Abraham Lincoln, in a despondent mood, wrote a little note to himself: "This morning, as for some days past, it seems exceedingly probable that this administration will not be re-elected. Then it will be my duty to so co-operate with the President elect, as to save the Union between the election and the inauguration; as he will have secured his election on such ground that he can not possibly save it afterwards."

There are two popular viewpoints on Joseph E. Johnston.

One is that he was a very capable, intelligent officer, popular with the men who served under him, a superb strategist, but, like McClellan, he would not actually fight. He traded ground for time, always promised that eventually he would counterattack but never did. During the Atlanta campaign, opportunities arose when he could have dealt severe blows at Sherman, but there was always some excuse for not doing so. Furthermore, it was said, he never won an offensive battle, and, excluding Seven Pines, he never tried to fight one.

The other viewpoint is that Johnston did the right thing.

With the Northern elections due in November, time was an important factor. If neither Richmond nor Atlanta were captured, Lincoln might not be reelected. Under these conditions Johnston could not afford to risk his army totally any more than Lee could. And, like Lee in Virginia, he inflicted greater losses upon his opponent than his own army suffered. When he finally reached Atlanta, there is where he planned to make his stand. At that point Johnston would have reacted sharply and vigorously.

The facts are that Johnston did not conduct as vigorous a defense in Georgia as Lee did in Virginia. However, it cannot be said that his was an inactive defense.

Twice during the Battle of Resaca he ordered an attack on Sherman's left but was forced to revoke those orders when he learned that Union troops were crossing the Oostanaula River in his rear. At that point Johnston had no choice but to cancel his orders and retreat, or risk losing his entire army at the very start of the campaign.

That case is not as clear-cut as what happened at Cassville. There he discovered an opportunity to turn on the Union armies when they were advancing on a very broad front, using both the Kingston and Cassville roads. Johnston's plan of attack miscarried entirely through the fault of General Hood. That officer received a report that the enemy was approaching in force along a road toward the right rear of his position. The report could not possibly have been accurate. It was manifestly untrue, but Hood fell back to that road and formed his corps across it, facing to the southeast. The enemy in question proved to be only some cavalry, but Johnston's best opportunity during the entire campaign to Atlanta to strike a severe blow at Sherman's armies was thereby completely lost.

Yet even after that episode he continued to impose delays on Sherman by active as well as inactive measures. For example, after confronting and stopping the Northern advance at New Hope Church, he knew that Sherman would then want to return to the railroad line to continue the advance on the main road to Atlanta. Johnston's method of slowing the Union armies there was to attack every time the Northern troops tried to disengage their forces.

There can be no doubt whatever that, when the armies reached Atlanta, the Confederate retreat would have stopped. Every move that had been made from the beginning of the campaign had been leading toward that climax. Whether there would have been one large battle or a series of battles followed by a prolonged siege would have depended on the actions of Sherman as well as Johnston. Judging not from what he said in later years, but rather from the advice that he had given as to how to conduct the Peninsular campaign, where he had wanted to fight the decisive battle near Richmond, one cannot help but feel that Johnston would have certainly attacked the enemy. Parenthetically, one cannot help but wonder what his next move would have been near Richmond if he had not been so severely wounded at Seven Pines. It could have been something similar to General Lee's Battle of the Seven Days.

On neither occasion, however, was Johnston given a chance to demonstrate what he would have done. At Richmond he was incapacitated. At Atlanta, on July 17, 1864, he was summarily relieved from command just as the time and the place for which he had planned for so many long months had arrived.

There Jefferson Davis relieved Johnston for fighting a campaign against Sherman similar to the campaign Lee fought against Grant. In Virginia there were the battles of the Wilderness, Spotsylvania, and Cold Harbor. In Georgia there were the battles of Resaca, New Hope Church, and Kennesaw Mountain with, in each case, almost the exact same results. Yet General Lee was praised to the skies by Jefferson Davis, who relieved Johnston.

In evaluating the Atlanta campaign, General Grant wrote: "My own judgment is that Johnston acted very wisely; he husbanded his men and saved as much of his territory as he could, without fighting decisive battles in which all might be lost. As Sherman advanced . . . his army became spread out, until, if this had been continued, it would have been easy to destroy in detail."

One cannot help but wonder what might have happened if Hood had not replaced Johnston. Two things are certain: The Battle of Nashville, resulting in a Confederate disaster, would not have been fought; and Sherman's "March to the Sea" would never have occurred.

Lee knew Johnston's worth, and it was Lee who brought him back at the last, in 1865, overcoming Davis' objections, to command the Army of Tennessee again and all troops in the Carolinas, Georgia and Florida.

The critics who indulge themselves in talking about the fact that Johnston never won an offensive battle and, with the exception of Seven Pines, never tried to fight one have ignored or overlooked the Battle of Bentonville. Yet it provides the positive definite clue as to what would have happened at Atlanta if Johnston had remained in command.

When, at the eleventh hour, General Lee was finally appointed general-in-chief of the Confederate armies, his first important decision had been to recall Joe Johnston to try to oppose Sherman's advance through the Carolinas. Both officers were well aware that neither had hardly a chance of success. Johnston's task of stopping Sherman's march was as impossible as Lee's was of saving Petersburg and Richmond. The forces under Johnston's command were a mixed aggregation of the survivors of the Army of Tennessee that were still with the colors after the terrible Battle of Nashville, the scattered troops assigned to the Departments of North Carolina and South Carolina, and some cavalry taken from states all over the South. All were widely dispersed, and there seemed little chance of making even a token effort to fight Sherman's powerful forces.

Within three short weeks Johnston gathered them together. Sherman's armies were expecting no further serious opposition when suddenly Johnston launched his attack, and he could not have picked a better time, for the Union troops were marching in two columns widely separated. The Confederate assault on

March 19, 1865, directed by Johnston, fell upon the Union left wing, turned it, and drove it to the rear. No soldier fighting strictly "by the book" would have considered such a risky endeavor. Yet the result was all, and more, than could possibly have been expected. At the end of the battle on the third day when the entire Union army was on the field, outnumbering Johnston by three to one, the Confederates were forced to fall back.

Lieutenant General Wade Hampton of Lee's Army of Northern Virginia, who took part in this Battle of Bentonville, concluded his account of it in *Battles and Leaders* with these words: "Few soldiers would have adopted the bold measure resorted to by General Johnston, and none could have carried it out more skillfully or more successfully than he did."

If with such odds against him and with such a conglomerate force Johnston did not hesitate to attack and even achieved partial success at Bentonville, it is impossible to doubt that under his command there would have been a furious struggle for the possession of Atlanta. The fighting would have been not only well planned, but ably directed and properly supervised. The city of Atlanta could still have been in Confederate hands as late as November, when the Northern people went to the polls to decide whether or not the war should be continued, while Johnston would today be universally recognized as one of the South's outstanding battlefield leaders.

Johnston was a general who proved himself more capable of commanding large bodies of troops than any of the other "three- and four-star" generals in the Confederacy except for those who can be classified as in the possible genius class. In that category I believe there were only three who fought for the South—Lee, Stonewall Jackson and Forrest. In the same category I would place Grant and Sherman. To illustrate, Johnston would have been incapable of splitting his army into two widely separated parts as Lee did at Second Manassas and at Chancellorsville. Johnston saw some of the possibilities inherent in leaving Jackson with a small force in the Shenandoah

Valley, with Ewell available in close support. He was responsible for making the initial dispositions which led to the famous Valley campaign, but he could never have executed it so brilliantly and dynamically as Jackson had, to produce such extraordinary results. Nor could he have brought himself to execute the Vicksburg operations as Grant had, cutting himself loose entirely from his line of communications and marching deep inland, bypassing Vicksburg to capture it later. In other words Johnston did not bear the hallmarks of genius, but, with the three especial exceptions named, there was no other lieutenant general or full general in the Confederacy who was as excellent as Johnston. Of all the mistakes ever made by Jefferson Davis perhaps his most fatal was in relieving Joseph E. Johnston from command just as the battles for Atlanta began.

9

John Bell Hood

FEW generals have taken command of an army under more peculiar, adverse circumstances. The mere fact of his appointment in place of General Joseph E. Johnston, who had been relieved from command for having failed to arrest the advance of the enemy to the vicinity of Atlanta, forced General Hood immediately to adopt an aggressive policy. He was committed to attack the larger, stronger army facing him, regardless of all odds and circumstances.

It has been recorded time and again that the men of the Army of Tennessee, who were wholeheartedly devoted to Johnston, were distressed, unhappy, bitter, angry, and discouraged when they heard the news. Although the vast majority stayed with the colors to fight for the cause, knowing that the climax of their great retreat was bound to come upon them soon, a number were so totally shocked by the loss of Johnston and his replacement by Hood that they threw away their arms and deserted, homeward bound.

Yet they knew that John B. Hood had a splendid reputation as a brigade and division commander in the Army of Northern Virginia, and they had witnessed his gallantry in action at the Battle of Chickamauga, where his division had played a prominent role in achieving that great Confederate victory, and where he had been so severely wounded that the surgeons had been forced to cut off his right leg.

Since the average man is not gifted with prophetic insight, one is tempted to ask why the army objected so violently and was so disheartened by the appointment of General Hood to command. First and foremost, every man knew in his heart that a terrible mistake had been made when Joseph E. Johnston had been relieved just as the battles for Atlanta were about to begin. Ever since Johnston had taken command of the army, six and one-half months before, he had been preparing them for this great coming struggle, and now he would not be there to lead them.

Secondly, even if General Johnston had to be relieved, a step with which no man in the army agreed, the troops would have much preferred his successor to have been Lieutenant General William J. Hardee, the senior corps commander, who had been with them ever since their first great battle at Shiloh. They would have put far greater faith in his leadership, not only because he was fifteen years older than Hood, with fifteen years longer service in the army, but because through all the battles they had fought together the men had learned to respect "Old Reliable" Hardee as an excellent corps commander.

Thus the officers and men of the Army of Tennessee bitterly resented not only the loss of their great commander but also the choice of his successor, a youngster of thirty-three, in whom they did not have confidence. Although mindful of his reputation for courage and valor on the battlefield, many of them knew that throughout the campaign to Atlanta he had been criticizing Johnston for timidity, yet he was the officer who had wrecked the plan of battle at Cassville by being too cautious.

The men of the Texas Brigade, one of the most famous in the Army of Northern Virginia, would not have agreed with the soldiers of the Army of Tennessee. Under the command of General Hood, inspired by his leadership, this brigade had rapidly acquired a remarkable reputation for hard fighting and dauntless courage, second to none. Time and again it was chosen for the most difficult, dangerous missions. Although other officers succeeded to command as Hood was promoted, the brigade was always a part of his division and was forever known as Hood's Texicans.

Surely John B. Hood must have been a Texan, but he was not. He was born in Owingsville, Kentucky, on June 1, 1831, so when the war began, he had not yet reached his thirtieth birthday. His West Point class of 1853 was graduated too late to participate in the War with Mexico, but before the War Between the States began, he had seen some active combat service. Initially commissioned a second lieutenant in the infantry, Hood was stationed for two years in California, then was assigned to the 2nd Cavalry, whose colonel was Albert Sidney Johnston, with Robert E. Lee second-in-command as lieutenant colonel. With this regiment he served for two years on frontier duty in Texas, where he was wounded in a battle with the Indians. After promotion to first lieutenant he was assigned as a cavalry instructor at West Point.

Promptly, in April, 1861, Hood resigned from the United States Army to offer his services to the South. Among his West Point classmates who served in the Northern armies, who would also become famous, and whom Hood would later face in battle were James B. McPherson, who had stood first in the class; and John M. Schofield, who was number 7; also Philip H. Sheridan, number 34, whom Hood would encounter, but only briefly, at Chickamauga. John B. Hood had been 44 in his class of 52 graduates.

Because his native state of Kentucky did not secede, Hood went to Montgomery, Alabama, then the capital of the seven states that had seceded, where he was given a commission as first lieutenant in the newly formed regular army of the Confederacy. It did not take him very long to rise above that rank. His first assignment was to report to "Prince John" Magruder on the Peninsula, who put Hood in command of all his cavalry companies and promoted him to captain. Then, since this still left Hood as junior to the other captains present, Magruder announced that Hood was a major, leaving it to the War Department to acquiesce in the decision.

Later, when a full colonel arrived to organize the cavalry into a regiment, Hood was left without a command but not for long. He was chosen to organize the 4th Texas Infantry, promoted to colonel, and then sent to Manassas to join the Texas Brigade, thus beginning his association with that famous unit which was to continue long as Hood remained with the army in Virginia. In March, 1862, just prior to the retreat from Manassas to the Peninsula, John B. Hood was promoted to brigadier general and assigned to command of the brigade. It then consisted of the 1st, 4th, and 5th Texas Infantry regiments, the 18th Georgia, and Hampton's (South Carolina) Legion. Later in the war the 3rd Arkansas Infantry became the fourth regiment of the brigade, replacing the other two units.

The first opportunity for Hood and his Texas Brigade to show their worth in battle came when General McClellan made his attempted envelopment up the York River. The brigade was part of the division that Johnston had selected to oppose the landing. It was Hood's and Wade Hampton's brigades that attacked the landing force and drove the enemy back to seek shelter under the protection of the bluffs by the river.

Although this was comparatively a minor action, it served to show the results that might be expected when Hood's Texans were committed to battle. In the Battle of Seven Pines they saw little action, but at the Seven Days' at Gaines' Mill on June 27, 1862, they earned the enduring reputation for superb valor and reckless courage that would follow them to the end of their days. Just before the attack, Brigadier General Hood was asked if he could take the extremely strong enemy position that faced him. He spoke for himself and for his men when he answered: "I don't know whether I can or not, but I will try." The result has been universally regarded as the most fierce, successful assault by any brigade in the entire Battle of the Seven Days. For several hours on that day, and throughout the entire preceding

day, the Union soldiers had firmly, strongly, and gallantly repulsed every Confederate attack. But when Hood's and General
Evander Law's brigades launched their assault, the Union line
finally gave way. Official battle reports are always full of praise
for officers and men who have done their duty well. This is to
be expected and perhaps sometimes taken with a little grain of
salt, but when the reticent Stonewall Jackson was impelled to
remark, "These men are soldiers indeed!" there can be no question in anyone's mind that the highest honor of the entire
Seven Days' belonged unequivocally to the Texas Brigade and
to their commander who had led them in their brilliant charge.

Not long after the conclusion of the Battle of the Seven Days,
Hood was given command of the division consisting of his own
and General Law's brigades and assigned to Longstreet's wing
of the army. In the campaign of Second Manassas, when Stonewall Jackson was sent on his famous long march around the
Union right flank to strike deep into the rear of Pope's Union
army, with Lee and Longstreet following behind, it was Hood's
Division that was the first of Longstreet's troops to arrive and
form line on Jackson's right. Leading Longstreet's wing that
day, his speed of marching had rivaled Jackson's own famous
"foot cavalry."

At the Battle of Groveton on August 28, and again on August 29, the first day of the Battle of Second Manassas, Jackson's
men bore the brunt of the fighting. After his hurried, forced
march, straining his men to the limits of their endurance, to
reach the battlefield on the morning of August 29, Hood (followed by Longstreet's other divisions) was forced to stand idly
by as a spectator while Jackson and his men fought the battle
by themselves.

It was only toward evening that Hood's Division took part in
a reconnaissance in force that penetrated the enemy lines, then
were withdrawn to the positions they had been occupying all
day. It was not until late in the afternoon of the second day of
battle that Longstreet's troops at last attacked. If they had been
brought into action upon arrival, the result would have been a

far more decisive victory for the Confederacy. An attack launched on August 29 would surely have captured the Henry House Hill and cut the enemy line of retreat across the Stone Bridge. On that earlier day, Union reinforcements marching from Alexandria would not have been present in sufficient numbers to take position with, and strengthen, Pope's retreating army on the heights of Centreville, just north of Bull Run. The result would have been a far more disastrous defeat for the Union.

The net effect of enforced waiting all day while the great opportunity slipped away, as Lee, contrary to his normal aggressive nature, yielded to Longstreet's cautious advice, could not have been lost on Hood. Nor could he hardly have avoided noting the contrast between his service under Longstreet and his next battle at Sharpsburg, or Antietam, September 17, 1862, where he fought under Stonewall Jackson. At the beginning of the campaign his division had been assigned to Longstreet, but as the troops reached the field, they had been placed where they were needed most. Thus Hood was on the left under Jackson's command. He and his division fought magnificently. In the midst of the most furious fighting, as the battle raged savagely around him, Hood was asked, by Jackson's aide, how the battle was going. The reply was reminiscent of Gaines' Mill. "Tell General Jackson unless I get reinforcements I must be forced back, but I am going on while I can."

Not for nothing has this day been called "the bloodiest day of the Civil War," and Hood's small division of only two brigades took an extremely large proportion of the total casualties. That night Lee called a meeting of his senior officers to discuss whether or not they should cross the river or stay and face the enemy. When he asked Hood about his division, the latter answered with some truculence, or perhaps a feeling of anger, or despair, "They are lying on the field where you sent them, for few have straggled. My division has been almost wiped out."

Because he knew McClellan, General Lee decided to stay

where he was, north of the Potomac. However, he must have wondered about General Hood until he learned of the magnificent fighting of Hood's Division at the Dunkard Church, where they had suffered a tremendous percentage of casualties. After the battle was over, although Hood was not one of his regularly assigned division commanders, "Old Jack" recommended his promotion to major general, and the words he used in his letter of recommendation were not words that came easily to him, for he was not one to lavish praise on his subordinates or anyone else. Quite the opposite was true in fact. Generally Stonewall considered it sufficient to tell an officer that he had done his duty. Yet of Hood's conduct at Sharpsburg, Jackson wrote that his "duties were discharged with such ability and zeal, as to command my admiration. I regard him as one of the most promising officers of the army."

Lee concurred, for by the Battle of Fredericksburg Hood had been promoted and his command enlarged to be a division of four brigades. Those who continually refer to Hood's Division as Texans should look more closely at the rosters of troops assigned. One gets the impression in reading about Hood and his division that the soldiers must have been primarily from Texas, whereas this was true only of the one brigade which now contained the 1st, 4th, and 5th Texas Infantry and the 3rd Arkansas. Law's brigade at this time consisted of three North Carolina regiments and two Alabama regiments. Later, at Gettysburg, Law would be commanding a brigade of five Alabama regiments. In addition, both of the other two brigades now assigned to Hood's Division were composed entirely of infantry regiments from the state of Georgia.

Fredericksburg did not turn out to be one of Hood's great battles. He was placed on the right of Longstreet's First Corps to connect with Jackson's Second Corps. Thus his division did not take part in defeating General Meade's attack on Jackson's front, and only one of his brigades was called upon to help repulse the fourteen separate attacks delivered by seven Union divisions against the sunken road with its stone retaining wall. After the arrival of these and other reinforcements the firing lines producing the slaughter were, in places, six ranks deep.

Nor was Chancellorsville a great battle for Hood, for his was one of the two divisions that had gone with Longstreet on the detached mission to the area southeast of Richmond and Petersburg. Hood missed Chancellorsville completely.

At Gettysburg, it is conceivable that if Hood had been the corps commander in charge of the attack on July 2, 1863, instead of Longstreet, who had been opposed to making an assault, the battle would have been a splendid Confederate victory. Hood might have captured Little Round Top in spite of the efforts of Major General Gouverneur K. Warren, who saved the day for the Union army.

That any attack at all aimed at Little Round Top was delivered that day was entirely due to Hood's own initiative. His orders had been to attack up the Emmitsburg Road, passing in front of Little Round Top, but Hood instantly recognized the importance of that hill as the key to the Union position. With his usual verve and audacity, and contrary to orders, he swung his division to the right and launched his assault on the Devil's Den and Little Round Top. If, on that day, Hood had been the commander of the corps, the attack could then have swept onward with no delay. But General Hood was wounded leading his division, and there was a measurable delay in transferring command to General Law, who continued the attack. It gave Warren sufficient time to bring in reinforcements, save the position, and become the hero of the day.

Hood's wound was so severe that he permanently lost the use of an arm and was not able to return to duty for two months. However he was back to lead one of the two divisions brought by General Longstreet to the Battle of Chickamauga in September, 1863, where Hood was wounded again, requiring amputation of his right leg.

At this point, in any modern army, he would have been declared incapacitated for further active duty. Yet, because of his outstanding service to the cause of Southern independence, despite his crippled condition, he was promoted to lieutenant general with his commission dating from September 20, 1863, the day he had lost his leg at the Battle of Chickamauga. He was then assigned to command a corps in Joseph E. Johnston's Army of Tennessee.

Regardless of the circumstances—personal, political, or otherwise, no matter what the reasons were—the appointment was a mistake that should never have been made. John Bell Hood was a proud and ambitious man. There is no doubt that he considered himself capable of performing the duties of a corps commander and assured everyone that he would be successful. Yet he had to be tied or strapped into his saddle, something which surely was humiliating and frustrating to a man of his nature; and the pain that he was forced to endure must, at times, have been excruciating. Furthermore, there was little the doctors could do for him. Medicine was in very short supply in the Confederacy, and opium was about the only thing the doctors could give him.

The further appointment of Hood as a temporary full general to take command of the Army of Tennessee was an even greater mistake. To ask an officer so physically handicapped to take command of a corps was bad enough, but to appoint him to command the second most important army in the Confederacy was inexcusable on the part of President Jefferson Davis. It shows clearly a lack of good judgment on the part of the Confederate President.

When Hood assumed command in Johnston's place on July 17, 1864, the composition and organization of the opposing groups of armies was the same as it had been at the beginning of the campaign. The only major changes that had occurred were among the Confederate leaders. Of these, General Hardee was still in command of his corps. The other corps of the Army of Tennessee was now entrusted to General B. F. Cheatham, who was appointed to command it when Hood relieved Johnston. The third corps, from the Army of Mississippi, also had a different commander than in the beginning. One month before, on June 14 at Pine Mountain, Georgia, north of Kennesaw, General Leonidas Polk, together with Generals Johnston and Hardee, had ridden to an exposed position on the crest of the hill. A hostile battery had opened fire on them at long range. On the third shot Polk was killed instantly, ending his dream of returning to the ministry when the war was over. His successor in command of the corps was now General A. P. Stewart.

On July 17, 1864, McPherson's Army of the Tennessee, of three corps, was on the Union left (east) flank. It was executing a wide turning movement toward Decatur. From there it was to move against Atlanta from the east, destroying the railroad as it advanced. Schofield's small Army of the Ohio, consisting essentially of only one corps, was next in line, approaching Atlanta from the northeast. The Army of the Cumberland, commanded by Thomas, containing the three largest and strongest corps, was to the north, preparing to cross Peachtree Creek.

The Confederate forces under General Johnston's command had retreated to positions in front of the main fortifications of Atlanta. They had not, however, moved into the strong entrenched lines and defensive works around Atlanta, which had been in the process of construction for several months. Johnston intended first to attack the enemy to the north while they were divided in attempting to cross Peachtree Creek. It was at this critical moment when General Thomas was about to undertake the dangerous crossing with the Union Army of the Cumberland that the change in Confederate command was effected.

General Hood immediately recognized the opportunity presented him and promptly adopted Johnston's attack plans. In fact, he asked General Johnston to remain at headquarters on the eighteenth of July to issue the necessary orders to place the troops in position, which Johnston readily agreed to do. The Confederate plan was excellent. Cheatham with his corps

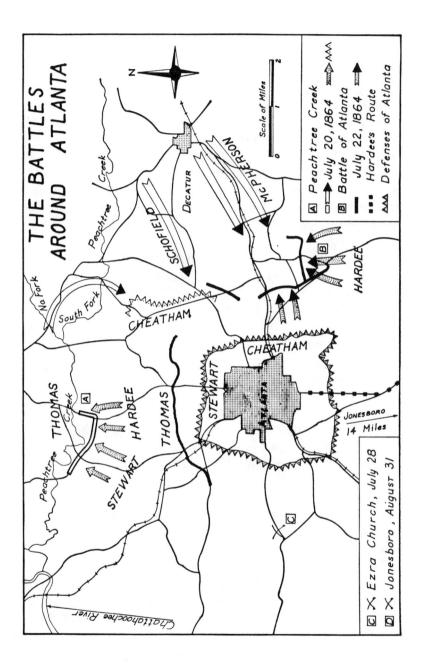

THE BATTLES AROUND ATLANTA

was to hold off the two Union armies advancing from the east and northeast, while Hardee and Stewart were to attack the Army of the Cumberland as it was in the midst of crossing Peachtree Creek. The point of attack was well chosen. It was to be on the east end of Thomas' line where a large gap had developed between the advancing Union troops. Initially the gap had been between Thomas' and Schofield's armies. In an attempt to close this interval, Sherman had sent two divisions from one of Thomas' corps eastward, but this had left another gap, two miles wide, between them and the rest of Thomas' troops, and it was directly at this point that Hood launched his attack.

Although some of Thomas' troops had crossed Peachtree Creek the evening before, and most of the army was across by early morning of the twentieth of July, if the Confederate attack had been launched at 1:00 P.M. as scheduled, the Union troops would have been caught in a most difficult position. They would not have had the opportunity to consolidate their positions, and with the nearest supporting troops two miles away to the east, the Confederate assault would have had an excellent chance of success.

However, the attack did not come until 4:00 P.M., three hours late. Although the fighting was severe and prolonged, the attack failed. And, in the midst of the action, just as General Hardee was about to commit his reserve (Cleburne's Division), it was taken from him and sent eastward because Hood had become worried about the approach of the Union troops from that direction. Thus the best division in the Confederate army saw practically no action at all that day. By the time it could reach its new position it was nearly midnight.

The Confederate troops who had fought at Peachtree Creek then withdrew into the fortifications of Atlanta. This retreat led General Sherman to believe that perhaps the city would be evacuated. When the news of Hood's appointment to command had reached him on July 18, two days before the Battle of Peachtree Creek, Sherman had inquired of the officers who had known Hood at West Point what kind of an opponent they were now facing. They all agreed that Hood was a courageous, determined, but reckless fighter. The new appointment meant only one thing: The Confederates would now be attacking and there would be a great battle. It had happened exactly as they had predicted. On the third day after assuming command, Hood had launched an attack at Peachtree Creek and been beaten back.

However, as the Union troops approached the fortified lines around Atlanta, they found them strongly held. It was apparent that the Confederate army had no intention of giving up the city so quickly. Sherman's orders now were to proceed with caution, but it is quite apparent that he was not expecting another attack so soon.

For many years it has been a popular pastime to accuse General Hood of being nothing more than an impetuous, courageous, determined officer who was too rash, erratic, and headstrong. As evidence, it has been common practice to point first to the Battle of Atlanta, fought only two days after Peachtree Creek. The critics will freely admit that Hood was forced to adopt an aggressive policy by the circumstances of his appointment. President Jefferson Davis had made it perfectly clear that he was dissatisfied with Johnston's continued retreats and expected Hood to fight aggressively. Thus Hood had no choice but to attack. However, after the losses suffered on July 20, the majority of the critics seem inclined to the opinion that no further attacks were necessary. Hood had done what was expected of him and should have stopped offensive operations at that point without taking any further chances of suffering additional heavy losses.

This is the "book" tactician's approach. It can be called the safe way to fight wars, and a cautious general would surely have adopted this method and simply retreated into the defenses of Atlanta to hold them as long as possible. However, to accuse General Hood of erratic, rash conduct because he promptly precipitated the Battle of Atlanta just two days after his defeat at Peachtree Creek completely ignores the very elements that were working in his favor. It was exactly the right moment to attack when his opponent, although approaching with some caution, was not expecting another assault.

Furthermore, the Union army was still divided into two parts, separated, with the two halves not within easy supporting distance of each other. The attack on the Army of the Cumberland had failed, but the moment had now come to attack the other half of Sherman's forces advancing on Atlanta from the east and northeast. Hood's plan was bold, well conceived, audacious, and worthy of a Jackson or a Lee.

Those who criticize General Hood for immediately turning around and suddenly attacking again on July 22 are generally the same critics who call Joseph E. Johnston overcautious. Yet in his official report of the campaign the latter made it perfectly clear that he himself intended to make a similar attack on the Union army. In fact, it has never been clearly established whether Johnston, when turning over command to Hood, outlined such a plan to him or not. The former stated that he did so; the latter denied it emphatically. The probabilities are that the idea of sallying forth from Atlanta was discussed in general terms but not in any detail, which makes both officers correct from their point of view. In any event the point is rather immaterial. The essential fact is that Hood, by that time, was the responsible officer in command and deserves the credit.

Hood's plan of attack was reminiscent of Stonewall Jackson's great flank march at Chancellorsville. While Stewart's and Cheatham's two corps held the lines at Atlanta, Hardee was to lead his corps on a long flanking march south through Atlanta, then swing wide to the east, thence north again to strike at the rear of General McPherson's Army of the Tennessee near Decatur. Major General "Joe" Wheeler's cavalry was to go with Hardee, and both were to attack at daylight, with the cavalry on Hardee's right.

Again the point of the attack was well chosen. The southern flank of McPherson's army was completely unprotected, for the cavalry that should have been guarding it had been sent on a raid far to the southeast. There was no one to give warning of the Confederate approach. The plan could have brought disaster to McPherson's army. The only impractical aspect was Hood's expectation that the assault could be delivered at daylight. The march did not begin until after dark, and when the troops left the main highway and turned east, the road became only a single narrow track. In the darkness progress was necessarily slow, and when it came time to deploy for the attack, it had to be done in dense underbrush, where it was difficult to see fifty yards in any direction.

Many of the soldiers had been fighting or marching for two days. All were wearied by the long, exhausting night march. Later, in his report of the battle, Hood criticized Hardee for being slow, but the real truth is that Hood miscalculated the time that the march would take. If Hood had been present at the Battle of Chancellorsville, waiting with Lee throughout almost the entire day of May 2, 1863, for Jackson to make his great assault, he would have had a far better idea of how much time such a difficult flank march would consume.

Considering the great distance involved, the fact that the march was made at night, the length of the column stretching over many miles on a single narrow road in the darkness, and the difficulties encountered in the approach to the Union position, Hardee's Corps made exceptionally good time.

In his book *Advance and Retreat* Hood complained bitterly that Johnston's policy of continuous retreat had destroyed the offensive spirit of the army. He devoted many pages to this subject, returning to it again and again. The action of Hardee's Corps on July 22, 1864, should have completely and utterly dispelled such a false notion. When the attack came shortly after noon, it burst with concentrated force and tremendous surprise upon McPherson's army. For a brief period it seemed that Hood's bold plan, so brilliantly executed by Hardee despite all the difficulties encountered, was to be a magnificent success. However, on that very morning, while the Confederates were approaching McPherson's open flank, two divisions of the Union army had been moved and were taking position to extend the Union line just as the Confederates struck. Almost by pure chance, these troops arrived in time to keep Hardee's men from hitting the rear of the enemy army and rolling up the Union line completely. Yet, in spite of the fact that the Confederates had struck a strong Union force, instead of the open flank they had expected, the attack continued forward with unabated fury into the Union lines. Clear evidence of the confusion caused among the Union troops was provided when General McPherson rode, totally unsuspecting, into a group of Confederate skirmishers and was killed while trying to escape.

Hardee's attack might yet have succeeded if Cheatham's Corps had been advanced immediately upon the front of McPherson's army, but the flank attack had spent itself before the frontal attack was launched. This also was delivered with great bravery and vigor, but it came three hours too late. Some Union troops were actually able to fight off Hardee's men, then turn about in their trenches and repulse the second frontal assault. As in the Battle of Peachtree Creek, the timing was again at fault. With simultaneous attacks by Hardee and Cheatham it would have been impossible for the defenders to have successfully fought in two directions at once. Thus passed Hood's great opportunity.

These two battles, Peachtree Creek and Atlanta, are remarkably similar in many respects. In each case, General Hood's attacks were bold, daring, and well planned. Each attack was directed against approximately one-half of Sherman's forces, which were divided. Both attacks, when launched, caught the enemy by surprise and should have achieved success. In neither case would Sherman's advance against Atlanta have been completely halted, but had the Army of the Cumberland been thrown back across Peachtree Creek or the Army of the Tennessee defeated at the Battle of Atlanta, Sherman would have been forced to fall back and regroup before continuing his advance toward the city. Had the Confederates won either battle, their losses would have been far less, and the Union losses correspondingly greater. A Union defeat at the outskirts of Atlanta in July would have been a great achievement. The Siege of Atlanta would have been postponed and prolonged for an indefinite period, although there is no doubt that, with their great preponderance of numbers, the Union armies could eventually have taken the city. Its capture, however, might have been delayed for many months, and there is the possibility that the voters of the North would have decided that the war should not be continued. These were the stakes for which Hood was fighting. No matter how audacious his plans were, they were certainly worth any risk.

If either Peachtree Creek or Atlanta had gone the other way, Sherman would not have received permission to make his "March to the Sea." Neither President Lincoln nor General Grant would have let him go, leaving in his rear an opponent who had shown himself capable of winning great battles.

Over the years, General John Bell Hood has been evaluated in two different ways. It has been said that he was a splendid brigade and division commander, perhaps an adequate corps commander, but unequal to the far greater task of commanding an army. Then we are told that he was too rash and reckless and took too little account of the odds against him.

It cannot be said that Hood was overwhelmed by a feeling of vast responsibility when the mantle of command of the second largest army of the Confederacy suddenly descended upon him, although many generals were so affected. The same phenomenon occurs daily in all walks of life when people suddenly find themselves confronted with assignments beyond their capabilities, none of which can possibly be compared with that of commanding an army. Feeling themselves unequal to the task, sensitive to the tremendous burden of responsibility weighing heavily on their shoulders, they feel crushed by it and, as a result, fail. The two best examples in the Civil War were Burnside and Hooker. The first knew nothing else to do but continue the useless slaughter he had begun at Fredericksburg. The second simply lost his nerve at Chancellorsville, faltered, and fell back.

In *Advance and Retreat,* referring to the evening of July 17, 1864, Hood wrote that "the totally unexpected order" directing him to assume command of the army "astounded me and overwhelmed me with sense of the responsibility thereto attached." However the rest of the book does not convey this feeling, nor do his actions while in command of the army. No one who felt overcome by too great a responsibility would have, immediately after the failure at Peachtree Creek, devised another even more daring plan than the first and promptly put it into action just two days later.

Hood's problem was not one of being overawed by the task assigned, or by the manifest difficulties that faced him. He had imagination and initiative and was perfectly willing and ready, even eager, to take his chances in battle.

The reason that both Peachtree Creek and Atlanta failed was, in each case, the same. The best of plans can fail if poorly executed. For years Hood tried unconvincingly to pin the blame for both failures on General Hardee. He also accused his officers and men of failing to charge vigorously enough against the enemy's breastworks. In fact, his book *Advance and Retreat* is a continuous series of accusations against others, blaming everyone but himself. The reason is not far to seek. He was only too well aware that his own excellent plans that deserved success had failed because he himself had not exercised proper control and coordination. And, again, the reason is not hard to determine. Hood knew full well that, because of his physical condition, he was not the leader he had been. Yet he could not afford to admit that the fault was his, since he had assured all and sundry that he was physically capable of command. But in his heart he knew that he was not the same man who had led the famous charge on Little Round Top that almost won Gettysburg.

Hood emphatically stated that he never required the use of

an ambulance either day or night, but this is not sufficient. Far more is necessary to exercise command. Control and constant supervision are essential; and because of the crippling wounds he had received at Gettysburg and Chickamauga, he could not properly fulfill the duties of an army commander in the Civil War. If armies of that day had been equipped with adequate staffs to see that the commander's orders and plans were carried out, General Hood might have been more successful. Yet even this is doubtful. The commanding general must still be able to move about freely, to make his presence known and his influence felt at critical times. He must be at the right place at the right time to seize opportunities as they appear, and he must be clearheaded at all times so that when emergencies develop, his decisions are the correct ones. This is difficult to do with one arm in a sling, using a crutch as a necessary aid in walking, or being strapped into the saddle. No one suffering from pain thinks too clearly at all times. Under the stress and strain of battle, when pain might be likely to strike, Hood cannot have been at his best.

At Peachtree Creek there is no question but that General Hood should have been with the main attack, *i.e.,* with Hardee's and Stewart's Corps. No one has ever completely established where he was throughout the battle. He was probably at headquarters in Atlanta, but in any event he was not where he was needed when the difficulties arose that caused the fatal three-hour delay. Orders had been issued prior to the attack requiring that both corps extend a half-division front to the right to connect with Cheatham's Corps. As General Hardee stated in his Official Report: "The delay . . . arose from the fact that Cheatham's Corps, with which I was to connect, was nearly two miles to my right instead of a division length. Had General Hood been on the field the alternative of delaying the attack or leaving an interval between Cheatham's command and my own could have been submitted to him for a decision."

At the Battle of Atlanta General Hood was in the proper place, with Cheatham's Corps on the right flank, where he could coordinate both attacks, but he was hesitant to act. He seems to have expected that the Union troops to his front would flee or fall back as soon as Hardee launched his attack, and he further seems to have expected that Hardee's Corps would do the entire job of routing the Union army even when totally unexpected resistance was encountered. He did finally send Cheatham into the battle but was three hours late in doing so. The frontal attack should have started forward as soon as Hardee made his flank attack, particularly so when it was seen that Hardee was encountering difficulties.

The Hood of Gaines' Mill, Second Manassas, Antietam, Gettysburg, and Chickamauga would never have dreamed of missing the action at Peachtree Creek. And assuredly he would have seen the absolute necessity of an immediate assault to aid Hardee at Atlanta. There is no question but that Hood was not the same man, either physically or mentally, that he had been when he was with the Army of Northern Virginia prior to his crippling injuries.

As for the charge of recklessness against General Hood, it can be substantiated in each of his two campaigns—Atlanta and Nashville—but only for a part of each. When he saw his plans go awry and failure occur when success should have been achieved, he became frustrated and angry. After losing Peachtree Creek and Atlanta, he should have retired into the defenses of the city with the object of prolonging the siege for the greatest possible length of time. In his first two savage battles he had taught his enemy to exercise due caution, but stung and irritated by his failures, he tried to make up for the lost battles by fighting another one. Ezra Church on July 28 resulted in nothing more than adding to the long list of casualties already incurred. In this instance there had been no plan of battle. It was just a head-on meeting engagement. A smaller army that has already suffered great casualties against a larger army cannot afford to fight this way. The net result of Ezra Church was simply to widen further the gap between the strengths of the two opposing armies and make the early capture of the city all the more probable.

Finally, late in August, after several heavy bombardments of the city and its defenses, Sherman started on another of his wide swinging movements to the west, striking at the railroad lines serving Atlanta. The Union armies were slow and deliberate in their advance and spent an entire day destroying the railroad. This delay and some false information misled Hood into believing that Sherman was retreating. Plans were laid for a grand victory ball at Atlanta, when suddenly Hood awoke to the facts. Despite all his previous and later accusations against General Hardee, he again selected that most capable officer for the mission of saving the army. Hardee encountered the enemy at Jonesboro, where, with little hope of success, he made a valiant attack. When this was repulsed, Hardee held off Sherman's armies long enough to enable Hood to save the rest of the troops from capture. On September 2, 1864, Union troops marched into Atlanta.

One month after the fall of Atlanta, Hood very neatly turned the tables on his victorious opponent. While Generals Wheeler and Forrest raided with their cavalry deep into Tennessee, Hood undertook an offensive against Sherman's supply lines which extended back for 400 miles to Louisville, Kentucky. He managed to lure Sherman all the way back to Resaca, Georgia, where the first battle of the Atlanta campaign had been fought, thence southwestward to the Alabama border. There Sherman gave up trying to catch the faster-moving Confederates. From that point onward the two armies marched in different directions—Sherman toward the sea, Hood west and northward into Tennessee.

In the Nashville campaign that followed, General Hood again came startlingly close to success. By skillful maneuvering he placed his army in a position where it could destroy the enemy. The Union army should have been destroyed, but it was not. The enemy was allowed to escape by marching past the

Confederate army at night within gunshot of the pickets and within the lights from their fires, yet no one made any move to stop them. Whereupon, although he had also been present, Hood lost his temper at his officers and men and the next day, in anger, ordered the disastrous assault at Franklin. Then, notwithstanding the tremendous casualties suffered there, he continued the advance to Nashville, where but one predictable result awaited.

It is perhaps a little unfair to General Hood, when on so many occasions he came so close to victory, to conclude this chapter with something so frivolous as a song. But at the end of the Battle of Nashville, as the soldiers of the Confederate Army of Tennessee left the field, they had a new song. Some wit had produced a parody on "The Yellow Rose of Texas." As the defeated army streamed southward, the soldiers, with irrepressible humor, their morale badly shaken but obviously not destroyed, were singing:

> So now we're going to leave you,
> Our hearts are full of woe;
> We're going back to Georgia
> To see our Uncle Joe.
> You may talk about your Beauregard
> And sing of General Lee,
> But the gallant Hood of Texas
> Played hell in Tennessee.

10

---◆◆◆---

George H. Thomas

MANY of the most capable generals on both sides in the Civil War could afford to fight drawn battles or be defeated if the odds were weighted heavily against them without fear of having their reputations tarnished or losing their command positions. There was one, however, who could not. He was suspect from the very beginning. Although his friends who knew him well and the officers and soldiers who fought under his command never for one moment questioned his loyalty to the Union, the country as a whole, and many of its more prominent leaders, regarded him with a feeling of great distrust. He was a *Virginian* who had elected to remain in the United States Army, and that fact was not forgotten. Even after two years of war had passed and he had established a reputation as one of the most outstanding, loyal generals of the North, many people still eyed him with suspicion. If at any time his fortunes had suffered a severe reversal, he could expect to be summarily relieved from command.

It is peculiar that this should be so, for he was not the only Southerner who fought for the North. There were many others who did so, just as there were several Northerners who fought for the South. Even that most fair-minded, just, and honest of all men, President Abraham Lincoln, seems to have been afflicted with the same unusual disease of distrust for this man from Virginia. It has previously been noted that General Sherman had to vouch personally to the President of the United States for the loyalty of his West Point classmate; and of no other officer has it ever been recorded that, when discussing promotions, the President said: "He is a Virginian, let him wait." No, this general could not afford to lose a battle.

George Henry Thomas was born near Newsoms in Southampton County, Virginia, not far from the North Carolina border, on July 31, 1816, the fourth of nine children, six girls and three boys. His father died when George was only twelve years old, leaving to his mother the burden of rearing the children and managing a large farm.

Unlike the case of Joseph E. Johnston, a great Virginian who fought for the South, the state of Virginia erected a historical marker to designate the birthplace of this other great Virginian who fought for the North. It is located on U.S. Highway 58, 1.7 miles southeast of Courtland (formerly Jerusalem) :

GENERAL THOMAS' BIRTHPLACE

GENERAL GEORGE H. THOMAS, "THE
ROCK OF CHICKAMAUGA," WAS BORN
ON JULY 31, 1816, ABOUT FIVE
MILES TO THE SOUTH. A GRADUATE
OF WEST POINT, THOMAS SIDED
WITH THE UNION DURING THE
CIVIL WAR AND WON DISTINCTION
IN THE CAMPAIGNS IN TENNESSEE.

Following his graduation from West Point in the class of 1840, George H. Thomas received a commission in the artillery and was sent to Florida to take part in the latter stages of the Second Seminole War. His classmate Sherman, who had been his roommate in their first year at West Point, was also stationed there. The latter saw very little action, but Thomas took part in an expedition that earned him a promotion to brevet first lieutenant. Then in 1842 both of them were assigned to duty at Fort Moultrie, Charleston, South Carolina, to serve there with Captain Robert Anderson. However, from this point onward, until they were both selected to serve together again in Kentucky under General Anderson's command, the two friends' careers differed widely.

Whereas Sherman missed the Mexican War completely and later resigned from the service, Thomas fought in the expedition commanded by General Zachary Taylor and took part in the battles of Resaca de la Palma, Monterey, and Buena Vista. At Monterey he was cited for gallantry and meritorious conduct and promoted to brevet captain. At the Battle of Buena Vista it was reported that he had more than sustained the reputation he enjoyed in the regiment as an accurate and scientific artilleryman and was again promoted for gallant and meritorious conduct to brevet major.

It would be tedious to enumerate all the various successive assignments to army posts and other duties given to Major Thomas between the Mexican War and the Civil War. These included a return to Florida, a tour of duty at Boston, Massachusetts, and a three-year assignment at West Point, where he met and was married to Miss Frances Kellogg of Troy, New York. There followed a short period of service in California; then he was transferred to the elite 2nd Cavalry, which included so many officers due to become famous in the Confederate States Army.

In 1860, while on duty with his regiment, he was wounded by an Indian arrow in an engagement with the Kiowas. Although he fearlessly exposed himself countless times in many dangerous situations during the Civil War, this was the only time he was wounded in action. In November of that year, while returning to the East on a leave of absence, he had a very serious accident that injured his spinal column to such an extent that he was confined to a hospital for six weeks. For a long while he was afraid that he might not be able to return to duty with his regiment. Thereafter he was careful not to exercise too strenuously and he was also cautious while riding a horse.

His army friends always called him Tom, but the soldiers

quickly dubbed him "Old Slow Trot." It has been said that this nickname came from the fact that he rarely rode his horse faster than a walk, due to his injury. Another version is that the name "Old Slow Trot" was given him by the cadets at West Point because this seemed to be his favorite command at equitation school. Neither explanation for the origin of the nickname sounds plausible. Every riding instructor at the academy followed the same general practice when first teaching new cadets to ride, usually preceding it with the command "Cross your stirrups in front of your saddles," then "Trot" or "Slow Trot." There is no more reason why Thomas should have been given the name "Slow Trot" than any other officer who taught equitation.

The soldiers were probably not referring to the speed of his horse at all. In the manner of all soldiers everywhere they were quick to recognize the qualities and talents of a commanding officer. From the very beginning they were aware of the fact that their commander was a deliberate, slow-speaking, careful person who was not to be hurried, no matter how great the crisis.

When the time came for Major George H. Thomas to make his fateful decision whether to go with his native state of Virginia or remain with the United States Army and fight for the Union, he never once hesitated or wavered but immediately renewed his pledge of allegiance to defend the federal government. Yet this decision must have been as difficult for him as it was for Colonel Robert E. Lee, although they took opposite stands. Their two cases have often been compared and rightly so. Most Southerners who cast their lot with the Confederacy did not face the immediate loss of their homes and possessions. The majority, since they expected to win the war, never took this factor into consideration at all.

However both Lee and Thomas faced this prospect. Lee, as a soldier, knew that his home in Arlington would be occupied immediately by Northern troops. On May 24, 1861, the very day that Virginia's secession became effective, Union troops crossed the Potomac River, seized Arlington and Alexandria, and Lee's home was lost to him forever. As soon as Thomas decided to fight for the Union, his home in Virginia was lost to him. It is doubtful, however, that he quite expected the violent reaction that his decision produced within his family. His two maiden sisters turned his picture toward the wall, never referred to him again, and after the war refused to give him the sword that had been presented to him by the citizens of Southampton County in recognition of his outstanding service in the Mexican War.

When Albert Sidney Johnston, Robert E. Lee, and William J. Hardee, all senior to him in the 2nd Cavalry, resigned to fight for the South, Thomas found himself the ranking officer in the regiment. He was soon promoted to colonel and ordered to join General Robert Patterson in an advance into the Shenandoah Valley. Thomas however, missed the First Battle of Bull Run, when General Joseph E. Johnston slipped quietly away from Patterson without letting his enemy learn the Confederates had gone, joined Beauregard at Manassas, and won the battle for the South.

One month later, in August, 1861, Thomas was promoted to brigadier general to serve with Sherman under their old Fort Moultrie commander, General Anderson, in Kentucky. This was the occasion for Sherman's personally declaring to President Lincoln that he knew Thomas to be completely loyal to the Union. The President would soon have occasion to be thankful that he had promoted Thomas and assigned him to duty in the Western theater, for on January 19, 1862, Thomas defeated a Confederate force at the Battle of Logan's Cross Roads, also called the Battle of Mill Springs or Fishing Creek, and, by some, the Battle of Somerset. It was only a small battle, with approximately 4,000 men engaged on each side, but it had far-reaching effects; it preserved eastern Kentucky from any invasion by the Confederacy for several months. At the time it also seemed to President Lincoln to be a great step forward toward his cherished goal of freeing east Tennessee, which he knew contained a large proportion of Union sympathizers.

It was after this battle that the President is supposed to have said, when the question was raised of promoting Thomas to major general: "He is a Virginian, let him wait." In all fairness to the President there were other factors to consider. If he had promoted Thomas, he certainly would have had to promote the department commander, General Don Carlos Buell, who had succeeded General Sherman when the latter had entered upon his peculiar period of despondency and been given an extended leave of absence to recuperate.

Promotion of Buell and Thomas would then have placed them both ahead of General Grant, which would have been a great injustice. For, less than a month later, Grant would deal the South a terrific blow by achieving the far greater success of seizing Forts Henry and Donelson, capturing 11,500 men and forty guns, breaking the whole Confederate line of defense across the entire state of Kentucky, and forcing a precipitate retreat into Tennessee. The one-day Battle of Mill Springs can hardly be compared with Grant's successful campaign, which many students consider to be one of the major events of the entire war.

The next critical episode in the career of General Thomas came in the fall of 1862, when General Kirby Smith and General Braxton Bragg undertook their joint invasion of Kentucky. During the campaign that followed, leading to the confused Battle of Perryville, the authorities in Washington became dissatisfied with Buell's conduct of operations. The command was offered to Thomas, who declined to accept it. He was far more aware than anyone in Washington could possibly be of the problems that General Buell faced. Thomas felt that it would be a supreme injustice to Buell to relieve him on the eve of the battle. This action on his part illustrates magnificently Thomas' innate qualities of fair-mindedness, honesty, and integrity. Many an overly ambitious man would have leaped at the chance to supersede his commanding officer, but Thomas refused to take advantage of his superior in his hour of difficulty. If he was to be promoted to higher command, he wanted it to come about as a result of his own proven merit, not at the expense of another.

Later, after the Battle of Perryville, fought on October 8, 1862, when the War Department did relieve Buell and appointed General William S. Rosecrans in his stead, Thomas felt then that he had been rebuffed because he had been offered the command once and had refused it for perfectly sound reasons. Now, when those reasons no longer applied, he believed that he was still the logical choice.

Yet the circumstances were totally different. If, while the campaign was in progress and the enemy close at hand, a change in commanders had to be made, the new commander must necessarily be someone who was on the ground and thoroughly familiar with the situation. At that moment, it would have been totally impractical to bring in another general from a distant field. Whereas after the battle had been fought and the prospect of immediate action had passed, the War Department could choose whomever it thought best suited for the assignment. In late 1862 the combat record of William S. Rosecrans was far more impressive than that of George H. Thomas. By then the facts concerning General McClellan's early victories in West Virginia, which had led to his being brought to Washington after the First Battle of Bull Run, to be given command of the Union armies, had become better known. Those early victories attributed to McClellan had actually been won for him by Rosecrans and others of his subordinates. Since then, also, Rosecrans had added to his reputation by victories at Iuka and at Corinth in Mississippi.

On December 26, 1862, Rosecrans advanced southward from Nashville toward Murfreesboro, Tennessee. The Union Army of the Cumberland was organized into three parts: the Right Wing, the Center, and the Left Wing, each composed of three divisions. The Center column was commanded by Thomas.

Although the distance was only thirty miles, it took the Union army three days to reach the outskirts of the city where the Confederate army commanded by General Braxton Bragg was awaiting it. The principal reason for the slowness of the Union advance was the excellent performance of General "Joe" Wheeler's Confederate cavalry, which opposed it every step of the way, constantly forcing the Union infantry to halt, deploy off the roads, struggle across country, then re-form on the roads, and deploy again. The Union cavalry seems to have been almost totally ineffective while Wheeler kept his superior, General Bragg, completely and accurately informed every step of the way.

The Battle of Murfreesboro, or Stones River, began on December 31, 1862. The plan of attack for each of the two armies was exactly the same. Unbeknown to each other, both the Union and the Confederate commanders planned an assault with the troops on their left against the right flank of the enemy. If each had executed his attack at the same time it could have produced a gigantic pinwheel effect, but the Confederates jumped off first in the early morning hours of December 31, shortly after dawn.

Although the Confederate army was outnumbered by about 45,000 to 38,000, the first day of battle was unquestionably a Confederate victory. A series of furious assaults rolled back the entire Union Right Wing. One of its divisions, commanded by General Sheridan, stubbornly held its ground and even counterattacked, but then it too was forced to retreat when its ammunition ran low, and the charging Confederates again pushed forward. The Union Center under General Thomas became heavily engaged in an effort to reinforce and halt the retreat of the faltering Right Wing. The planned Union attack on the opposite flank had long since been canceled, and its troops sent hurriedly toward the battle.

The final Union position at the end of the day, where the troops were to make their last stand, was alongside, just in front of, and parallel to the Nashville Turnpike. If this road were to be cut on the next day, the line of retreat for the Union army would be gone.

That night a conference of his senior generals was held by a very worried Rosecrans. It is an old military axiom that a council of war never fights, but this was an exception, and its outcome was due almost entirely to the presence of one man. Several accounts have been written of this meeting, but almost all agree in one particular. Many of those present were fearful of the outcome if the Confederates attacked again on the morrow. They argued that their line of retreat would be cut and the result could be a terrible disaster. Others were undecided, while a few wanted to stay and fight. Throughout this discussion, Thomas seemed to be paying but little attention. Some officers present were unkind enough to say that he actually went to sleep until called upon for his opinion. His firm statement that the army would remain in position and fight was then made in such a calm, imperturbable, assured manner, with no apparent questioning whatever of the outcome, that all present were so impressed that they returned to their commands confident of success, despite their previous fears and worries.

On the next day, January 1, 1863, the two armies stood facing each other. Bragg made no move to follow up his victorious advance of the day before. On the third day he made an effort to dislodge the Union troops on the opposite (eastern) side of Stones River but was stopped by massed Union artillery fire. Bragg then retreated on the night of January 3, yielding Murfreesboro to the Union army. Both sides claimed to have won the battle.

It had been a definite Confederate victory on the first day; twenty-eight Union guns had been captured and some 3,700 prisoners. The total Confederate losses in the three-day battle were about 10,000 men compared with the Union losses of 13,000 killed, wounded, captured, or missing. However General Bragg's decision to retreat gave credence to the Northern claim of a strategic victory, and the credit for it must go primarily to General Thomas, who insisted that the Union army not retreat.

In the months following the Battle of Stones River, as the men of his command, now redesignated the Fourteenth Army Corps, gradually came to appreciate the stalwart, solid qualities that their leader had displayed in those crucial, desperate hours of that first day of battle on December 31, when stark defeat had stared them in the face, they began referring to General Thomas in a more affectionate way than before. They started calling him Pap Thomas. The old nickname Slow Trot did not completely disappear from their vocabulary; it was, after all, so very appropriate and so completely descriptive of his careful, methodical, deliberate nature; but "Pap" became their favorite term. None knew, as spring and summer passed and September approached, that shortly he would acquire a new title that would become famous in history and by which the entire United States and countless people in foreign lands would know him for as long as men and women ever read about the American Civil War.

The date would be September 20, 1863, the occasion the second day of the Battle of Chickamauga, when the Confederate Army of Tennessee unexpectedly broke through a huge gap opened by mistake in the Union line of battle. General Rosecrans, two of his corps commanders, and a third of the Northern army were swept from the field.

Thomas was left with various assorted elements of the three Union corps, something fewer than 40,000 of the original 60,000 men of the Army of the Cumberland, to face the full fury of the Confederate onslaught. At Murfreesboro he had held the center of the Union line, but at Chickamauga he faced a far more frightening task. Grimly, tenaciously, and stubbornly, he clung to his position against the entire Confederate Army of Tennessee, which in the beginning had numbered 66,000 troops and now outnumbered him heavily by odds of well over three to two. Attack after attack was repulsed. Although the Confederates slowly gained ground, they were facing a very stubborn opponent; George Thomas was a methodical, determined man who was not to be driven from a position he had decided to maintain. Until almost dark his lines held, when he was forced back still fighting stubbornly for every yard.

The Battle of Chickamauga was the greatest Confederate victory in the Western theater during the entire war, and but for one man, it would have been a complete disaster for the Union Army of the Cumberland. From that day forward, George H. Thomas has been known to history as The Rock of Chickamauga.

Rarely in warfare was Napoleon's famous statement *"A la guerre, les hommes ne sont rien; c'est un seul homme qui est tout"* ("In war, men are as nothing; it is the leader who is everything") applied so forcibly and dramatically to both armies and to both leaders. While George H. Thomas was saving the Union Army of the Cumberland from an unprecedented disaster, Braxton Bragg was sitting in his tent (like General Horatio Gates at the Battle of Saratoga) apparently unable to comprehend the fact that he had at last won a battle. As a result the attacks of the Left and Right Wings of the Confederate army on the position held by Thomas were uncoordinated, delivered separately and piecemeal.

On the following day the victors made no pursuit except for that conducted by a Confederate brigadier general of cavalry on his own initiative. Reaching the crest of Missionary Ridge and climbing to the top of a tree from which he could overlook the entire Union army, he sent back messages, urging the victorious Confederates to come forward. All that day his little cavalry force held their position, expecting the army to appear. Two weeks later this officer, who had no formal education and no military training, who had enlisted as a private and would before the war was over be promoted to lieutenant general in the Confederate States Army, received an order transferring his troops to another command. He stormed into Braxton Bragg's tent, told him what he thought of him, called him a "damned scoundrel," and flatly announced that he would never serve under his command again. One could wish for the sake of history that Nathan Bedford Forrest had been in command of the Army of Tennessee on that twentieth day of September, 1863, to see how the Battle of Chickamauga might have ended.

After his failure to pursue the Union army General Bragg then began a siege of that army in Chattanooga. Union reinforcements, comprising the greater part of two corps of the Army of the Potomac, were hastily dispatched by rail from Virginia. General Sherman was started from Mississippi with a large force from the Army of the Tennessee, and General U. S. Grant was placed in command of all these troops. His orders were handed to him personally at the Galt House in Louisville, Kentucky, by the Secretary of War. There were actually two sets of orders, identical in all respects but one. The first left Rosecrans still in command of the Army ot the Cumberland; the other relieved Rosecrans and assigned Thomas to take his place. Naturally, Grant chose Thomas.

With all these forces gathering against him, Braxton Bragg then made the incredible mistake of sending Longstreet with his two divisions from the Army of Northern Virginia to east Tennessee to besiege Burnside at Knoxville. Thus Bragg was weakening the size of his army just at the same time that Grant was strengthening his. The result was predictable, although not the manner of achieving it. The battles around Chattanooga were fought in three successive phases on three consecutive days: Orchard Knob on November 23; Lookout Mountain on November 24; and Missionary Ridge, November 25. When the Army of the Cumberland was ordered to advance on the third day of battle, the soldiers were supposed to take the trenches at the foot of Missionary Ridge, then stop and await orders. Instead, to the surprise of all their commanders, they kept on going and never stopped. That phase of the battle, which constituted the final decisive action, was not ordered by any general, nor can any senior officer claim the credit. It was a soldiers' battle in which the junior officers and enlisted men took the initiative into their own hands and, contrary to orders, kept moving forward and upward until they had seized the heights. The battle was suddenly and dramatically finished by the men themselves within the short span of one hour's time.

In the 1864 campaign that resulted in the capture of Atlanta, the Army of the Cumberland, commanded by General Thomas, always far outnumbered the other two armies. Some writers have claimed that General Sherman disliked Thomas, was unfair to him in reports to higher authority, and never gave Thomas sufficient credit for his achievements.

Sherman's operations in the Atlanta campaign constitute proof positive that such claims are false. If he had tried to reduce the size of the Army of the Cumberland and increase the strength of the other armies, it might have showed some distrust of Thomas' ability, but no such effort was ever attempted. It is perfectly obvious that Sherman was completely satisfied with the existing arrangement and with the fact that his friend Thomas was in command of far more troops than either of his juniors McPherson or Schofield.

Any student of the Atlanta campaign will, however, notice almost immediately that when it came to making those wide swinging movements toward the east or west flank, McPherson was generally chosen, or sometimes Schofield was given these missions, but never Thomas. The reason that such assignments were not given to the larger Army of the Cumberland was simply that it, being the largest body of troops, was always needed near the center to form the base around which the smaller armies swung.

In addition, however, it is true that Thomas was not noted for his ability to move rapidly. He was thoroughly reliable and trustworthy, but he was slow; and speed was always desirable when executing a wide flanking movement.

Those persons who accuse Sherman of not liking Thomas and being unfair to him usually point to correspondence between Sherman and Grant in which Sherman criticized Thomas, and particularly to one paragraph in which Sherman said:

> My chief source of trouble is with the Army of the Cumberland which is dreadfully slow. A fresh furrow in a plowed field will stop the whole column and all begin to entrench. I have again and again tried to impress on Thomas that we must assail and not defend; we are on the offensive and yet it seems that the whole Army of the Cumberland is so habituated to be on the defensive that from its commander down to its lowest private I cannot get it out of their heads.

If this had been written to someone who did not know both Sherman and Thomas well, it would have been considered terribly derogatory. However, Grant knew Thomas very well indeed, was thoroughly acquainted with his good qualities, and believed him to be suited admirably to remain as commander of the Army of the Cumberland. Grant had indeed chosen him for that position in preference to Rosecrans.

As for Sherman's method of expressing himself, Grant knew very well that his chief subordinate was prone to exaggeration, in fact enjoyed expressing himself in unusual fashion, had a real gift of gab, and a lively sense of humor. After the war these qualities of Sherman's made him the most popular after-dinner speaker in the country. His schedule was so full that it was difficult for him to keep track of his appointments. He practically never prepared a speech in advance and indeed would not have had time to do so. Sherman never knew what he was going to talk about ahead of time, but never failed to delight his audience. Furthermore, he sometimes did not recall exactly what he might have said. Such was the case with his statement that "war is hell." It was not until he read the newspapers the next day that Sherman learned that he had made that now famous statement.

Therefore when Grant read what Sherman had written about Thomas' being slow, it did not come as a shock to him. It would have surprised him if Sherman had not made some such complaint. That both Grant and Sherman trusted Thomas was to be proven very shortly after the fall of Atlanta, when Sherman made his "March to the Sea," leaving Thomas to face Hood's army. Sherman would never have proposed that Thomas be chosen for that assignment, nor would Grant have approved it, if they had not thought highly of him. It may also be assumed that, when they both agreed to place Thomas in charge of defending against an attack by Hood, they fully expected Thomas to be successful, although his methods of accomplishing his mission might be more cautious and methodical than they themselves would have employed.

For the student of military history the Nashville campaign holds a special interest. From beginning to end it differed in countless ways from any other campaign of the war. For nearly six months the principal armies of the North and South had been fighting each other. Four months had been consumed in a struggle for possession of the city of Atlanta. Then, after a pause, there had come another short campaign in which General Hood had struck against Sherman's long line of communications, causing him to retrace his route almost back to its starting point. The two opponents had finished facing each other along the Georgia-Alabama border. Then they had completely separated, going in opposite directions, Sherman on his way through Georgia to the sea, Hood to embark on his invasion of Tennessee.

General Thomas had missed this last, short campaign between the two armies. While it was in progress and there appeared to be a threat against Chattanooga, Thomas had been placed in charge of the defense of that city. Then he had been sent back to Nashville to prepare to combat the invasion.

The infantry and artillery of Hood's Confederate army reached Tuscumbia, Alabama, on the last day of October, 1864. There Hood had expected to find supplies awaiting him, but the railway line needed to be repaired and heavy rains were delaying the work. At this time also he had no cavalry. He had been ordered to leave Wheeler's cavalry to oppose Sherman, and General Forrest had been ordered to join him. This took time and there were further delays, so it was not until November 21 that Hood had his whole army marching northward.

Of all the blessings that ever descended on George H. Thomas in his lifetime, this long three-week delay by Hood at Tuscumbia was surely the most welcome. To oppose Hood's 40,000 (including Forrest's men) he had only about 30,000 soldiers badly scattered in detachments stretching from Chattanooga to the Ohio River. These could have presented but little resistance to a Confederate advance. Thomas' principal combat elements ordered to join him were, for the most part, still en route. These consisted of the Fourth Corps from the Army of the Cumberland, Schofield's Twenty-third Corps, and A. J. Smith's Sixteenth Corps. The last-named, however, had a long way to go. It was in western Missouri and did not reach Nashville until the last day of November, completing its move on the first day of December.

To wait so long in one place, postponing his invasion, was not like the bold, audacious Hood. He could have moved forward without waiting for all his supplies, counting on obtaining what he needed from the surrounding countryside as he advanced. Nor need he have waited for Forrest to join him. The latter was in north-central Tennessee and should not have been required to march all the way south to Tuscumbia, Alabama. They could have met each other in southern Tennessee and saved at least two weeks. Hood's decision to wait was to prove fatal to his campaign. Furthermore, when he did finally move, the weather turned bad. He was met by rain, sleet, snow and terrible roads that slowed his march to an advance of ten miles a day.

Meanwhile General Thomas had been slowly gathering his forces without seeming to realize the urgency of the situation. Admittedly, there was nothing he could do to hasten Smith's corps coming from Missouri, but he was slow to bring in his detachments. If Hood had advanced as late as the second week, he would still have found only the Fourth Corps and one division of the Twenty-third Corps to block his way. These had been concentrated at Pulaski, Tennessee, in the southern part of the state, and counted fewer than 25,000 men.

By the time Hood did advance, after a three-week delay, the other division of the Twenty-third Corps had reached Pulaski and the Union cavalry had been greatly strengthened. This army under the command of General Schofield numbered approximately 34,000 men. His mission was to block the Confederates and delay their advance for as long as possible to give Thomas the maximum amount of time to concentrate all the troops he could at Nashville.

At this point all the accounts of the Nashville campaign produce a peculiar impression. It would seem that 34,000 Union troops constituted a force of reasonable size sufficient to delay the Confederate army of 40,000 men, but everyone involved in the campaign acted as if the Union army was terrifically outnumbered and would be extremely lucky if it escaped capture or annihilation. This is also the way almost every one of the accounts is written. Practically no one asks why a Union force of 34,000 should run so precipitately from 40,000 Southern soldiers. The difference in strength was not that great. Yet that is how the campaign was fought.

Pulaski is due south of Nashville, whereas Tuscumbia is to the southwest. Pulaski is not on the main road between Nashville and Tuscumbia; General Schofield was therefore out of position to oppose a direct advance by Hood. When the Confederate army moved forward, it passed well to the west of Pulaski. Suddenly Schofield realized that Hood's army was heading for the town of Columbia on the Duck River in his rear, a little less than half the distance between him and Nashville. Hastily he fell back to that point. His troops arrived at Columbia just in time to stop Forrest's cavalry from seizing the bridges over the river. One hour later Forrest would have completely blocked the road.

The next move was for Hood to swing to his right flank and

cross the river east of Columbia. General Forrest led the way on the evening of November 28. Early the next morning the Confederate infantry began crossing while Forrest hastened onward to meet the Union cavalry of Major General James H. Wilson. In very short order Wilson was sent flying up the road to the north, completely cut off from the rest of the army. By this time Schofield had learned of the Confederate advance and had started troops marching toward the rear to seize the vital road junction of Spring Hill. That night the remarkable episode occurred, when the Confederate army let its enemy escape untouched.

On the following day, November 30, Hood took up the pursuit. He found Schofield in a strongly entrenched position at Franklin, less than twenty miles from Nashville. Furious on account of his failure at Spring Hill, General Hood hurled his two corps against the Union position without waiting for his third corps to reach the field. Far too little attention has been paid to this battle. The great Confederate charge of the Civil War is still "Pickett's Charge," yet it suffers by comparison in almost every respect. In the charge at Franklin, more Confederate generals and soldiers were killed, the troops had a greater distance to advance across open fields, yet they broke through the center of the fortified line and were stopped only by a heroic counterattack.

At this point General Hood should have halted. The casualties at Franklin had been terrific and there was no hope of replacement, while his adversary, General Thomas, was waiting for him at Nashville and the Northern army was growing stronger all the time. Yet Hood kept on, and when he arrived at Nashville, he made the same incredible mistake that Bragg had made in front of Chattanooga. In the same way that Bragg had depleted his forces there, by sending Longstreet to Knoxville in east Tennessee, Hood now sent Forrest to besiege Murfreesboro. If that redoubtable leader had been present at the Battle of Nashville, he and his men would probably not have been able to snatch victory from defeat, but at least the battle would not have become the great disaster that it was.

If anyone has any doubt as to whether or not the Confederate invasion of Tennessee caused excitement, alarm, and concern in the North, he has only to read the series of telegrams that flashed back and forth over the wires between Washington and Nashville after Hood reached that point. Of course Secretary of War Stanton was excited and upset; that was normal and to be expected. But the President became greatly concerned, and, for the first and only time in the war, General Grant lost his normal, calm, unruffled manner. As a result, while Thomas was making his preparations for attack, he found himself besieged with telegrams accusing him of being slow to move and urging him to attack immediately.

Because of this flurry of telegrams drawing attention to the days immediately preceding the Battle of Nashville, most students of the war and the majority of historians have accepted as fact the idea that Thomas was unduly slow and cautious in his preparations for battle. Throughout his career Thomas had often demonstrated these qualities. General Grant should have known, and undoubtedly did know, that persuading "The Rock of Chickamauga" to move rapidly before he considered himself ready in all particulars was a little like trying to move the Rock of Gibraltar.

In this instance, however, General Thomas, although deliberate and methodical in his preparations, did not actually lose much time. Schofield's army had, by marching almost all night on the eve of the Battle of Franklin, struggled into Nashville on December 1. Most of A. J. Smith's corps had only reached the city on November 30, with the remainder arriving on December 1. Also a considerable part of the army that Thomas had assembled consisted only of detachments and "casuals" that needed to be organized into units. In addition, and this was a factor of overriding importance, Wilson's cavalry had proved at Spring Hill to be totally inadequate to confront Forrest's troops. Time was needed to reorganize, mount, and equip the Union cavalry quickly. To accomplish all this work took a few days. Thomas had been very slow in concentrating his forces at the beginning of the campaign, but in those early days of December at Nashville he actually wasted little time.

It is one of the twists of fate that there should have been so much more excitement and concern in Washington and at Grant's headquarters in Petersburg over Thomas' being slow at Nashville than at any other time in his career when in fact on this occasion he was organizing his army, preparing it for battle, making plans, and issuing orders about as fast as anyone could. On December 8 Thomas was ready to attack, the assault to be launched on the tenth, when a terrible storm of freezing rain struck, converting the whole countryside into a sheet of ice.

In the meantime, urged by the President and goaded by the Secretary of War to take action, General Grant had directed that an order be prepared relieving Thomas from command. Schofield was to supersede him; but the order was never sent, presumably because on that day Thomas' telegram arrived telling of the sleet storm. However, while Thomas was waiting as patiently as he could for the weather to improve, Grant, along with the President and the Secretary of War, again became anxious. Major General John A. Logan, who was in Washington at the time, was told to go to Nashville and take command in place of Thomas unless upon his arrival he found that a battle had been fought. Grant himself then determined to go to Washington and thence to Nashville.

On the morning of December 14 the weather broke. On the next day Thomas attacked. The Battle of Nashville is one of the very few battles in history that went almost exactly according to plan. It was a classic example of a holding attack (against Hood's right) with the main effort striking with almost overwhelming force against Hood's left, the cavalry swinging wide toward the rear.

The first day, December 15, the defenders held their lines

until almost dark, then gave way before the greatly superior numbers attacking them. A new position was selected and entrenched farther to the rear. With the same plan of battle, the attacking force again came forward, and this time broke through completely. Pursuit, however, was delayed because Wilson's cavalrymen had been fighting on foot and had to go back to get their horses. A Confederate cavalry division, at tremendous sacrifice to itself, saved the army from further disaster.

Of all the really great generals of the Civil War Thomas was the only one who achieved resounding success by fighting strictly "by the book." There was no occasion throughout his military career when it was essential or advisable to do otherwise. Except at Chickamauga he always had superior numbers, so there was no reason for him to depart from the accepted principles of war. He was never confronted by a situation such as Grant found facing him at Vicksburg. Great boldness, audacity, and the willingness to take risks were not required of him. If he had been asked to fill the shoes of Lee, Jackson, Johnston at Bentonville, or Hood, it is doubtful that he would have been willing to take the same risks they did, for Thomas' greatness lay not in that direction. Instead he will be remembered as a master in the application of the proper principles of strategy and tactics.

Epilogue

<hr style="width:20%"/>

It is totally impractical to summarize the qualities of each of the ten leaders who have been presented or to compare them in any detail. None of them would have reached the positions they attained if they had not had outstanding ability of one sort or another. George B. McClellan was the worst battlefield commander of the ten. The old story that General Lee is supposed to have said that McClellan was by all odds the best of the Union generals he opposed has long since been effectively disproved.* Yet McClellan was almost certainly the most outstanding organizer and trainer of troops to appear on either side during the Civil War.

Success on the battlefield must be the final criterion. By this standard, Lee, Jackson, Grant, and Sherman were outstandingly successful. So was Thomas, but it is doubtful that he would have achieved the same degree of success as the first four if he had been as thoroughly tested as they in situations requiring great boldness or rapidity of decision.

By this same harsh standard, Longstreet and Meade were likewise successful, but their great achievements were generally confined to defensive operations. The same might be said of Joseph E. Johnston, although he would have become far more famous

---

* The best discussion on this subject is contained on pages 478 and 479, Volume II, of Kenneth P. Williams' *Lincoln Finds a General.*

as a general if he had not been prevented from taking the offensive, first by a severe wound, then by direction of President Jefferson Davis. Likewise Hood was never given a fair test, having been placed in command only after he was severely incapacitated physically, but it is more difficult to make an accurate judgment in his case.

It had been mentioned repeatedly that those officers who were supremely successful were the ones who, when necessity arose, did not fight "by the book." It must be steadily borne in mind, however, that they did so only when the occasion demanded. In almost every other instance they followed the teachings of warfare, realizing full well that their education and training were based on solid precepts. Risks were taken at their peril; it takes proper training, practical experience, and a certain amount of genius to tell when such risks should, and must, be taken.

In *American Campaigns,* while discussing Nashville, Major Steele had this to say:

> The two chief actors in it, Thomas and Hood, were the exact opposites of each other. One was slow, apparently timid in taking the initiative, but sure in execution; the other was quick and bold to act, but uncertain as to the outcome. One apparently weighed the odds against him too carefully; the other gave no heed to them at all. If the characters and talents of the two men could have been combined in a single general, it would be hard to pick his better.

When he wrote these sentences, Major Steele probably had no particular person in mind, but of all the generals in the Civil War his words seem to fit Stonewall Jackson best.

Bibliography

Of all the books studied over the years describing military leaders, their campaigns and battles (ancient and modern) that influenced the viewpoints expressed in this work, only those applying specifically to the individuals and events described are listed. Nor is this a complete listing of all the Civil War sources utilized. Only those that were frequently consulted or that proved to be of material value or benefit in the preparation of this study have been cited.

ALEXANDER, E. P., *Military Memoirs of a Confederate*. New York, Charles Scribner's Sons, 1907.

BADEAU, ADAM, *Military History of Ulysses S. Grant*. New York, D. Appleton & Company, 1868-81.

BARNARD, JOHN G., *A Report on the Defenses of Washington to the Chief of Engineers, U.S. Army*. Washington, U. S. Government Printing Office, 1871.

BOATNER, MARK M., III, *The Civil War Dictionary*. New York, David McKay Company, 1959.

BRADFORD, GAMALIEL, *Lee, the American*. Boston, Houghton Mifflin Company, 1912.

————, *Confederate Portraits*. Boston, Houghton Mifflin Company, 1923.

BUCK, IRVING A., *Cleburne and His Command*. Jackson, Tennessee, McCowat-Mercer Press, 1959.

Campaigns of the Civil War. New York, Charles Scribner's Sons, 1881-83. New York and London, Thomas Yoseloff, 1963.

Bibliography

CATTON, BRUCE, *Grant Moves South*. Boston, Little, Brown & Company, 1960.

———, *Grant Takes Command*. Boston, Little, Brown & Company, 1968.

CODDINGTON, EDWIN B., *The Gettysburg Campaign*. New York, Charles Scribner's Sons, 1968.

CULLUM, GEORGE W., *Biographical Register of the Officers and Graduates of the U.S. Military Academy*.

DABNEY, R. L., *Life and Campaigns of Lieut.-Gen. Thomas J. Jackson*. New York, Blelock & Company, 1866.

DAVIS, JEFFERSON, *The Rise and Fall of the Confederate Government*. New York, D. Appleton & Company, 1881.

Dictionary of American Biography, Allen Johnson, ed. New York, Charles Scribner's Sons, 1927-36, 1943.

EVANS, CLEMENT A., ed., *Confederate Military History*. Atlanta, Confederate Publishing Company, 1899.

ESPOSITO, VINCENT J., ed., *The West Point Atlas of American Wars*. New York, Frederick A. Praeger, 1959.

FIEBEGER, G. J., *Campaigns of the American Civil War*. West Point, United States Military Academy Printing Office, 1914.

FREEMAN, DOUGLAS S., *R. E. Lee: A Biography*. New York, Charles Scribner's Sons, 1934-35.

———, *Lee's Lieutenants*. New York, Charles Scribner's Sons, 1942-44.

FULLER, J. F. C., *Grant & Lee*. Bloomington, Indiana University Press, 1957.

———, *The Generalship of Ulysses S. Grant*. Bloomington, Indiana University Press, 1958.

GOVAN, GILBERT E., and LIVINGOOD, JAMES W., *A Different Valor, the Story of General Joseph E. Johnston, C. S. A.* Indianapolis, Bobbs-Merrill, 1956.

GRANT, ULYSSES S., *Personal Memoirs of U. S. Grant*. New York, Charles L. Webster & Company, 1885-86.

HASSLER, WARREN W., *General George B. McClellan, Shield of the Union*. Baton Rouge, Louisiana State University Press, 1957.

HENDERSON, G. F. R., *Stonewall Jackson and the American Civil War*. London, New York and Toronto, Longmans, Green & Company, 1932.

HENRY, ROBERT S., *The Story of the Confederacy*. New York, Grosset & Dunlap, 1936.

——, *"First with the Most" Forrest*. Indianapolis, Bobbs-Merrill, 1944.

HOOD, JOHN B., *Advance and Retreat*. New Orleans, published for the Hood Orphan Memorial Fund, 1880.

HORN, STANLEY F., *The Army of Tennessee*. Indianapolis, Bobbs-Merrill, 1941.

——, *The Decisive Battle of Nashville*. Baton Rouge, Louisiana State University Press, 1956.

JOHNSON, ROBERT U., and BUEL, CLARENCE C., eds., *Battles and Leaders of the Civil War*. New York, Century Company, 1884-87. New York and London, Thomas Yoseloff, 1956.

JOHNSTON, JOSEPH E., *Narrative of Military Operations*. New York, D. Appleton & Company, 1874. Bloomington, Indiana University Press, 1959.

LAMERS, WILLIAM M., *The Edge of Glory, a Biography of William S. Rosecrans, U. S. A.* New York, Harcourt, Brace & World, 1961.

LEE, ROBERT E., *Recollections and Letters of General Robert E. Lee*. New York, Doubleday, Page & Company, 1904.

LEWIS, LLOYD, *Sherman, Fighting Prophet*. New York, Harcourt, Brace & Company, 1932.

——, *Captain Sam Grant*. Boston, Little, Brown & Company, 1950.

LIVERMORE, THOMAS L., *Numbers and Losses in the Civil War in America 1861-65*. Boston, Houghton, Mifflin & Company, 1901.

LONGSTREET, JAMES, *From Manassas to Appomattox*. Philadelphia, J. B. Lippincott Company, 1896. Bloomington, Indiana University Press, 1960.

MCCLELLAN, GEORGE B., *McClellan's Own Story*, W. C. Prime, ed. New York, Charles L. Webster & Company, 1887.

MEADE, GEORGE G., *The Life and Letters of George Gordon Meade*. New York, Charles Scribner's Sons, 1913.

MICHIE, PETER S., *General McClellan*. New York, D. Appleton & Company, 1901.

MITCHELL, JOSEPH B., *Decisive Battles of the Civil War*. New York, G. P. Putnam's Sons, 1955.

———, and Creasy, Edward S., *Twenty Decisive Battles of the World*. New York, Macmillan, 1964.

———, *Discipline and Bayonets: The Armies and Leaders in the War of the American Revolution*. New York, G. P. Putnam's Sons, 1967.

Patch, Joseph D., *The Battle of Ball's Bluff*. Leesburg, Virginia, Potomac Press, 1958.

Pemberton, John C., *Pemberton, Defender of Vicksburg*. Chapel Hill, University of North Carolina Press, 1942.

Porter, Horace, *Campaigning with Grant*. New York, Century Company, 1897.

Ropes, John C., *The Story of the Civil War* (continued by William R. Livermore). New York, G. P. Putnam's Sons, 1933.

Sandburg, Carl, *Abraham Lincoln: The War Years*. New York, Harcourt, Brace & Company, 1939.

Sherman, John, *Recollections of Forty Years in the House, Senate and Cabinet*. Chicago and New York, Werner Company, 1895.

Sherman, William T., *Memoirs of General William T. Sherman*. New York, D. Appleton & Company, 1875.

Sorrell, G. Moxley, *Recollections of a Confederate Staff Officer*. New York and Washington, Neale Publishing, 1905.

Stackpole, Edward J., *They Met at Gettysburg*. Harrisburg, Pennsylvania, The Stackpole Company, 1956.

———, *The Fredericksburg Campaign*. Harrisburg, Pennsylvania, The Stackpole Company, 1957.

Steele, Matthew F., *American Campaigns*. Washington, D.C., Byron S. Adams, 1909.

Stephenson, Nathaniel W., *Abraham Lincoln and the Union*. New Haven, Yale University Press, 1918.

———, *The Day of the Confederacy*. New Haven, Yale University Press, 1919.

Swinton, William, *Campaigns of the Army of the Potomac*. New York, Charles B. Richardson, 1866.

Thomas, Benjamin P., *Abraham Lincoln*. New York, Alfred A. Knopf, 1952.

Thomas, Wilbur, *General George H. Thomas, the Indomitable Warrior*. New York, Exposition Press, 1964.

"Today and Yesterday in the Heart of Virginia." Farmville *Herald*, Farmville, Virginia, 1935.

TUCKER, GLENN, *High Tide at Gettysburg*. Indianapolis, Bobbs-Merrill, 1958.

——, *Lee and Longstreet at Gettysburg*. Indianapolis, Bobbs-Merrill, 1968.

VAN HORNE, THOMAS B., *History of the Army of the Cumberland*. Cincinnati, Robert Clarke & Company, 1875.

——, *The Life of Major General George H. Thomas*. New York, Charles Scribner's Sons, 1882.

War of the Rebellion, Official Records of the Union and Confederate Armies. War Department, U. S. Government Printing Office, 1880-1901.

WILLIAMS, KENNETH P., *Lincoln Finds a General*. New York, Macmillan, 1949-59.

WILLIAMS, T. HARRY, *Lincoln and His Generals*. New York, Alfred A. Knopf, 1952.

WYETH, JOHN A., *Life of General Nathan Bedford Forrest*. New York, Harper & Brothers, 1899.

Index

Index

(Ranks given are the highest attained during the war)

Advance and Retreat (Hood), 207, 210
Allatoona Pass, 163
Allegheny Mountains, 49, 50
American Campaigns (Steele), 179, 237
American Revolution, 172, 185
Anderson, Lt. Gen. Richard H. (CSA), 78, 80, 219
Anderson, Maj. Gen. Robert (USA), 154, 155, 156, 217
Antietam campaign, 35, 39, 60, 85, 88, 91, 92–93, 95, 135, 198, 212
Appomattox River, 130
Aquia Creek, 72, 76
Army of Mississippi, 159, 162, 201
Army of Northern Virginia, 30–31, 32, 35, 65, 82, 86, 88, 91, 104, 105, 107, 126, 129, 130, 137, 144, 147, 159, 186, 193, 194, 212, 226
Army of Tennessee (CSA), 158, 174, 175, 185, 186, 190, 193, 194, 201, 214
Army of the Cumberland, 158, 202, 204, 206, 208, 221, 225, 226, 227, 228, 230
Army of the Ohio, 158, 202
Army of the Potomac (CSA), 174
Army of the Potomac (USA), 23, 25, 26, 28, 30, 31–32, 34, 68, 72, 85, 93, 96, 97, 115, 127, 133, 135, 136, 137, 142, 150 151, 159, 226
Army of the Shenandoah, 174, 177
Army of the Tennessee (USA), 122, 158, 171, 172, 202, 206, 226
Army of Virginia, 59, 69, 71, 75, 77
Atlanta campaign, 160, 165–66, 187–91, 202, 205–9, 210, 211–12, 213, 227

Baker, Col. Edward D. (USA), 21
Ball's Bluff, Battle of, 21, 23
Baltimore, Maryland, 140
Baltimore and Ohio Railroad, 81
Banks, Maj. Gen. Nathaniel P. (USA), 41, 42, 45, 46, 47, 48–49, 50–51, 54, 55, 56, 69, 75, 124–25
Barksdale, Brig. Gen. William (CSA), 98
Baton Rouge, Louisiana, 124
Battles and Leaders (Hampton), 191
Beauregard, Gen. P. G. T. (CSA), 15, 31, 33, 154, 177, 178, 219
Belmont, Battle of, 111
Benjamin, Judah P., 39–40, 179–80
Bentonville, Battle of, 190, 191
Big Black River, Battle of, 126
Black Hawk War, 175
Blair, Francis P., Sr., 63

Blenker, Brig. Gen. Louis (USA), 47, 51
Blue Ridge Mountains, 49, 50, 51
Bonaparte, Napoleon, 37, 225
Boonsboro, Maryland, 83
Bragg, Gen. Braxton (CSA), 81, 104, 105, 106, 154, 158, 183, 185–86, 225–26, 232
Brandy Station, Battle of, 138, 140
Buell, Maj. Gen. Don Carlos (USA), 220, 221
Bull Run, Battles of. *See* Manassas
Burnside, Maj. Gen. Ambrose E. (USA), 73, 96, 209–10

Cameron, Simon, 63, 156
Carrick's Ford, Battle of, 18
Cashtown, Pennsylvania, 142
Cassville, Battle of, 188, 194
Cedar Mountain, Battle of, 75
Chambersburg, Pennsylvania, 142
Champion's Hill, Battle of, 126
Chancellorsville, Battle of, 60, 91, 102–3, 135, 136, 137, 191, 200, 206, 207
Charleston, Virginia, 81
Chase, Salmon P., 134
Chattahoochee River, 165
Chattanooga, Battle of, 104, 113, 157–58, 160, 226–27, 229
Cheatham, Lt. Gen. B. Franklin (CSA), 201, 202, 206, 208, 211, 212
Chickahominy River, 29, 30, 65
Chickamauga, Battle of, 104, 105, 106, 185, 193, 195, 200, 211, 212, 235
Cleburne, Maj. Gen. Patrick R. (CSA), 158
Cold Harbor, Battle of, 189
Congress, USS, 55

Conrad's Store, Battle of, 51, 52, 53, 59
Cooper, Gen. Samuel (CSA), 177, 179
Coosa River, 163
Corinth, Battle of, 221
Couch, Maj. Gen. Darius N. (USA), 101
Crampton's Gap, Battle of, 85
Crater, the, Battle of, 127
Crimean War, 19
Cromwell, Oliver, 61
Cross Keys, Battle of, 58, 59
Culpeper, Virginia, 72, 96, 138
Cumberland, USS, 55
Cumberland Church, Battle of, 130
Custer, Brig. Gen. George A. (USA), 107

Dalton, Georgia, 162
Davis, Jefferson, 32, 49, 62, 64, 66, 89, 105, 128, 129, 165, 176, 178, 179, 180, 181, 183, 184, 185, 186, 189, 190, 192, 201, 205, 237
Doubleday, Maj. Gen. Abner (USA), 99
Dunkard Church, Battle of, 199

Early, Lt. Gen. Jubal A. (CSA), 103–4, 114, 115, 116
Etowah River, 163
Evans, Brig. Gen. Nathan G. (CSA), 21
Ewell, Maj. Gen. Richard S. (CSA), 51, 52, 53–54, 55, 56, 57, 58, 72, 103, 129–30, 136, 138–39, 141, 142, 146, 153
Ewing, Thomas, 153
Ezra Church, Battle of, 212–13

Fair Oaks, Battle of. *See* Seven Pines

Farmville, Virginia, 130, 131, 176
Five Forks, Battle of, 113, 129
Forrest, Lt. Gen. Nathan Bedford
(CSA), 159, 184, 191, 213, 226,
230, 232, 233
Fort Donelson, 23, 111, 220
Fort Henry, 23, 111, 220
Fort Moultrie, 154, 216
Fortress Monroe, 24, 25, 26, 27, 73
Fort Stevens, 114, 116
Fort Sumter, 18, 63, 155
Franklin, Battle of, 214, 232, 233
Franklin, Maj. Gen. William B.
(USA), 97, 98, 99, 100
Frayser's Farm, Battle of. *See* Glen-
dale
Frederick, Maryland, 82, 139, 142
Fredericksburg, Virginia, 51, 54, 59,
72, 73, 96, 136, 138; Battle of, 91,
93, 95, 97–102, 135, 199–200, 210
Freeman, Douglas Southall, 129
Frémont, Maj. Gen. John C. (USA),
46, 47, 49, 51, 52, 53, 55, 56, 57,
58, 59, 69
French, Maj. Gen. William H.
(USA), 101
From Manassas to Appomattox
(Longstreet), 106
Front Royal, Virginia, 50, 53, 54,
55, 56

Gaines' Mill, Battle of, 33, 135, 196,
198, 212
Galena, Illinois, 110
Gates, Maj. Gen. Horatio, 225
Gettysburg, Pennsylvania, 35, 103,
142; Battle of, 80, 104, 106, 135,
144–50, 151, 199, 200, 210, 211,
212
Gibbon, Maj. Gen. John (USA), 99
Glendale (Frayser's Farm), Battle
of, 34, 135

Grant, Fred, 126
Grant, Julia Dent, 89, 110
Grant, Lt. Gen. Ulysses S. (USA),
25, 34, 78, 87, 88–89, 103, 106,
108–32, 151, 158, 159, 160, 162,
166, 184, 189–90, 191, 192, 209,
220, 226, 228–29, 233, 234, 235,
236
Grierson, Maj. Gen. Benjamin H.
(USA), 123, 124
Groveton, Battle of, 80, 136, 197

Hagerstown, Maryland, 83, 85
Halleck, Maj. Gen. Henry W.
(USA), 71–72, 82, 116, 121, 125,
126, 133, 135, 156, 157
Hampton, Gen. Wade (CSA), 191,
196
Hancock, Maj. Gen. Winfield Scott
(USA), 101, 143, 146, 148
Hardee, Lt. Gen. William J. (CSA),
159, 194, 201, 202, 204, 206, 207,
208, 211, 212, 213, 219
Harpers Ferry, West Virginia, 39,
41, 42, 50, 56, 82, 83, 85, 86
Harrisburg, Pennsylvania, 139, 140
Harrison, James, 141
Harrisonburg, Virginia, 50, 51, 56
Harrison's Landing, Virginia, 72,
73
Henderson, Col. G. F. R., 78
Hill, Lt. Gen. Ambrose Powell
(CSA), 85, 136, 138, 143
Hitler, Adolf, 185
Hood, Gen. John B. (CSA), 159,
163, 165, 166, 188, 190, 193–214,
229–33, 234, 237
Hooker, Maj. Gen. Joseph (USA),
97, 98, 99, 101, 135, 138, 139, 142,
143, 210
Howard, Maj. Gen. Oliver O.
(USA), 101

Howe, Gen. Sir William, 172
Hunt, Maj. Gen. Henry J., 97
Huger, Maj. Gen. Benjamin (CSA), 91

Illinois Central Railroad, 19
Iuka, Battle of, 221

Jackson, Mississippi, 125, 184
Jackson, Lt. Gen. Thomas J. "Stonewall" (CSA), 15, 30, 32, 33, 37–61, 72, 75–76, 77, 78–80, 83, 87, 91, 92, 96, 98, 100, 102, 103, 126, 136, 143, 155, 159, 179, 180, 184, 191, 197, 198, 199, 206, 207, 236, 237
James River, 25, 27, 30, 34, 113, 127
Johnson, Maj. Gen. Edward (CSA), 51, 52, 53
Johnston, Gen. Albert Sidney (CSA), 177, 195, 219
Johnston, Gen. Joseph E. (CSA), 21, 24, 28, 29, 30, 34, 40, 44, 49, 51, 65, 66, 129, 157, 158–59, 160, 162, 163, 164, 165, 170, 171–72, 173, 174–92, 193, 194, 201, 202, 206, 219, 236
Jonesboro, Battle of, 213

Kennesaw Mountain, Battle of, 164, 189
Kernstown, Battle of, 45–48
Knoxville, Battle of, 105, 226

Law, Brig. Gen. Evander M. (CSA), 197, 199, 200
Lee, Gen. Robert E. (CSA), 30, 31, 32, 34, 35, 42, 49, 51–52, 53, 60, 62–87, 91, 92, 93, 96, 97, 102, 104, 105, 107, 113, 128, 132, 134, 137–38, 139–40, 141–42, 143, 144, 146, 147, 148, 150, 159, 160, 162, 174, 175, 176, 178, 180, 182, 183, 189,

190, 191, 195, 197, 198–99, 218–19, 236
Leesburg, Virginia, 21
Letcher, John, 40, 63
Lincoln, Abraham, 17, 18, 23, 24, 25–26, 28, 46, 47, 48, 55, 57, 63, 69, 70, 71–72, 96, 109, 114, 115–16, 117, 121–22, 127, 133, 138, 166, 170, 187, 209, 215, 216, 219, 220, 233, 234
Lincoln, Maj. Gen. Benjamin, 185
Logan, Maj. Gen. John A. (USA), 234
Logan's Cross Roads (Mill Springs), Battle of, 219–20
Longstreet, Lt. Gen. James (CSA), 78, 80, 85, 88–107, 136, 141, 146–47, 181, 182, 183, 197, 198, 200, 226, 236
Longwood, Virginia, 176
Lookout Mountain, Battle of, 158, 185, 226
Loring, Maj. Gen. W. W. (CSA), 39, 40
Louisiana State University, 154
Luray, Virginia, 50, 51, 54

Magruder, Maj. Gen. John B. (CSA), 27, 28, 38, 181, 195
Malvern Hill, Battle of, 34, 66
Manassas (Bull Run), First Battle of, 18, 21, 23, 38, 39, 44, 64, 89–90, 155, 177, 196, 219; Second Battle of, 60, 80, 91–92, 135, 191, 197–98, 212
Manstein, Field Marshal Erich von, 185
"March to the Sea," 166–71, 190, 209, 229
Martinsburg, West Virginia, 82
Maryland campaign, 82–87, 92, 138–50

Massanutten Mountains, 50, 54, 57

Maury, Matthew F., 176

McCall, Brig. Gen. George A. (USA), 59

McClellan, Maj. Gen. George B. (USA), 15–36, 38, 41–42, 44, 46, 47, 48, 51, 52, 55, 57, 59, 68, 72–73, 74, 75, 80, 82, 83–86, 95–96, 115, 155, 181, 182, 187, 196, 198, 221, 236

McClernand, Maj. Gen. John A. (USA), 122

McDowell, Battle of, 52–53

McDowell, Maj. Gen. Irvin (USA), 18, 26, 28, 29, 30, 32, 48, 51, 54, 55, 56, 57, 58, 60, 69, 96

McLaws, Maj. Gen. Lafayette (CSA), 83

McNair, Lt. Gen. Lesley J., 27

McPherson, Maj. Gen. James B. (USA), 122, 158, 162, 163, 195, 202, 206, 207, 208, 227

Meade, Maj. Gen. George G. (USA), 93, 99, 100, 133–51, 159, 236

Mechanicsville, Battle of, 33, 59, 66, 135

Mechum's River Station, Virginia, 52

Memoirs (Grant), 89, 120–21

Memoirs (Sherman), 165, 171–72, 173

Merrimack, CSS, 25, 30, 55

Mexican War, 18, 38, 62–63, 74, 89, 109–10, 134, 154, 172, 175, 217, 219

Mill Springs, Battle of, 220

Missionary Ridge, Battle of, 185, 225, 226

Mississippi River, 111, 117, 122, 157

Monitor, USS, 25

Moorefield, Virginia, 51

Murfreesboro, Battle of, 221–23, 232

Narrative of Military Operations (Johnston), 171

Nashville, Battle of, 190, 212, 213–14, 229–35

New Hope Church, Battle of, 164, 188, 189

New Market, Virginia, 50, 51, 54

Norfolk, Virginia, 30

North Anna River, 102

Ohio and Mississippi Railroad, 19

Oostanaula River, 162–63, 188

Ord, Maj. Gen. Edward O. C. (USA), 56

Pamunkey River, 29

Patterson, Maj. Gen. Robert (USA), 177, 219

Paulus, Marshal Friedrich von, 185

Peachtree Creek, Battle of, 165, 202–5, 208–9, 210, 211, 212

Pelham, Maj. John (CSA), 99, 100

Pemberton, Lt. Gen. John C. (CSA), 124, 183

Peninsular campaign, 27–36, 41, 90–91, 135, 181, 187, 189

Pennsylvania Railroad, 81

Perryville, Battle of, 220–21

Petersburg, Battle of, 103, 115, 127, 129

"Pickett's Charge," 148, 149, 232

Pine Mountain, Battle of, 202

Pinkerton Detective Agency, 23

Pipe Creek, 144, 146

Polk, Lt. Gen. Leonidas (CSA), 159, 162, 165, 202

Pope, Maj. Gen. John (USA), 59, 69–74, 75, 76–80, 85, 96, 197

Porter, Adm. David D. (USN), 119, 122, 123, 124

Porter, Maj. Gen. Fitz-John (USA), 33

Porter, Brig. Gen. Horace (USA), 132

Port Republic, Battle of, 52, 58–59

Potomac River, 21, 22, 23, 39, 42, 50, 55, 82, 95, 96, 139, 142

Randolph, George W., 40, 180, 181

Rapidan River, 80

Rappahannock River, 70, 96, 97, 136

Raymond, Battle of, 125

Reconstruction period, 106, 171

Resaca, Battle of, 162–63, 164, 188, 189, 213

Reynolds, Maj. Gen. John F. (USA), 143, 146

Richmond, Virginia, defense of, 17, 24, 29, 32, 51, 52, 59, 64, 65, 66, 68, 76, 90, 96, 103, 128, 129, 138, 160

Rich Mountain, Battle of, 18

Rome, Georgia, 163

Romney, Virginia, 39, 179

Rosecrans, Maj. Gen. William S. (USA), 221, 226, 228

Savage's Station, Battle of, 34

Sayler's Creek, Battle of, 129–30

Schofield, Maj. Gen. John M. (USA), 158, 162, 195, 202, 204, 227, 230, 231, 232, 234

Scott, Lt. Gen. Winfield (USA), 18, 19, 22, 62, 63, 66, 89, 110, 134, 175

Sedgwick, Maj. Gen. John (USA), 35, 143, 149

Seminole Wars, 134, 154, 175

Seven Days' Battle, 33–34, 59, 60, 65, 66, 67, 91, 92, 135, 182–83, 189, 196–97

Seven Pines (Fair Oaks), Battle of, 30–31, 62, 90, 182–83, 187, 189, 190, 196

Sharpsburg, Battle of, 85, 88, 198, 199

Shenandoah River, 39, 50

Shenandoah Valley, 30, 39, 41, 49–50, 82, 103, 104, 114, 116, 169, 180, 191–92

Shenandoah Valley campaign, 42–60

Sheridan, Maj. Gen. Philip H. (USA), 113–14, 169, 195

Sherman, Eleanor Ewing, 154

Sherman, John, 155, 173

Sherman, Maj. Gen. William Tecumseh (USA), 122, 123, 124, 125, 129, 152–73, 184, 189, 190, 191, 204–5, 206, 208, 209, 213, 215–16, 217, 219, 226, 227, 228–29, 236

Shields, Maj. Gen. James (USA), 45, 46, 53, 54, 55, 56, 57, 58, 59

Shiloh, Battle of, 111, 152–53, 157, 194

Sickles, Maj. Gen. Daniel E. (USA), 149

Sigel, Maj. Gen. Franz (USA), 69

Smith, Maj. Gen. Andrew J. (USA), 230, 233

Smith, Maj. Gen. Gustavus W. (CSA), 181

Smith, Gen. E. Kirby (CSA), 81, 220

South Mountain, 83, 85

Special Order No. 191, Lee's "Lost Order," 35, 83–85, 86, 92

Spotsylvania, Battle of, 112, 127, 189

Spring Hill, Battle of, 232, 233

Stanton, Edwin M., 17, 35–36, 46, 47, 48, 49, 51, 52, 53, 55, 57, 170, 172, 179, 233, 234

Steele, Maj. Matthew F., 119, 155, 179, 237
Steuben, Maj. Gen. Friedrich Wilhelm von, 27
Stewart, Lt. Gen. Alexander P. (CSA), 202, 204, 211
Stone, Maj. Gen. Charles P. (USA), 21–22
Stones River, Battle of, 222–24
Strasburg, Virginia, 48, 50, 53, 56
Stuart, Maj. Gen. J. E. B. (CSA), 32, 76, 77, 82, 140–41, 142, 176
Sturgis, Maj. Gen. Samuel D. (USA), 101
Sumner, Maj. Gen. Edwin V. (USA), 97, 98, 99
Susquehanna River, 139
Swift Run Gap, Virginia, 51, 52

Taylor, Lt. Gen. Richard (CSA), 54
Taylor, Maj. Gen. Zachary, 89, 110, 134, 217
Tennessee River, 152, 157
Texas Brigade, 194, 196, 197, 199
Thomas, Frances Kellogg, 217
Thomas, Maj. Gen. George H. (USA), 153, 155–56, 158, 162, 202, 204, 215–35, 236, 237
Turner's Gap, Battle of, 85, 135
Tuscumbia, Alabama, 229
Tyler, Brig. Gen. Erastus B. (USA), 58

United States Military Academy, 18, 38, 62, 88, 108, 109, 134, 153, 172, 175, 177, 195, 205, 216, 217, 218
Urbana, Virginia, 24

Vicksburg campaign, 113, 116–26, 151, 157, 183–85, 192, 235
Virginia Military Institute, 38

Walker, Maj. Gen. John G. (CSA), 83
War of 1812, 22
War Order No. 3, Lincoln's, 47
Warren, Maj. Gen. Gouverneur K. (USA), 200
Warrenton, Virginia, 72, 96
Washburne, Elihu B., 109, 112
Washington, D.C., defense of, 21, 24, 25, 26, 29, 42, 48, 55, 80, 81, 114, 115, 140
Washington, Gen. George, 74
West Point. *See* United States Military Academy
Wheeler, Lt. Gen. Joseph (CSA), 206, 213, 230
White House, Virginia, 29, 34
Wilderness, Battle of the, 103, 127, 189
Williamsburg, Battle of, 28–29, 90
Wilson, Maj. Gen. James H. (USA), 232, 233, 235
Winchester, Battles of, 39, 41, 42, 44, 45, 55, 139
Woodstock, Virginia, 49
World War II, 185
Wright, Maj. Gen. Horatio Gates (USA), 116

Yazoo Delta, 117, 119, 123
Yazoo Pass Expedition, 119
Yazoo River, 117
York, Pennsylvania, 139
York River, 25, 27, 29, 182, 196
Yorktown campaign, 15, 27, 29, 33, 181